THE DEVELOPMENT OF

Behavioral States
AND THE
Expression of
Emotions
IN
Early Infancy

THE DEVELOPMENT OF

Behavioral States

AND THE

Expression of Emotions

IN

Early Infancy

New Proposals for Investigation

PETER H. WOLFF

The University of Chicago Press · Chicago and London

Peter H. Wolff is professor of psychiatry at Harvard Medical School and senior associate in psychiatry at Children's Hospital, Boston.

The University of Chicago Press, Chicago 60637
The University of Chicago Press, Ltd., London

Library of Congress Cataloging-in-Publication Data

Wolff, Peter H.
  The development of behavioral states and the
expression of emotions in early infancy.

  Bibliography: p.
  Includes index.
  1. Infants—Development.   2. Emotions in infants.
I. Title.
RJ134.W65   1987   155.4′22   86-16066
ISBN 0-226-90520-9

For Carol

Contents

Introduction

This monograph describes the behavioral development and daily events in the lives of healthy infants who were observed for extended periods each week during the early months after birth. Nonintrusive home observations under free field conditions served as a point of departure for planning informal experiments; and the experiments were designed to examine boundary conditions under which the observed behavior was stable, as well as changes in behavior when the boundary conditions were exceeded. The studies were thus modeled after the *methods* of ethology (Hinde, 1983), i.e., to describe the spontaneous behavioral repertory of normal infants in their species-typical environment, as a precondition for planning and carrying out focused experiments. In contrast to the main emphasis of many ethological *theories*, the present investigations focused on developmental transformation of behavioral forms rather than on the constraints imposed by evolution on species-typical behavior. The observational strategies adopted for these studies therefore represent a significant departure from currently accepted methods of collecting and analyzing behavioral data on human infants; and the reasons for this departure may require some explanation.

Over the past twenty-five years, developmental psychology has become a scientific discipline in its own right, generally adopting the well-accepted research strategies of hypothesis testing which are consistent with the procedures of experimental psychology. At the same time, the hypotheses tested on *infants* are typically generated from notions about behavioral organization in the *adult,* or else by concerns about the etiology of clinically significant variations in developmental outcome, rather than by an interest in behavioral phenomena which are specifically relevant for understanding behavioral organization in neonates and young infants. Consistent with their essentially experimental orientation, the majority of current de-

1

velopmental studies on infants have therefore abandoned "naturalistic" observation as a method that is unsuitable for testing hypotheses about the organization of infant behavior, or for predicting the course of clinically significant deviations in behavioral development. Consequently, what infants actually do in their species-typical environment has become an issue of secondary interest.

From a different perspective, the psychological disciplines had by the early twentieth century made a concerted effort to expunge the mentalistic vocabulary of philosophical psychology, on the premise that such terms smacked of metaphysical speculations (Stich 1983). To achieve a truly scientific psychology they substituted what were considered theoretically neutral and operationally defined primitive terms such as "stimulus," "response," and "reflex," as the self-evident givens of experience which would require no a priori assumptions. The great enthusiasm engendered by the environmentalist perspective and by the scientific theories of behaviorism derived from it also captivated the field of developmental psychology; and the latter adopted experimental manipulations under a learning theory paradigm as the preferred basis for investigating the development of behavior in human newborns and infants (see Kessen et al. 1970, for a review).

By the late 1950s it was readily apparent, however, that the behaviorist program of applying the same general laws of learning to all species of animals at all ages was not particularly useful for investigating the development and causation of species-specific adaptation. More generally, there was a growing suspicion that the environmentalist program contributed nothing of interest to our understanding about the origins and organizational properties of uniquely human attributes like logical thought, the grammatical usage of natural languages, skilled tool-usage and historically informed social interactions.

At around the same time, renewed interest in Darwin's evolutionary biology gave rise to the hypothesis that selective pressure operates on socially relevant behavior as much as it operates on physiological functions, morphological structures, and the timing of embryological sequences (Tinbergen 1951; Eibl-Eibesfeldt 1970; Lorenz 1971; Gould 1977). To test this hypothesis concretely, ethology codified a set of explicit procedural guidelines for cataloguing the genetically programmed behavioral repertories of various animal species. These guidelines prescribed the nonintrusive observations in natural or near-natural conditions are an essential prerequisite for any functionally meaningful experimental manipulations under controlled conditions in restricted environments. Otherwise one can never exclude the possibility that the results are experimental artefacts of the manipulation which have no adaptive significance for the species. Proceeding by this method, ethologists demonstrated biologically and functionally significant differences in courtship and mating behavior, care of the young, territorial defense against predators, and the like between closely related species, even when such species differences were not apparent from morphological analysis. The method also provided the data base for an experimental causal analysis of behavior that focused on patterns which had previously been shown to have adaptive significance for the species.

The ethological method has been used extensively for studying the behavioral repertory of birds, fish, and nonhuman mammals. However, until recently it has not been applied systematically to the nonintrusive observation and experimental analysis of behavior in human infants or adults (for exceptions, see Hinde 1983). By contrast, the *theoretical constructs* of ethology concerning the proximal causation of behavior (innate releaser mechanisms, fixed action-patterns, imprinting, critical periods) were quickly, and perhaps prematurely, assimilated by perspectives on human psychology, indicating that the findings of ethology were well known to students of human behavior. On the other hand, the sequence of procedural guidelines prescribed by ethology may have been ignored by investigators of human infancy on the assumption that we already have sufficient knowledge about the repertory of human behavior under free field conditions in order to justify the next step of experimental manipulation and hypothesis testing.

In fact, however, we do not have such knowledge in nearly the same detail as we have, for example, about the social behavior of the herring gull and three-spined stickleback. There is, at present, no comprehensive "ethogram" of human infancy that could serve as a basis for carrying out biologically relevant experimental manipulations. Consequently we can also not assume that hypotheses and categories of behavioral organization inferred from observations of human adults are at all pertinent to the causal analysis of behavioral development in early infancy. On the contrary, grafting adult categories onto the behavior of infants may inadvertently introduce serious theoretical biases about continuity and discontinuity of form-function relationships during psychological development from infancy to adult life.

The derivative character of hypotheses tested on infants but generated from inferences about the behavioral organization of adults, is

3

suggested, for example, by the bewildering range of new specialties that have emerged in the field of infancy over the past twenty years (see, for example, Mussen 1970, 1983). These are an almost direct copy of corresponding specialties in adult human psychology. By now infant research includes areas of concentration in visual and social perception, cognition, information processing, nonverbal communication, affect development, mother-child interaction, developmental psycho- and sociolinguistics, psychosomatics, and neuropsychology. The behavioral criteria required to define each of these fields as a distinct specialty almost certainly did not emerge from observations of infants. Instead such specialties were probably created by a backward projection from inferences about behavioral organization in children and adults.

The derivative character of experimental studies on infants is also illustrated by neuropsychological investigations on the ontogeny of hemispheric specialization for psychological functions. Leaving aside the broader conceptual question of whether it is ever legitimate to conclude that any psychological function is localized in a particular anatomical structure of the central nervous system (for example, that "language is localized in the left hemisphere," when the left hemisphere is made up only of neurons that either do or not fire in various combinations), the phenomenology of infant behavior per se would probably generate no testable hypotheses concerning functional specialization of the cerebral hemispheres. Yet a substantial research effort, motivated in part by the attempt of neuropsychology to resolve the "nature-nurture controversy," is now devoted to the question of whether "language" is preferentially programmed in the left hemisphere and "music" and the recognition of emotional expressions in the right hemisphere of young infants, leaving it entirely unclear what exactly "language" and "music" mean during the first three months after birth.

Similar backward projection from adult categories to experiments on young infants are apparent in contemporary research on the prefunctional status of "basic emotions" and the "organizing" function of affects on perception, cognition, and social transactions. Such questions are not generated from nonintrusive observations of infants but from theoretical debates that may be relevant for the human adult but have no operative status in early infancy. As an unintended consequence of this one-sided emphasis, many theoretically important questions concerning the organization of behavior and mechanisms of development been ignored and will probably continue to be overlooked as long as our observations and experiments about early infancy are guided primarily by adult categories and adult units of measurement.

Skilled naturalists had already collected a detailed repertory of "spontaneously" occurring behavior of infants recorded in diaries, long before there was an established specialty of developmental psychology to impose "adultomorphic" categories on free field observations (Darwin 1877; Preyer 1882; Baldwin 1895; Moore 1896; Dennis and Dennis 1937; as well as some of the studies reported by Piaget, 1951, 1952, 1954). These records suggest that many of the most interesting behavioral phenomena unique to early infancy are readily accessible to direct observation without experimental manipulation and without preconceptions about what should be the relevant categories for psychological analysis. Moreover, the phenomena are eminently suitable for causal experimental analysis (see, for example, Baldwin 1897; Piaget 1951, 1952, 1954), and could have provided the basis for a human "ethogram," if they had not been essentially ignored by contemporary research on infants. Since many of the diary accounts remained in the form of single-case anecdotes they are probably most useful as points of departure for more detailed investigations. In planning these studies, I therefore proceeded on the assumption that it would be important to replicate such observations on larger numbers of infants and to examine how spontaneously observed behavioral patterns can be tested critically by experimental manipulations.

In sum, the studies for this monograph were organized according to the *methods* prescribed by ethology for examining the species-typical behavioral repertory of human infants. However, their theoretical orientation departed in important ways from some comprehensive formulations of ethology about the proximal causation and developmental invariance of behavioral mechanisms (Tinbergen 1951; Eibl-Eibesfeldt 1970; Lorenz 1971). These departures may also require some clarification. A consensus has emerged over the past twenty years that the full-term infant is neither an empty black box, nor a device for recording, storing, summating, and compiling changes of stimulus-response sequences (Stone et al. 1973; Osofsky 1979). An extensive body of empirical evidence indicates that naive newborns are selectively sensitive to the perceptual parameters of auditory, visual, and kinesthetic stimulus arrays which have adaptive significance for the species; and that infants are equipped with a limited but nevertheless finely tuned array of neuromotor mechanisms for the production of coordinated consumatory and other goal-directed actions, as well as of socially relevant vocal and gestural communication signals (Bower 1974; Wolff and Ferber 1979; de Vries et al. 1984).

The concept of the "competent infant" (Stone et al. 1973) which emerged from such findings has laid to rest the once popular perspective that the human infant is a biologically neutral recording device that initially operates by reflexes or stimulus-response sequences, reflexes being the only biological constraint on the otherwise infinite plasticity of the naive organism. The concept has also shifted the focus of research away from primary concerns with learning paradigms toward an exploration of prefunctional structures that make the course of human behavioral development uniquely human, and to research questions such as how prefunctional structures contribute to, and are transformed by, later acquisitions; and by what mechanisms novel behavioral forms that cannot be reduced to their antecedent conditions are *induced* during ontogenesis.

Yet this shift in perspective was motivated partly as a reaction against the earlier environmentalist perspective, and may therefore have gone too far in the opposite direction, imposing a biological reductionist perspective on development that can be as misleading for developmental research as environmentalism was in its time. There is, for example, a world of difference between the interactionist perspective of the infant as equipped at birth with a limited repertory of behavioral mechanisms that undergo extensive and qualitative transformations during ontogenesis; and the competing perspective emerging from recent theoretical restatements of preformationism, which attributes to the young infant all the essential computational rules and structural competencies that the organism will require to become a logically, linguistically, historically, and socially competent adult. The latter perspective reduces development to a trivial process of stabilizing and fine tuning preformed structures merely for the purpose of adapting them to local variations in environmental demands. Under the latter perspective the central research task for a psychology of infancy becomes a detailed description of surface manifestations from which the developmentally invariant underlying cognitive, linguistic, and social universals can be inferred. Since the latter can never be inferred unambiguously from the former, the far more important theoretical work becomes a rational deduction of the essential underlying structures and computational rules from their mature performance characteristics.

Having proposed a program of investigations that intended to avoid the pitfalls of forcing infant behavior into the categories that are relevant for children and adults, I was obliged to specify a set of observational criteria that are relevant to the phenomenology of infant behavior and are at same time not unduly biased by my own perspectives on behavioral organization in the human adult. However, for obvious methodological reasons, it was impossible to proceed as if I were a totally neutral naive observer whom the true categories of behavior would reveal themselves as self-evident; I had to specify some categories at the start. These were for the most part derived from my previous observations of infants in the newborn nursery (Wolff 1966). Instead of settling beforehand on a fixed protocol of items that would be recorded in all infants at all ages and to the exclusion of all other categories, I also left the study protocol open so that new behavioral categories could be added, others discarded or redefined as the observations progressed. By this route, my implicit theoretical biases may well have influenced the choice of novel categories to be included in the protocol.

The general categories for observations and experimental analysis with which I started were *behavioral states*—with emphasis on states of wakefulness; the *expression of emotions*—with emphasis on the universals of human nonverbal communication (in other words, emotional expressions that have been reported in all cultures studied to date); the emergence of novel expressive motor patterns not evident during the neonatal period; and the interaction between *behavioral state* and *expressions of emotion*—as a possible avenue for inferring the "meanings" of observable emotional expressions in nonsymbolizing infants. To these I subsequently added a general category on the infant's *relation to persons and things*—as a context for examining whether the behavior patterns that would later be classified separately as social-emotional and intellectual adaptations are clearly distinguishable in the newborn period; whether they are instead the emergent properties of a differentiation from a common matrix; or whether the distinction has no operative meaning in the early months after birth. For reasons to be detailed below, *motor coordination* was the unit of measurement by which all other categories were described. Each of the broad categories, in turn, was broken down into operationally defined units of observation which will be described in the body of the text.

An observational and essentially descriptive study of healthy human infants covering only a brief span of the early growth years can obviously not resolve any of the enduring problems that confront all of the developmental sciences. Nor can it hope to "explain" the origins of uniquely human capacities for logical thought and social transaction from infant data. Such a study can, however, provide an "ethogram" of human infancy that serves as a first step towards the functional analysis of species-typical human behavior. It can help to identify testable hypotheses about behavioral development that are specifically relevant for human infants and which do not rely exclusively on categories derived from psychological functions of the adult. Finally, I hoped that such a study might provide a frame of reference for integrating the somewhat parochial field of human infant studies into the broader theoretical perspectives on developmental biology, neurology, and evolutionary theory.

1

Method and Categories

Sample

The core sample of subjects selected for longitudinal study were twenty-two full-term infants. Only one infant and its family were studied at any one time; and each infant was observed for an average of thirty hours each week, for either one, three, or six months. At the start of the project I was justifiably concerned about the effect which my prolonged presence in the home might have on family members who were at home, and the concerns it might cause fathers who were away for most of the day. As one partial safeguard against these potential disruptive effects, I limited the sample to second and third children in the family, so that the parents would already have established their routines of child care firmly; mothers would feel more confident about their ways of doing things; and they would therefore feel less flustered by what they considered my "expert" knowledge. As an additional safeguard, I always made sure that fathers had had ample time to consider whether they wanted their wives to participate.

Potential volunteers were identified with the help of their pediatricians, who had known the parents for some time and could select the families least likely to be affected by my extended home observations. During the last trimester of the mother's pregnancy, I visited families who expressed an interest in participating and explained to them the rationale of the study and the amount of time I would be in the home each week. I also outlined what I proposed to do, stressing how important it was for the study that both parents should adhere as closely as possible to their usual routines. Families were paid small stipends to offset the incidental expenses of a sandwich or cup of coffee, and to objectify the aims of the study by a contractual arrangement; but the amount of money was never enough to become an unfair inducement if parents were otherwise reluctant to participate. All parents were informed that I would discontinue the study if

9

my presence created personal difficulties that could not be resolved by a simple adjustment; but none of the families felt the need to call on this option. They were also informed (correctly) that the primary purpose of my study was to investigate how normal infants develop in their homes; in other words, that the mother-child interaction was not one of my central interests.

Further, I acknowledged (again correctly) that I had no privileged information about the best way of bringing up infants; and that I was not in any position to offer gratuitous or requested expert advice about child-rearing practices. These caveats were important even then. Child-rearing experts were already professing a bewildering array of contradictory recommendations and prescriptions about the best way to raise babies. By implication they had created the impression that the technology of infant development had progressed sufficiently so that parents who wanted to do right by their children could no longer afford to rely on common sense, historical precedent, or their own autonomous decisions. So as not to compound this false impression, I therefore disclaimed any privileged knowledge. However, when infants had a medical condition which warranted medical attention, I informed the parents of my opinion and referred them to their own pediatricians. On the other hand, when some of the mothers raised questions about their or their family's psychological difficulties, I tried to steer the conversation to neutral topics, or again suggested that they might wish to consult their family physician.

The recruitment procedure proved to be remarkably successful. Most of the anticipated difficulties never arose. Three families refused participation once they learned about the nature of the study. In addition, I excluded seven families because I thought that my extended visits in the home would place them under too much stress. All other volunteers remained in the study for the duration, and several actually encouraged me to extend my observations beyond the time specified. After the first week of home observations, nearly all families seemed sufficiently comfortable with my presence to go about their business without excessive concern for my welfare or the baby's safety. Siblings sometimes became so involved in what I was doing that they wanted to "help," and I finally had to encourage them to play in the other room so as not to "disturb the baby." Some mothers also relied on my scheduled visits to run errands or visit friends, leaving me in charge of the household with instructions on how and when to (bottle) feed the baby.

The final sample for the longitudinal study included twenty

families and twenty-two infants. Several families notified me a year or two after I completed my observations that the mother was pregnant again, and that I was welcome to observe the next baby as well. I accepted two of these invitations in order to have the opportunity to study two infants in the same family, and to follow children observed during the newborn period at a more advanced stage of development. I made no effort to restrict the sample to one homogeneous cultural subgroup, or to randomize it, so that there were considerable variations in the cultural background and socioeconomic status of families studied. However, either by self-selection or because of hidden biases in the recruitment procedure, the final sample was limited to lower-middle and middle-class, white Caucasian families, including blue- and white-collar workers, graduate students and young professionals, but no other ethnic groups.

The study schedule was structured so that the first six infants were observed for a one-month period; the next ten infants for a three-month period; and the last six for six months. By this schedule, the findings on infants studied for one month served as a basis for an expanded, revised, and refined protocol for the three-month observations, and so forth. Four additional infants were observed for a ten-hour period one day each week over the first six months, in order to increase the sample size for planned experiments requiring longitudinal follow-up. Two or more of these infants could be observed concurrently. In addition, I have included results of several cross-sectional experiments carried out on infants who were not part of the longitudinal sample. In these experiments I tested hypotheses that had emerged from the longitudinal observations but required examination under better-controlled environmental conditions, and on different study populations.

Units of Behavioral Description and Analysis

Most generally, the thirty hours each week of longitudinal observations were subdivided into two main categories, whose data were always analyzed separately. On four days each week, infants were observed from four to five hours a day by methods that interfered as little as possible with the infant's or the mother's daily routine. These periods were distributed equally over the morning, early afternoon, and early evening hours, to test for diurnal variation in daytime sleep-waking patterns; and so that I could observe the infant's behavior while the father and siblings were at home. On the fifth day each week, every infant was observed for a continuous ten-hour period, and the time was devoted to informal experiments that complemented the nonobtrusive observations. These were intended as first steps toward a causal-functional analysis of behavior in human infants. Many of these experiments had not been formulated a priori, but were planned during observations under free field conditions. Others, however, had been planned on the basis of my observations in the neonatal nursery (Wolff 1966); or else they were planned on the basis of general hypotheses taken from various theories of mental and behavioral development that served as a formal frame of reference for the study. For example, during my graduate training I had studied the developmental theories of Werner, Piaget, and psychoanalysis in some detail (Wolff 1960), while my medical school education and postgraduate research training in neurophysiology added a neurological and psychobiological dimension or bias to the studies. Although providing an essential frame of reference, these theories also constituted a potential source of biases that could have distorted the selection of behavioral categories for the study. To minimize these potentially biasing effects, I made a systematic effort to examine the theoretical implications of each major phenomenon from at least two very different theoretical perspectives, rather than attempting to combine them into one eclectic formulation. Each internally coherent and complete theoretical perspective was intended to have a corrective effect on the distortions that might inadvertently be imported by relying exclusively on other frames of reference or theories.

Under this general orientation, informal experiments were planned in keeping with methods of observation used by Piaget to study sensorimotor intelligence in infants and young children. He called his procedure the "clinical method" (Vinh-Bang 1966), which in practice turned out to be quite similar to the methods of ethology, even though their respective empirical aims and theoretical assumptions are obviously quite different. For example, when more than one infant was noted to carry out a discrete and readily definable behavior pattern repeatedly, which I considered to be of importance in relation to one or another theory, I systematically varied the environmental conditions associated with the behavior until the pattern was either disrupted or qualitatively altered. In this way I hoped to establish the boundary conditions under which the behavior pattern remained stable, and the range of variations in behavioral organization resulting from the experimental manipulation.

A full ten-hour day turned out to be necessary and sometimes barely sufficient to carry out the planned experiments. Particular experiments, for example, could only be carried out when the infant was in the appropriate behavioral state, and state transitions are notoriously under the infant's, rather than the experimenter's control. Therefore I frequently had to wait until the infant was in the right state before starting or completing an experiment. At the start of the study, the experimental protocol was relatively short; but as new phenomena of theoretical interest were discovered during nonintrusive observations, they also required experimental confirmation. Near the end of the project, the ten hours were therefore sometimes barely enough to complete the entire protocol each week.

By prior arrangement I accompanied the baby wherever it was sleeping, playing in its own crib, being fed, bathed, or diapered. A place was designated for me in the kitchen, bedroom, and living room where I could make entries in the running record, having an unimpeded view of the baby, who could not see me. All observations were entered in a running record with reference to a continuously running clock. However, the times of entries were determined by the actual occurrence of the behavior pattern in real time, and not by an arbitrary time-sampling procedure. A stopwatch was also used to measure the exact duration of behavioral states and other time-distributed events, and to quantify the temporal organization of rhythmic motor patterns.

One major category of description was, as already indicated, the infant's *behavioral states*. In earlier reports, I had defined the infant's behavioral states as mutually exclusive organismic dispositions like wakefulness and sleep, that apparently had a causal relation to, or were at least correlated with moment-to-moment fluctuations in the type and frequency of spontaneous-movement patterns as well as to variations of input-output relationships in response to environmental events. During the intervening years, refined polygraphic studies by many investigators have generally confirmed the initial conclusion that behavioral states are an essential ordering principle for all infant studies, whether their orientation is primarily clinical or experimental (Prechtl and O'Brien 1982). However, most of our systematic information about behavioral states in young infants comes from the study of newborns in the nursery; and we still know remarkably little about the development of the behavioral states and particularly of states of *wakefulness* that undergo dramatic changes during the early months after birth. Yet these are in effect the organismic dispositions within which infants carry out most of those transactions with their social and intellectual environment that will have a direct and probably a causal bearing on their intellectual and social-emotional development. Considerable space and time will therefore be devoted to a description of waking states and their differentiation during the first six months.

In other reports I had outlined the natural history of two "universal" *emotional expressions*—smiling and crying—over the first three months after birth (Wolff 1963, 1969). During the intervening years, emotions, affects, and emotional expressions have again become a major focal point of infant research (Campos et al. 1983), as well as a topic for elaborate theoretical speculations. Empirical observations by others indicate that the repertory of emotional expressions in young infants is far richer than was once thought, and greater than my previous descriptions might have implied. Expansion of the repertory of "basic" emotions in young infants confirmed the impression that considerable ambiguity still surrounds the term "emotion." Even today a great deal of confusion remains about what exactly emotions are or do; whether the term connotes observable motor expression, measurable processes of the autonomic nervous system, nonobservable feelings including "unconscious affects," temperament, moods, states, or all of these. Without risking still another a priori definition of emotion, I will attempt a more detailed developmental description and experimental analysis of smiling and crying. Further, I will describe other motor patterns generally classified as expressions of emotion; and with some hesitation I will propose one strategy for exploring the presumed functional significance or "meaning" of emotional expressions in infants, that does not, I hope, succumb to untestable speculations or appeals to self-evidence and "clinical experience."

Motor coordination remains a relatively neglected field in contemporary investigations of human infants, despite its central position for all observational studies of infants. Carmichael's manual and Mussen's *Handbook of Child Psychology* are probably the most extensive and detailed English-language reviews of the empirical literature in infant and child studies. Yet they devote no chapter to motor processes in infancy; even their indices contain only a few explicit references to motor behavior (Mussen 1970, 1983). This omission does not come as any surprise if we accept the premise that the categories of behavioral description for infants have come, by and large, from psychological theories about adult behavior; and that the conduct of systematic studies of motor coordination and performance in adults has until recently been isolated almost completely from university departments of psychology. The omission becomes more surprising when we consider that such systematic investigations of motor control have become an important growing point of research in human brain-behavior relationships (Bernstein 1967; Kelso and Tuller 1983). However, with respect to infant studies, the omission becomes glaring when we consider that movements are our only source of information about what infants perceive, do, feel, or think (Wolff 1982) and therefore they constitute a category that should in principle be of critical interest for any study of behavioral development in human infancy. Throughout the chapters to follow, I will use units of motor coordination in order to examine the organizational features of behavioral states, expressions of emotion, and the infant's relations to persons and things. The use of motor coordination as the source of behavioral units has numerous strategic advantages. Motor processes provide a natural bridging framework for investigating human brain-behavior relations in adults (Lashley 1951; Sperry 1951), and perhaps in infants (Thelen 1985). Units of analysis appropriate for studies of motor coordination can be stated, on the one hand, in physiologically plausible terms relevant for the neurological sciences; on the other hand, in behaviorally plausible terms relevant for the psychological and developmental disciplines. Such bridging concepts are particularly useful for the study of early infancy where it is always difficult to make any clear separation between the psychological and biological domains of behavioral organization.

The infant's relation to *persons and things* served as a frame of reference for discrete observations and experiments on the early differentiation between social-affective and intellectual development. Some current theories hold that the naive infant's repertory of social-adaptive behavior patterns is rigorously controlled by genetic factors, such behavior patterns running their course relatively independent of intellectual or cognitive development. Competing theories assume a priori that the development of social relationships is intimately and indissociably linked with processes of cognitive development, while still other theories hold that age-related changes in the infant's relation to physical objects and to persons conform to the same general laws of learning, so that the conventional distinctions between social-affective and goal-directed instrumental behavior become meaningless. These competing claims are largely based on evidence from the experimental analysis of behavior in children and adults rather than in infants, and infant observations are usually made to fit with what we know, or think we know, about the end stages in the development of emotions and social processes. The observations I have summarized under this heading were not intended either as a detailed replication of previous studies on the sensori-

15

motor intelligence during the first six months (Piaget 1952, 1954), or as a test of specific hypotheses about early affective relations between the infant and significant persons in its proximal environment. Instead they were designed to reexamine some of the strong claims that have been made about similarities and differences in the infant's relation to inanimate objects and persons.

In keeping with my general purpose of presenting a comprehensive natural-history account of behavioral development in healthy human infants, it would have been a serious omission to leave out all references to the infant's transactions with mother, father, siblings and pets (as well as with my constantly looming presence). There is a considerable body of clinical and normative observation to indicate that the quality of the social context is a critical determinant of early human development, certainly more important than the studies to follow would suggest, but perhaps not as crucial as current fashions of infant research would suggest. The "mother-child interaction" that has become so central to so many contemporary studies in infant development was not chosen as a focus of investigation or experimental analysis. For one thing I knew little enough about what infants actually do in their home environment, so that the added burden of describing the behavioral characteristics of another individual whose motives and causes for action were even more complex, and then to characterize the new units of behavior emerging from their interaction (Fentress 1976), would have seriously interfered with the main goals of the study. For another thing, there are, as far as I can tell, no formal procedural guidelines or units of measurement at present which reliably and validly identify the *interactants* in any interaction, in contrast to those discrete action patterns that may be observed when two individuals happen to be acting on each other and responding to each other in linear sequence (Dawkins 1976; Wolff 1981). Dyadic relationships as dynamic processes are now considered to be a central issue in all studies of infant development, but the confusions commonly resulting from any effort to study such relationships in terms of essentially linear models have, as far as I can tell, not been resolved to date, despite repeated efforts to remedy the problem. (e.g., Lewis and Lee-Painter 1974; Brazelton et al. 1975; Stern 1977).

Objective Recordings

Technical recording equipment was kept to a minimum to preserve the nonintrusiveness of the observations. Since the time when infant studies were first incorporated into systematic programs of developmental psychology, there have been major technical advances in methods of objective data collection, polygraphic recording, and telemetry, some of which are directly relevant for the units of observation for the present study. Prechtl's refined studies on behavioral states in the full-term newborn and premature infant, for example, illustrate the great advantages that can be derived from a combination of carefully controlled polygraphic recordings and behavioral observations. Yet these methods are useful primarily when applied under the controlled environment of the laboratory or neonatal nursery. If introduced into the home, the same methods would probably have yielded unreliable data, while at the same time disrupting precisely those behavioral sequences that were central to the proposed studies. Moreover, polygraphic recordings are considerably less reliable as criteria for classifying *waking* than sleep states, even during the newborn period. At the same time one cannot overlook the fact that there are obvious advantages to using objective recording methods. Without them, for example, the quantitative data on behavioral state duration, state transitions, and the like are certain to be less reliable than measures of state duration based on meter readings (Prechtl 1974; Prechtl and O'Brien 1982).

Some relatively simple methods of instrumental recording were, however, introduced, particularly on days of experimental manipulations, and these included a pneumotachograph to monitor respirations during sleep; pressure transducers to investigate nutritive and nonnutritive sucking patterns; audio tape recorders to collect samples of cry and noncry vocalizations for off-line spectographic analysis and to prepare auditory stimulus sequences to play back to the infant; and high-speed 16mm film sequences for the detailed analysis of particular behavior patterns.

Data Reduction

Many of the discrete observations could be reduced to frequency counts within and across babies; in some cases, such data also lent themselves to nonparametric statistical analysis. However, in many other cases, even frequency counts would have been meaningless, and efforts at statistical analysis would have served no purpose. For example, a number of the observations described below refer to events that were apparently unique to a particular child, and could not be demonstrated as a stable phenomenon in other infants. The conservative strategy might therefore have been to discard these observations. However, when such behavior patterns were analyzed for their presumed "underlying function," theoretically relevant similarities across infants emerged, even when the surface features of the behavior patterns were radically different across individual infants. Such observations were therefore left in raw form and are reported as individual case histories, occasionally supplemented by informal experiments; but for obvious reasons they were not reported as group data.

The number of infants observed longitudinally was small relative to the number of behavioral categories scored on each infant. Furthermore, new items (both categories in the running record and experimental manipulations) were added to the protocol during the course of the project, and the number of data points for any behavioral category was not always the same during the course of the project. Whenever the total number of infants tested on a particular category departs significantly from the total sample of infants studied over one, three, or six months, the departures are noted in the text. Another limitation on the use of statistical analysis was that experimental interventions could be carried out systematically only while infants were in a particular behavioral state appropriate for that experiment, so that a full schedule of observations could not always be completed on each baby every week.

Firm conclusions about early behavioral development based on these findings must therefore be limited to the infants who were actually observed; and without further experimental investigation and independent experiments on different samples, no general conclusions can be drawn. On the other hand, the refined experimental analyses of behavioral development in large samples of young infants under controlled conditions, and based on hypotheses derived from comprehensive theoretical formulations about psychological organization in the adult steady state, may yield results that are irrelevant and misleading, even if they are statistically reliable. Detailed description of spontaneously occurring behavior in the infant's "natural environment," supplemented by informal experiments, therefore seemed the best compromise for the present time.

2

Behavioral States

The category of behavioral states overlaps extensively with all other categories of behavioral development, and will therefore serve as a bridging concept throughout this work. When applied to human infants, the term "behavioral state" has been used in at least two distinct senses: as an "independent variable" or reference criterion which allows one to impose order on otherwise unexplained variations in many physiological and behavioral dependent variables within as well as across healthy and impaired infants; and as a dependent variable that refers to the inherent dynamics of the organism, and by inference to human brain-behavior relationships. In the latter sense, behavioral-state concepts provide the means for analyzing nonlinear input-output relationships between organism and environment; and for analyzing state transitions that are determined by discontinuous relationships among ensembles of state variables rather than as linear changes along a quantitative continuum of levels of arousal or excitation.

In commonsense language, behavioral state refers to the question of whether the infant is awake, asleep, or crying. Polygraphic recordings and detailed observations have refined this taxonomy by identifying different kinds of sleep and different kinds of waking, according to objective criteria which provide the basis for predicting the distribution of spontaneous motor activities as well as variations in the nonlinear input-output relations of human infant behavior. Nearly all contemporary studies of normal and functionally impaired infants have found it both convenient and methodologically essential to adopt some classification of state variables. However, the periodic state fluctuations that can critically influence spontaneous action and alterations of input-output relations in children and adults are so much a part of our everyday expectation, that we are inclined to take the state variable in the adult more or less for granted. Consequently,

19

there is at present no theoretically based taxonomy of behavioral states in older individuals, and no concerted effort to investigate how state variations might influence actions and performance in normally functioning adults. Yet clinical observations on states of consciousness (Rapaport 1951a,b), ego states (Rapaport 1967), and "state-dependent learning" suggest that the state variable is also a critical factor in the behavioral organization of adults.

In young infants, changes of behavioral state are obvious because they are usually abrupt and unpredictable, and they frequently disrupt ongoing spontaneous activity. Moreover, many environmental events can destabilize at least some of the behavioral states of the young infant. In the adult, by contrast, the interdependence of state and behavior is less fragile and therefore less obvious. Yet a *developmental* analysis of behavioral states beyond infancy may be as important for understanding the nonlinearity of organism environment interactions as it is during infancy.

Whereas the behavioral states of infants are usually defined as independent or classifying variables whenever other dependent measures are under investigation (Hutt et al. 1969; Parmalee and Stern 1972; Anders et al. 1971), the concept of state changes has also been used to connote arbitrary shift along a physiological continuum of arousal or activation. Explicitly or implicitly, this use of the term connotes a central executive or agency such as the ascending reticular activating system, the instincts, or motivational drives that generate, inhibit, modulate, or intensify the expression of particular sensorimotor patterns *but are extrinsic* to the motor patterns they control (Pratt 1937; Sokolov 1963; Birns et al. 1965). Of the many reasons that militate against this usage, which in effect introduces a theoretically unspecified "ghost in the machine" to "explain" behavior and development, some will be discussed in detail below. Probably the most important reason for rejecting this conception of state are empirical observations demonstrating that state fluctuations modify the organism's input-output relations not as linear but as essentially nonlinear functions. The assumption of nonlinearity is critical for any coherent attempt to account for the causes of spontaneous motor patterns and their state dependence, and it will serve as the conceptual basis for integrating the many observations indicating dramatic differences in the self-correcting or self-equilibrating potential of the various behavioral states in response to exteroceptive stimulation. Linearity, which will be contrasted with nonlinearity throughout the discussion of findings, can be defined informally as a direct one-to-one correspondence between input (stimulus) and output (response). The more intense the input, the greater the output in a near-linear relationship. Linear dynamic systems (those which evolve in time in a well-defined way) conform to a fundamental "superposition property," such that if one can describe numerically the different ways in which such a system behaves and adds any two or more numerical descriptions, their sum will also describe a possible behavior of the system. Physical examples of such linear dynamic systems are common, and they usually conform to the behavior of machine models. In the psychological disciplines, experimental psychophysics and behaviorism constitute familiar explicit examples. Many important and interesting functional properties emerging from the interaction of biological systems are inherently nonlinear, so that the systems exhibit no one-to-one correspondence between input and output and do not conform to the superposition property. Very small perturbations, fluctuations within the system, or stimuli from the outside can be amplified into massive changes, "catastrophes," or "bifurcations" (Prigogine and Stengers 1984). Dynamic nonlinearities may also account for the many observations indicating that relatively minor stimuli or perturbations will, in some behavioral states but not in others, generate disproportionately large effects, resulting either in "chaos" or qualitative state changes.

In behavioral studies on young infants, the effect of nonlinear transfer functions is made evident by the observation that physically identical stimuli may produce very different motor outputs in different behavioral states, and that *spontaneous* motor patterns are asymmetrically distributed across the various states. A slight jar to the crib of the infant will, for example, produce a massive startle response when the infant is in "deep," regular, or state I sleep, but the same stimulus will produce either no response or a minor movement in "light," irregular, or state II sleep, or when the infant is fully awake (Wolff 1966). Prechtl and his colleagues (Prechtl et al. 1967; Lenard et al. 1968) have presented many controlled observations that illustrate the same nonlinearity of input-output relations as a function of state (see also Richmond et al. 1953). Such observations were the empirical basis for defining states as discontinuous ensembles of self-organizing variables rather as conditions corresponding to differences in levels of arousal or excitation along a continuum of linear input-output relations. They were also the basis for planning concrete experiments designed to address questions such as how behavioral states of the infant are organized, maintained, or altered in the

21

presence of extrinsic perturbations; along what parameters states alter organism-environment interactions; and how new states are induced during ontogenesis.

This second definition of behavioral state as a dependent variable rather than as an independent classifying criterion does, however, raise technically difficult questions. For example, why do we identify five rather than two, seven, or twelve states when there are no logical constraints on the number of state criteria that can be selected, and therefore no self-evident limitation on the number of possible combinations among variables that may coalesce as stable ensembles? In practice, however, there are only a limited number of discontinuous states, or a limited number of ways in which collectives of essential state-variables are aggregated as self-organizing conditions exhibiting discontinuous properties of nonlinear input-output relationships. These properties, rather than the variables themselves, provide the most direct window on human brain-behavior relationships.

Addressing very different theoretical problems of motor coordination in voluntary action, Kelso and Tuller (1983) proposed a formulation of states which may be directly relevant to the issues considered here: "Systems at many scales of magnitude exhibit transitions from one state to another that are continuous even though the factors controlling the process change continually. Transitions from one mode to another are discontinuous, not because there are no possible intervening states but because none of them is stable. Thus transitions from one state to another are likely to be brief compared to the time spent in stable states. . . . there may be a relatively small number of ways for it to change *discontinuously*. We associate the discontinuity with nonlinear properties that are revealed when the system is scaled to some 'critical value'."

Prechtl and his colleagues (Prechtl 1974; Prechtl and O'Brien 1982) have formulated a logically consistent and operationally defined classification of behavioral states that is biologically valid and clinically feasible. By combining the data of direct observation and physiological recording, and without either insisting that behavioral states are fixed entities to be discovered by empirical investigation or denying that such categorization is to some extent arbitrary, they have recommended that the number of essential state criteria should be limited to four or five. Moreover, the discriminating variables should be continuous, whereas the *patterns* among variables should be discontinuous and clearly distinguishable. In this way a formal scale of behavioral states for full-term infants could be constructed which requires binary decisions on each of four variables, and the definition of combinations among the four variables which are mutually exclusive and readily distinguished from one another.

The five behavioral states of the newborn infant that will also serve as a first approximation for the present studies were taken primarily from Prechtl's taxonomy for newborn infants, and they include:

State I (regular, quiet, synchronous, or non-REM sleep). The infant is at rest, and resistance of the limbs to passive movement is low. There is little diffuse motor activity except for intermittent myoclonic jerks ("spontaneous startles") and occasional bursts of rhythmic mouthing. The eyelids are firmly closed and at rest; spontaneous eye-movements observed through the eyelids are rare. The face is relaxed and symmetrical; there are no or few facial grimaces, chewing, or gross mouthing movements. The skin is pale or light pink. Respirations are regular in rhythm and constant in amplitude. Their mean frequency is 36 per minute, and the frequency varies from 30 to 40 per minute.

State II (irregular sleep, paradoxical REM sleep, etc.). The eyes are closed and may be pinched or relaxed. Intermittent eye movements in the horizontal and vertical directions can be observed through the eyelids. Respirations are irregular and their amplitude and frequency vary continuously; but the mean rate of respiration is faster during state I (average: 48 per minute), and brief apneic spells may interrupt the overall pattern of respiration. The face is relaxed except for intermittent grimaces that range in type from "smiling" to sneering, frowning, puckering, pouting, or making of pre-cry faces. The infant may chomp or tongue but the mouthing follows no orderly sequence and can be readily distinguished from the rhythmic mouthings usually observed in state I. Resistance of the limbs to passive movement is greater than during state I. Motor activity varies from general limb movements to occasional voluptuous stirring that involves the trunk and one or more limbs and head. Limb movements follow no obvious temporal sequence, and periods of relative inactivity vary randomly with periods of stirring. The skin is usually pale or pink but may become flushed during a burst of activity.

State III (alert inactivity). The limbs and trunk are at rest except for occasional small movements. the face is relaxed but the eyes are open and have a "bright, shiny appearance." Respirations are more

23

variable and faster than in state I but generally constant in amplitude and rate. While alert, the infant scans the environment with directed or undirected intricate eye movements; it usually maintains a stable posture and after a general readjustment posture usually comes to rest again.

State IV (waking activity). This state is characterized by frequent bursts of generalized motor activity involving the limbs, trunk, and head which varies in intensity and duration. The eyes are open and the infant may be silent or moaning, grunting or whimpering, but it does not cry for sustained periods. The face is relaxed during periods of inactivity and may be pinched into a precry face when the limbs are moving. When the infant is active, the skin becomes flushed. Respirations are grossly irregular, and on the polygraph respiratory movements are obscured by motor artifacts. The eyes may scan the environment intermittently but only during periods of relative motor inactivity.

State V (crying). Cry vocalizations are the essential defining criterion; they may vary in intensity from persistent whimpering to loud screaming. Vigorous cry vocalizations are accompanied by diffuse motor activity or a rigid posture of the trunk in partial extension. During vigorous crying, resistance of the limbs to passive movement is high; the face is contorted into a cry grimace and may be flushed bright red. Except during the early stages, patterns of respiration are subordinate to crying. Even during the first twenty-four hours after birth, some infants show tears when they cry vigorously.

These five states constitute the basic taxonomy of organismic conditions that recur repeatedly in the young infant and can be recognized easily when they occur again. They are present in all healthy newborns and organized in predictable temporal sequences. Were one to apply only one or two state-criteria it would be possible to classify a large number of other "dispositions" of the infant. In fact, a number of such conditions have occasionally been included in extant behavioral-state taxonomies, but they are usually of short duration and do not fulfill the generic definition of coherent ensembles of mutually exclusive constellations. Therefore they were classified as transitions rather than as states for purposes of this study.

The classification of sleep states remains generally applicable throughout the first six months and beyond (Roffwarg et al. 1966), but the taxonomy of nonsleep states that is appropriate for classifying waking conditions of the neonate proves to be unsuitable for the description of waking and crying states in older infants. For the developmental analysis of wakefulness I therefore included at least one other waking-state wakefulness that does not satisfy the criteria of states III or IV, but does fulfill the generic definition of a behavioral state specified earlier.

Alert Activity. This category is not readily observed in the neonate, but takes up increasing periods of time after the second month. The infant engages in controlled motor actions of limited intensity and frequency that may sometimes have a rhythmical character, or may be goal-directed, while the eyes are open and have a "bright, shiny appearance" and may scan the environment concomitant with ongoing movement patterns. The face is relaxed, visual pursuit of globally directed actions is not associated with inhibition of limb movements, unlike during the neonatal period when infants will either spontaneously or in response to environmental inputs involve in only one goal-directed activity. Alert activity is characterized by capacity to engage in two or more acquired goal-directed actions at once. The definition of alert activity proposed here departs from the procedural guidelines recommended by Prechtl for classifying behavioral states of the newborn; it thus violates the prescription of limiting the criteria to continuous variables scaled at different parameters across states by identifying a feature that is unique to one state and not observed in others. For the sake of consistency it might therefore be parsimonious to include alert activity as a variation of state III. My reasons for breaking with convention will, I hope, become apparent in the substantive chapters to follow in which I will also suggest that a broader theoretical formulation of behavioral states of wakefulness and sleep is required (Wolff 1984) that may partially address developmental questions concerning the emergence of new behavioral forms and functions during ontogenesis.

For similar reasons the question of state-transitions will be examined in greater detail than has been the custom in discussions of behavioral states during the neonatal period. Transitions are points in the daily cycle of sleep and waking when one can most clearly observe the self-organizing and disequilibrating features of behavioral states which may be clues as to how novel behavioral forms are induced during development. A number of observations and some of the discussion will be devoted directly to descriptions of drowsiness and fussing, as conditions of the infant that do not qualify as behavioral in any sense but nevertheless can provide important clues about the organismic substrate that facilitates the emergence of new behavioral forms.

Sleep States

Of all the behavioral states of human infants, sleep has been most thoroughly studied and is probably best understood, because neonates spend the better part of the twenty-four-hour day asleep during the first five days in the nursery. During that time they are also a captive population that is readily available for polygraphic studies under the carefully controlled laboratory conditions of the nursery. By contrast, little is known about the *development* of behavioral states after infants go home from the nursery. Polygraphic studies in the home are not satisfactory because infants rapidly adapt to the daily routine of their familiar surroundings; and the experimental manipulations required for polygraphic recordings become an irritant that interferes with the phenomenon being studied (Emde and Harmon 1972; Sosteck and Anders 1975), whereas bringing infants into the laboratory for polygraphic examination simply exaggerates this disruptive effect. Extended home observations therefore provided a unique opportunity to fill in missing information about the development of sleep states during the daytime, even though direct observations alone do not achieve the degree of quantitative precision that is possible with physiologic recordings.

Global Quantitative Data

In the running record all notations on behavioral sleep states lasting three minutes or longer that were not disrupted by maternal interventions or environmental disturbances were tabulated for duration and temporal sequence. The results were computed first as percentages of total observation time. As figure 1 indicates, infants as a group spend three-fourths of the day asleep during the first week at home, and one-fourth of the day awake. By the end of the third month, however, they were awake for 65 percent of daytime observations, and the amount of daytime sleep decreased correspondingly in near linear fashion from the first to the third month. Despite considerable intra- and inter-individual variations in daytime sleep duration, which are not accurately reflected in figure 1, the overall trends described in that figure were the same across infants, regardless of baseline values at which they started. Biweekly and monthly decreases in daytime sleep duration were statistically significant (p<.001,

% TOTAL OBSERVATION TIME

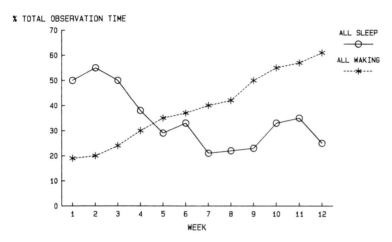

Figure 1: Daytime Sleep and Waking

by Friedman two-way analysis of variance). With two exceptions the many potential sources of the individual variations in daytime sleep could not be inferred from the observations alone. The exceptions were that when infants were mildly ill with a cold or other infection, they usually slept much longer than when they were healthy. Similarly, when they had gastrointestinal upsets such as "colic" they were more restless and their sustained daytime sleep was shorter.

The duration of daytime sleep also differed significantly between bottle and breast-fed infants. Bottle-fed infants slept less overall (as percentage of daytime observations) and were awake and alert for longer periods, than breast-fed infants during the first and second months ($p < .02$, by Mann-Whitney-U Test). By the third month, such group differences had essentially disappeared.

For reasons of convenience and the parents' privacy, I never observed infants during the nighttime hours from 10 P.M. to 8:30 A.M., hours that would have yielded a very different pattern of rest-activity and sleep-waking cycles than those indicated here. I did, however, request all parents to keep diaries of the frequency and time during the night when they were awakened by their infants; what they did for the baby at the time; and what the effect of their intervention was. From such records I was able to reconstruct the approximate nighttime sleep-waking patterns of infants, although parents recorded only occasions when they were awakened by the babies

27

crying or stirring, so that the data do not reflect periods when the infant might have been awake at night without awakening their parents. The diaries indicate that the mean duration of uninterrupted nighttime sleep increased from 210 minutes (3.5 hours) during the first week at home, to 370 minutes (6 hours) by the end of the twelfth week (see also Kleitman 1963). The type of feeding again had a significant influence on the duration of nighttime sleep. Breast-fed infants, who usually came home from the hospital on a demand schedule, slept for an average of two and a half to three hours during the night and did not sleep through the night (i.e., for six hours or more of uninterrupted sleep) until the end of the ninth week. By contrast most bottle fed infants were already on a stable four-hour schedule when they returned from the hospital. They slept without waking their parents for four and a half hours during the night in the first week at home, and by the eighth week were sleeping for an average of seven hours through the night. Differences of sleep patterns between feeding groups were significant during the first six weeks, but had disappeared by the tenth week.

The mean duration of daytime sleep was also used to determine the distribution of rest-activity cycles during the day, and to test whether these cycles followed any distinct (ultradian) pattern. A comparison of time spent asleep and awake during morning hours (8 A.M.–12:30 P.M.), early afternoon hours (12:30 P.M.–5 P.M.), and evening hours (5 P.M.–9:30 P.M.) during the first, second, and third month indicated that no clear pattern or cycling pattern developed either within or across babies. The parents' own sleep-waking habits, the environmental activity level (siblings coming home from school) and the fathers' work schedules apparently influenced the rest-activity cycle of the infants sufficiently so that no "intrinsic" cycling of sleep, waking, or crying at different points during the daytime emerged from these tabulations.

Duration of Sustained Sleep

Cumulative tabulations of total daytime sleep do not disclose the distribution of sustained sleep periods. All individual sleep periods lasting 3 minutes or longer were therefore tabulated separately, and then computed as interval histograms. Infants slept for a mean of 70 minutes without interruption (SD=12.8) in the first week at home; and for a mean of 42 minutes (SD=8.7) by the twelfth week. The mean length of individual periods of uninterrupted sleep decreased significantly from the first to the third month (p<.02). Bottle-fed infants slept significantly longer *at any one time* than breast-fed babies, but their total sleep time was less. The type of feeding as well as the duration of individual periods of daytime sleep both affected the overall amount of sleep, but in opposite directions. By eight or ten weeks these group differences had again disappeared.

During the first month at home the most common duration of single sleep episodes was between 20 and 40 minutes, and this remained the preferred duration until the third month. After the first month long periods of uninterrupted *daytime* sleep lasting 80 minutes or more were no longer observed, while the frequency of relatively short naps of 20 to 40 minutes remained essentially unchanged. In contrast to bottle-fed infants, breast-fed infants slept for many shorter naps disrupted by frequent waking and crying. Breast-feeding mothers also offered their infants the breast on the average two to three times as often as the other mothers offered the bottle, but from the data, I could not determine whether infants awoke frequently because they were never fully satisfied, or whether mothers offered the breast more frequently for reasons of child philosophy and ideology, in this way altering the baby's sleep-waking cycle.

Specific Sleep States

The discussion so far refers to sleep as an undifferentiated disposition, and does not take into account the sleep types which are the point of departure for the classification of behavioral states. My earlier observations of neonates, as well as the polygraphic studies of newborns by others, have repeatedly demonstrated that in the controlled environment of the nursery, two distinct patterns of sleep can easily be recognized. These refer to different organizations among essential behavioral variables, earlier defined as state I and state II. The duration of state I sleep typically lasted for a well-defined period of approximately 20 or 21 minutes; and there was relatively little variation around this central periodicity within or across healthy full-term infants. Sometimes the infants remained in state I for less than 21 minutes, but during the neonatal period they rarely exceeded this preferred duration. By contrast, the duration of state II sleep was quite variable and lasted anywhere from 3 to 45 minutes.

To determine whether the stability of state I sleep persists into the later months, and whether the variability of state II sleep diminishes over time, I again tabulated all sleep episodes from the running record and computed the mean length and variability of each sleep state over the first three months. Figure 2 indicates that the mean duration of individual periods of state I remained remarkedly constant over the first three months (from 20.5 minutes, in the first two months, to 22.0 minutes, in the third month). In infants observed for the first six months the preferred duration of state I was still 21 minutes. This peak duration was characteristic for breast- as well as bottle-fed infants, and for individual babies over time. Its temporal boundaries were sufficiently stable so that the end of any episode of state I could be predicted within two minutes or less from the time of its onset.

By contrast the duration of individual periods of state II sleep remained variable throughout the first six months ranging in duration from three minutes (the lower boundary for defining a behavioral state) to more than seventy minutes, without any central tendency and only a slight trend toward stabilization from the first to the third month (see figure 2). Unobtrusive observations suggest that state I and state II differ qualitatively in their self-organizing potential. In later sections I will amplify this distinction by comparing the degree to which the two sleep conditions are "self-equilibrating" or susceptible to disruption by environmental influences.

Sleep Cycles

The evolution of human sleep, from birth to maturity, has been summarized in detailed reviews by Roffwarg et al. (1966), who used very different terms and relied exclusively on polygraphic criteria to classify sleep but identified essentially the same two kinds of sleep. More recently, observational, polygraphic, and ultrasonic imaging studies

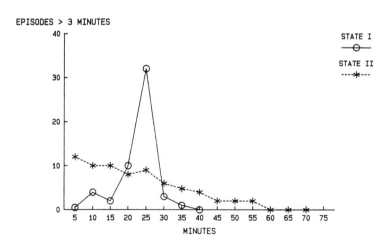

Figure 2: Individual Periods of State I and State II Sleep

30

Table 1: First-Order State Sequences during Sleep

Month	State II–I–II Percent Sequences	State II–I–Drowsy Drowsy–State I–II Percent Sequences	All Other Percent Sequences
1	59.8	25.8	14.4
2	66.2	23.4	8.1
3	46.0	42.8	11.2

have shown that the same two patterns of sleep are established at least six weeks prior to term; and that the same ensembles of behavioral variables that characterize states I and II in the full-term newborn, can already be recognized as mutually exclusive conditions in healthy infants born at thirty-four or thirty-five weeks. By ultrasonic imaging, the component features of respiration, spontaneous motor activity, and perhaps eye movements can also be discerned as isolated events or as more limited coalitions long before thirty-five weeks of gestation (Nijhuis et al. 1984). Most of the systematic data on the development of sleep cycles during early infancy have, however, been reconstructed from cross-sectional observations. The longitudinal home observations again provided a unique opportunity to trace the ontogenesis of *daytime* sleep. When all periods of state I lasting 15 minutes or longer were used as a reference point, and the behavioral states immediately preceding and following this reference point were tabulated, more than half of the state I episodes within and across babies were preceded and followed by a period of state II (see table 1). Another 15 percent of state I periods were either preceded or followed by a period of drowsiness. The sequence: state II–state I–state II, was by far the most common pattern of state sequences observed during the first week after birth; and it remained the preferred pattern of sequences until the end of the third month. Thereafter the sequence was modified to some extent. State I might be preceded by a sequence of waking and drowsiness without a preparatory phase of state II. Similarly a state I episode was sometimes followed directly by drowsiness and waking without an intervening episode of state II. Direct transitions from full waking to state I, without an intervening period of either state II or drowsiness, were very rare at any time during the first six months. Abrupt shifts from state I to full waking without an intervening phase of either state II or drowsiness, comprised at most 7 percent of all transitions, even in the fifth and sixth months.

An extension of this reconstruction of state sequences from the running record that would include the "next but one" condition before or after state I as a reference point, was complicated by the fact that sustained periods of daytime sleep commonly included two complete cycles of state II–state I–state II (10 percent of all occasions of prolonged sleep). The initiation of state I from waking by way of state II was also frequently facilitated (and for purposes of observation distorted) by parental interventions such as a feeding or the efforts to wake a baby from state II for a change of diapers and an overdue feeding. The extended reconstruction of state sequences supports the impression that during the early months, infants almost never shifted from wakefulness to state I without an intervening period of state II lasting at least three minutes. By the end of the third month, the elapsed time between the end of the full waking and the onset of state I sleep had shortened considerably, and much of the decrease in latency was accounted for by shorter transitions or conditions of drowsiness. By contrast, the latency of transition from the end of state I to the onset of full waking did not decrease over the first three months, in part because the duration of drowsiness in the transition from sleep to waking did not decrease in length. Figure 3

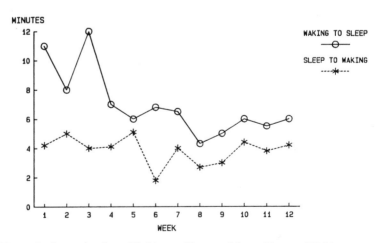

Figure 3: Latencies from Waking to Sleep and from Sleep to Waking

summarizes such observations for all occasions not modified by parental intervention or environmental disturbances which might have accelerated such a transition. The interval from waking to sleep decreased significantly from the first to the second to the third month (p<.01, Friedman two-way analysis of variance), but the interval from sleeping to waking did not show any similar developmental trends over the first six months. In each month, the infants needed more time to fall asleep (i.e., to enter state I) than they needed to wake up (to enter an alert state) from state I. Such differences would suggest that the time "needed" to assemble the component behavior elements constituting state I as a self-equilibrating condition was longer than the time needed to disrupt the conditon of state I in preparation for a period of wakefulness.

Discrete Motor Events during Sleep

The sleep patterns of young infants differ markedly from those of children and adults by the discrete or generalized spontaneous-movement patterns observed during sleep. Such differences pertain not only to the overall amount of movement but also to the kinds of movement patterns, their distribution in behavioral sleep states, and their temporal organization. Such movements are identified here as "spontaneous" because they were not induced by any obvious or known external stimulus, they were observed consistently across all infants at least during the early weeks, and they could at the same time be provoked by environmental stimuli in essentially the same form when the appropriate stimulus parameter was presented in the appropriate behavioral state. The term "spontaneous" therefore is used simply to indicate that there were no obvious causal conditions. The distributions of spontaneous-movement patterns during sleep was clearly state-related; and an analysis of the distribution of spontaneous movements as a function of state provides some hints about the characteristic behavioral patterns that distinguish state I and state II sleep.

Spontaneous Startles. During the first five days after birth, all full-term infants demonstrated intermittent generalized muscle jerks which involved the trunk and limbs as well as the head in various combinations. Such jerks started from a condition of complete rest, they were sudden in onset, and after two or three seconds of movement they were usually followed by a return to the state that preceded the jerk. Spontaneous startles varied in intensity as well as in the component motor elements involved. Some were limited to an extension of the arms, shoulders, and elbows; others included a partial flexion of the wrist and a hyperextension of the fingers as well as an occasional hyperextension of the head and an arching of the trunk. In form these "spontaneous" startles were very similar to the elicited Moro reflex of the neurological examination, except that they occurred in absence of any obvious stimulus and were more variable in intensity and their component motor elements. During the first twenty-four hours after birth in full-term infants, spontaneous startles were widely distributed across state I, state II, drowsiness, and occasionally in waking states. By the second day, 85 percent of all startles occurred in state I; the residual 15 percent were distributed between state II and drowsiness, where they were never as forceful or complete (see table 2).

When spontaneous startles occurred toward the end of an episode of state I sleep, they seemed to precipitate a change of state, but

Table 2: Spontaneous Startles and Sighing Inspirations in State I Sleep (Mean Intervals between Motor Events in Minutes)

Week	Startles	Sighs
1	5.03	6.0
2	10.3	7.1
3	13.3	7.7
4	12.1	8.1
5	19.0	7.9
6	12.3	10.9
7	13.9	8.8
8	(118.7)	(39.6)
9	—	(20.7)
10	—	7.7
11	—	14.1
12	—	11.8

this association was noted only after the infants had already been in state I for at least sixteen to eighteen minutes. Many periods of state I sleep ended without any startle, whereas many startles occurred in the middle of state I sleep without disrupting sleep, the infant settling back to stable sleep after a brief stir. The potentially disruptive effect of spontaneous startles was more clearly demonstrated during drowsiness, when infants showed relatively frequent and forceful spontaneous startles. In some infants spontaneous startles had the paradoxical effect of "preventing" them from falling asleep exactly at those times of complete motor arrest that should have facilitated the transition from waking to sleep. The possible reasons for such spontaneous startles are discussed below.

As long as spontaneous startles in state I were a common occurrence they tended to occur at near periodic intervals of about three minutes; as their overall frequency diminished during the first month at home, their periodicity was also no longer apparent. By seven weeks spontaneous startles during state I had become a chance event (see table 2).

Rhythmic Mouthing. All healthy full-term infants, most pre-term infants after thirty-six weeks of gestation, and many infants with severe central nervous system pathology responded to a blind pacifier with sucking movements that are typically organized as alternations of bursts and rest periods (Wolff 1968a; see figure 4a). Such *nonnutritive* sucking patterns differ in both function and temporal organization from nutritive sucking (Wolff 1972a). Nonnutritive sucking was of particular interest in the present context because its overall temporal organization was remarkably similar to the spontaneous mouthing movements observed during sleep when infants had no nipple in the mouth (see also Salzarulo et al. 1980). The hypothesis that nonnutritive sucking on a blind nipple and spontaneous mouthing in sleep may be homologues sharing common mechanisms of temporal regulation, is suggested by a fine-grained analysis of polygraphic data indicating that nonnutritive sucking patterns and spontaneous mouthing are typically organized in bursts of six to twelve sequential mouthing movements followed by a rest period of four or five seconds. Although there are some quantitative differences, the organization of spontaneous mouthing during state I sleep is essentially the same. When infants are alert, or in state II, the constant alternation of bursts and rest periods with a pacifier in the mouth can continue for up to fifteen minutes (see figure 4a), whereas *nutritive* sucking has very different temporal organization. At the start of a feeding when the infant is hungry, nutritive sucking is usually organized as a continuous stream of sucks at half the mean frequency of nonnutritive sucking (Wolff 1972a). It is not organized in well-defined sequences of bursts and rest periods until near the end of a feeding, when the drowsy infant may periodically break the vacuum seal around the nipple and switch back and forth between nutritive and nonnutritive patterns of sucking. The formal distinction between nutritive and nonnutritive sucking patterns may be blurred unless their respective temporal patterns are analyzed by a fine time-window, instead of being averaged across one-minute ep-

Nonnutritive Sucking

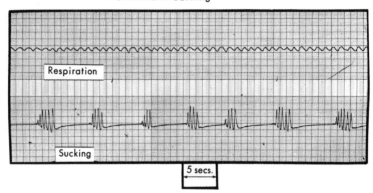

Nutritive sucking

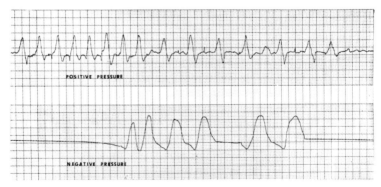

Figure 4: a. (above) Nonnutritive Sucking in State I

b. (below) Shift from Nonnutritive to Nutritive Sucking as Nipple Delivers Milk (Time-scale Doubles That of 4a)

36

ochs or for an entire meal (Crook and Lipsit 1976; see figure 4b). The analysis of serial order in human sucking becomes of broader theoretical interest when we consider that nonnutritive sucking as a coordinated motor pattern with a temporal organization distinct from that of nutritive sucking, is probably unique to the human species.

Nonhuman mammals, including the great apes, do not exhibit two distinct temporal patterns of sucking corresponding to the nutritive and nonnutritive functions, although some species of mammals will suck in the "nutritive mode" on nipples which produce no nutrient (Wolff 1968c).

Observation on human infants, children, and adults with major neurological impairment indicated that all healthy infants up to the age of three or four months, as well as older children who have been accustomed to the pacifier, will respond to the blind pacifier in the typical rest-burst pattern at a mean frequency of 2.0–2.4 sucks per second within each burst. Normal adults cannot produce a stable pattern even if they know what the expected performance should be and make a concerted effort to reproduce the pattern. By contrast, individuals at all ages can easily reproduce the usual nutritive pattern when asked to take fluid through a feeding nipple. After the sixth month, infants not accustomed to the pacifier no longer respond in the typical rest-burst pattern at the specified frequency, although the original pattern can be reinstated in these infants during early stages of surgical anesthesia when the anesthesia is administered rectally while sucking patterns are recorded orally (Wolff 1972a). Among adults, only severely impaired decorticate neurological patients will exhibit the nonnutritive pattern at a mean frequency of 2.4–2.5 per second within bursts, and will continue in this pattern for extended periods without evidence of the fatigue that rapidly sets in among normal adults who attempt to reproduce the pattern. These comparison studies suggest that the temporal organization of nonnutritive sucking reflects a highly specialized neuromotor timing mechanism which is unique to the human species, and is usually suppressed during development or "maturation" but can reemerge in adults under conditions of severe neurological dedifferentiation.

Nonnutritive sucking on a pacifier was described in such detail because it is similar, and perhaps homologous, to the pattern of spontaneous oral activity observed during state I sleep. Healthy infants frequently show small lip-movements during sleep with the same rhythmical rest-burst patterns and approximately the same frequency of movements per burst as nonnutritive sucking on a pacifier

37

in other states, even though there are slight differences in the mean number of sucks per burst, the duration of rest periods, and the frequency of mouthing movements per burst due to a rubber nipple which introduces changes in the biomechanical properties of the motor pattern.

Of the twenty-two infants in the longitudinal study, only eight showed such spontaneous mouthing in state I during the first five days, but by the second week twelve of the infants showed it consistently; and by the end of the fifth week fifteen did. Two of the infants were never observed to mouth rhythmically in state I sleep, although they sucked in the usual temporal pattern on a blind pacifier; the remaining infants showed spontaneous mouthing only on occasion. The mean rate of spontaneous mouthing was remarkably stable over the period of observation; it was slightly, but consistently, faster than the same infants' nonnutritive sucking rate (mean rate of 2.4 sucks per second per burst without a pacifier, as compared to a mean rate of 2.2 sucks per second with the pacifier). Salzarulo et al. (1980), who used surface electromyography to compare spontaneous mouthing and nonnutritive sucking, came to essentially the same conclusion I had reached; namely, that the two oral motor patterns probably utilize a common timing mechanism.

Sighing Inspirations. Respirations during state I sleep approximate a sinusoidal wave pattern, with a relatively constant rate and amplitude; but by polygraphic recording, the breathing patterns were not invariant from the start to the end of any one 20–22 minute period. Instead, breathing frequency and amplitude decreased gradually, although slightly, from the start to the end of a 21-minute period, which was visually represented as a flattening of the peaks and valleys of the breathing curve, suggesting that when parameter changes on certain physiological variables reach a critical value (in this case, regular respiration), a behavioral state may be terminated "spontaneously."

In addition, the pattern of breathing showed a variation of respiratory movements that was periodically superimposed on the continuous breathing curve. These sighing inspirations during state I may be of theoretical interest as a physiological mechanism that prevents premature termination of state I by resetting the respiratory rhythm. The amplitude and rise time of sighing inspirations are considerably greater than the usual respiratory movements. During sleep, they corresponded exactly to those occasions when infants made a deep, sighing, sobbing sound, and these were sometimes followed by a slight shudder of the trunk. Sighing inspirations were present in full-term infants, and remained a stable feature of state I sleep, at least until the end of the sixth month, although their frequency gradually diminished. At least by anecdotal observations of sleeping young children and adults, they probably remain a constant feature of deep sleep throughout life.

During the early weeks after birth, the sighing inspirations occurred at a preferred rate of about every three to five minutes. Immediately after a sigh, the infant stirred and changed its posture but then returned to a stable respiratory pattern of larger amplitude and faster rate, similar to that observed at the beginning of a state I sleep episode.

Using pneumometric impedence pneumography, Fleming et al. (1984) recorded respiratory patterns and sighs in infants ranging in age from twenty-two hours to six months. The aim of the study was to examine changes in ventilation as well as the characteristics of brief apneic spells that followed after such sighs. Its results suggested that the infant's respiratory control operates like a linear second-order system during the period immediately following the transient perturbations of sighing. Thus, sighing may intermittently "recalibrate" the rate and amplitude of regular respirations, in this way maintaining the intrinsic stability of state I sleep.

Facial Grimaces. Premature and full-term infants exhibited a wide range of facial expressions during state II sleep which were not related to any obvious environmental events; they followed no particular temporal sequence and were apparently instigated by intrinsic or "spontaneous" mechanisms. Such sleep grimaces have sometimes been interpreted as precursors of emotional expressions in waking infants. In fact, according to their surface appearance, they run the gamut of emotional expressions from smiling to frowning, sneering, surprise, contempt and disgust, that can also be observed in adults (see, for example, Darwin 1873). Of the various facial expressions that can be observed in the premature and full-term infant, "endogenous" or spontaneous smiles in sleep, which have been described in greatest detail, have sometimes been referred to as "precursors" of social smiling (Emde and Koenig 1969). What exactly might be meant by precursor is unclear since it seems to be only the face, and not the baby, that is smiling; and one would presumably have to make similar assumptions about these grimaces for an extensive repertory of other expressions of emotion.

A weekly tabulation of the frequency and temporal sequence of various facial grimaces during sleep indicated that they predominated in state II. There was also a close temporal contiguity between "smiling" or other "emotional" grimaces and mouthing and tonguing movements, so that it was often difficult to distinguish between mouthing and smiling. A smile sometimes preceded a distinct mouthing or tonguing movement; at other times the order was reversed, and by behavioral criteria it was impossible to distinguish between the two.

Apart from the fact that these are apparently spontaneous phenomena, similar to other motor patterns in sleep, it is difficult to draw any inference about the functional significance of such spontaneous grimaces, or about their presumed developmental relations with emotional expressions in older infants. In keeping with Darwin's thesis that the human facial musculature has evolved specifically for the expression of a limited number of distinctive emotions, one could conclude that the individual facial muscles are not combined in arbitrary ensembles varying randomly from one infant to another, but even in the neonate comprise discontinuous collectives of muscle synergies which will later during ontogenesis be utilized for the expression of emotions and further refined by experience. Without such an a priori assumption, it would be hard to imagine how a limited set of expressions of emotion achieve a near universal status in humans from very different cultures with different social sanctions and rules of nonverbal communication. From a developmental perspective, the assertion would be of theoretical interest only if it the facial grimaces of newborn infants could be shown to be identical in form with those of older infants and children. By fine-grained electromyographic analysis it might be possible, for example, to test whether the muscle synergies of emotional expression observed in early infancy are developmentally invariant or qualitatively transformed during the early months. In this way it should be possible to avoid exclusive reliance on pattern perception as a basis for drawing far-reaching conclusions about the developmental invariance and genetic basis of human emotions.

Mouthing Movements. Aside from the rhythmic or periodically repeating mouthing pattern observed primarily in state I, infants also showed nonrhythmical tonguing, chewing, or mouthing movements that could be clearly distinguished from rhythmic mouthing, and were concentrated primarily in state II sleep and drowsiness. They, too, seemed to serve no specific adaptive function, except perhaps of helping the neonate to get rid of inspissated mucus during the first eight hours after birth.

Generalized Movements. Diffuse motility or generalized movements were one criterion by which I distinguished state I from state II, and alert inactivity from waking activity or crying. The term "generalized movements" refers to a heterogeneous collection of motor patterns involving any or all limbs as well as the trunk and head in various combinations, but conforming to no stable spatial configuration or recognizable temporal order. Such movements are prominent aspects of the young infant's motor repertory but diminish over the first six months. Within the context of the "Coghill Windle controversy" on the origins of goal-directed action of human and other animal species (Carmichael 1970), some early investigators of infant behavior assumed that all or nearly all motor activity of the young organism is organized in reflexes or discrete stimulus-response sequences. These comprise building blocks for coordinated action, whereas "mass activity" was reserved as a wastebasket category for movements not conforming to reflex patterns. The assumption holds that the reflex is a neurologically valid entity, and that all later motor acquisitions are in fact composed of reflexes in various combinations (Dennis 1934). A competing perspective on the origin of coordinated movements assumed that mass activity or global movements are a primary condition of the immature motor system, differentiated and integrated actions gradually emerging from mass activity, either under the guidance of an overriding maturational plan or under the pressure of practice and experience (Irwin and Weiss 1930; Pratt 1937). A recent compromise solution proposes that both discrete-movement patterns and generalized movements are inherent characteristics of the immature motor system, but that generalized movements are ontogenetic adaptations which gradually drop out of the developing organism's motor repertory as discrete-action patterns differentiate (Hopkins and Prechtl 1984).

Generalized movements have been measured extensively as an index of the infant's sensitivity to environmental events, as a response to organic stimuli such as hunger and other discomforts, and as a marker variable for clinically relevant individual differences in the choice of psychiatric symptoms. The boundaries of what constitutes generalized movements, and what should be identified as coordinated action, remain ambiguous. For example, the earlier descriptions singled out spontaneous startles, facial grimaces, and

41

rhythmic mouthing for separate discussion while reserving the category of generalized movements for various limb displacements and head/trunk rotations. One approximate distinction that might justify such an arbitrary separation is the hypothesis that generalized movements conform neither to constant spatial configurations nor to recognizable temporal order, whereas spontaneous startles, rhythmic mouthing, and facial grimaces partially fulfill one or both of these criteria (Hopkins and Prechtl 1984). The possibility cannot be excluded that the human capacity for pattern perception is limited, and that a not yet specified time-series analysis would detect complex temporal order in what currently appears to be a random sequence of capricious movement. Moreover, spontaneous startles, for example, are a global term for a wide range of superficially different (more or less "complete" muscle jerks) that have in common only their rapid onset from total rest and their rapid termination.

A distinction between generalized motor activity as spontaneous, and discrete movements as environmentally caused reflexes (Capute et al. 1978), is also not a satisfactory solution. The term "spontaneous" applies equally to well-organized action patterns, such as rhythmic mouthing, and to generalized movements. Recent advances in developmental neurology have demystified the term "spontaneous" by indicating that the central nervous system is always active in all of its parts (Lashley 1951; Weiss 1955; Jeannerod 1985), and that motor activity can be conceived of as the consequence of shifts in the relation between competing component systems or dynamic "bifurcations," as the parameters of one or more state variables are scaled up or down. Similarly, experimental studies on motor coordination demonstrate that the reflex concept is essentially an abstraction of isolated movements produced by arbitrary stimuli, and that the muscle components designated as reflexes are simply elements in a coherent ensemble of movements and postural adjustments widely distributed across the motor system (Greene 1972). Because generalized movements are one of the essential criteria for classifying behavioral states, their surface characteristics will be considered again in other sections. For the present, the categories are used primarily to distinguish state I from state II sleep.

The frequency of mouthing movements, hand-face and hand-mouth contacts, hand sucks, self-initiated rooting, and kicking was counted for five-minute periods in twelve infants of the longitudinal sample. As table 3 indicates, state II was, in fact, an "active" form of sleep, the number of most motor events being significantly greater during state II than state I. The methods of data collection were not

Table 3: Motor Activity Counts as a Function of State (N = 12; Age 1–4 Weeks)

Behavioral Condition	Mouthing/ Tonguing	Hand to Face	Hand to Mouth	Hand Suck	Rooting to Own Hand	Kicking
Sleep State I	0.6	0.1	0.2	1.0	0	0.3
Sleep State II	8.8 (6.0)	4.1 (6.2)	1.6 (2.3)	0.3 (0.9)	0.2 (0.3)	1.2 (2.4)
Drowsy	9.5 (3.6)	5.4 (5.7)	4.0 (5.8)	0	1.6 (2.8)	17.1 (18.3)
Alert Active	19.0 (12.8)	6.3 (4.4)	8.1 (10.6)	2.6 (6.5)	1.3 (4.4)	8.3 (13.3)
Fussing	12.1 (7.7)	15.8 (16.2)	12.1 (10.7)	3.5 (4.2)	2.1 (1.7)	53.1 (33.9)
Crying	6.0 (8.7)	17.5 (16.5)	10.3 (8.8)	2.9 (4.7)	2.7 (3.1)	71.8 (30.1)

precise enough to draw any firm conclusions about the temporal or spatial organization of individual motor patterns, but a tabulation of intervals between individual motor events indicated that there was no obvious regularity or rhythmicity in their temporal distribution. Such a conclusion is consistent, I believe, with the tallies conducted by Prechtl and his colleagues, using ultrasound imaging (de Vries et al. 1984).

The Experimental Manipulation of Sleep States

The findings so far pertain exclusively to unobtrusive observations of sleep during the four days each week set aside for the purpose. Results from these observations were always tabulated separately from experimental observations and manipulations performed in the ten-hour day reserved for that purpose. My unobtrusive observations, and polygraphic studies by others, converge on the conclusion that the "self-organizing" and self-equilibrating properties of the two sleep states differ considerably from each other. State I was characterized by strong "homeostatic" constraints which, by some theoretically undefined process, determined the overall length of individual episodes. Presumably, the essential behavioral state criteria and physiological concomitants were tightly phase-coupled, so that state I could not be easily disrupted by massive muscle jerks or spontaneous startles or environmental perturbations were usually followed by a rapid return to the prestartle condition in which the respirations, heart rate, posture, motility, and input-output relations were reconstituted as a stable ensemble (Prechtl 1974; Prechtl and O'Brien 1982). By contrast, state II sleep appears to have less efficient self-correcting mechanisms. The duration of individual episodes was far more variable, and the infant was much more responsive to adventitious environmental perturbations or organismic stimuli. The greater or lesser self-equilibrating features of the two sleep states were therefore tested directly on days reserved for experimental manipulations, to determine whether and how state I and state II could be either prolonged or terminated prematurely by environmental interventions.

Sleep Prolongation. Traditional cultures have long used continuous, monotonous, or repetitive stimulation to soothe crying babies and, in this way, to facilitate the transition from waking to stable sleep. Modern-day mechanical rockers and sound generators that presumably mimic the human heartbeat are simply commercial exploitations of traditional cradles, rocking chairs, and lullabies. The sleep-inducing effect of monotonous stimulation is a widespread phenomenon extending to adult life (Oswald 1962), and it may also be reflected in the continuous stereotypic movements of psychotic or severely retarded children (Wolff 1968c). As early as 1887, Pavlov (1928) had noted that repetitive conditioning trials induce a hypnotic like state in experimental animals which renders them relatively unresponsive to further conditioning trials; he referred to this effect as active inhibition, and implied that it signaled a shift in behavioral state of the animal itself. From a methodological perspective, this phenomenon of "active inhibition" as a response to conditioning stimuli is of practical importance for the interpretation of "learning experiments" on young infants because the response decrement after repeated stimulus presentations may not demonstrate either habituation or early indications of learning, but may simply reflect a change of behavioral state after repeated stimulation. At the least, the variable of state transitions must be carefully controlled before one can draw any inferences concerning habituation and learning from such observations.

The particular sensory modality in which the infant is presented with monotonous or repetitive stimulation is probably of less importance than the monotony or repetition itself (Brackbill et al. 1966). The effect is one of "soothing" the baby—i.e., modifying its behavioral state from a condition in which it is motorically active to one in which the infant is relaxed, whether such relaxation refers to the quiet alertness that facilitates attending to the environment (as in older infants) or the induction of sleep (as in young infants).

In studies of newborn infants I had previously observed that continuous white noise without any distinctive acoustic or temporal features, as well as monotonous auditory stimulation can convert state II to state I within less than a minute. Once state I had been induced experimentally, it became "self-organizing," persisting for an average duration of twenty-one minutes even when the monotonous sound was turned off. The white noise was also used in home observations one day a week to test whether its stabilizing effect persists after the neonatal period, and whether it can still buffer the infant against disruption by intermittent environmental stimuli (see also Wolff and Simmons 1967). The effect of white noise was also compared to those of cradle rocking and pacifier sucking.

For these observations, the white noise was always turned on five minutes after the infant had fallen asleep (state II) following a period of waking; and it was continued either for five minutes altogether or for two minutes after respirations had shifted to a regular pattern; but it was always turned off after five minutes, even when there was no effect on behavioral state. Trials were reported as effective when there was a shift to state I within the designated time which continued for at least ten minutes after the white noise had been turned off. Whenever the white noise did not induce state I sleep within five minutes, the trial was scored as a failure. To distinguish the effects of white noise from spontaneous state transitions, similar periods of state II were selected from the running record on days of unobtrusive observation, and the mean duration of state II before a spontaneous shift to state I was compared to transitions after white noise was turned on. According to these criteria, white noise accelerated the transition to state I sleep significantly in each of the first five weeks, but by the sixth week it had lost its effect, and the duration of state II before the transition to state I with white noise could no longer be distinguished from the mean length of spontaneous transitions to state I sleep. Even in the first five weeks, monotonous sound had little effect when it was turned off as soon as the breathing pattern had smoothed out.

The effect was therefore biphasic, including an initial reduction of motility and change in respirations, and a subsequent transition to a new state that maintained itself after the white noise was turned off and usually lasted for a mean twenty-one minute period. The actual transition to new state apparently required a period of relative immobility or nonvariable proprioceptive input during which the state I variables could be coordinated into a dynamic and self-organizing coalition.

Cradle rocking involves a heterogeneous summation of stimulus modalities from many sources as well as a rhythmical rather than a monotonous temporal pattern. Its effect, which lasted well into the third month, was demonstrated in thirteen infants who were accustomed to sleeping in beds that could be easily rocked. On appropriate days each week, while infants were in state II or crying, they were rocked at a steady rate of forty to sixty half-cycles per minute along their longitudinal body axis, by a paradigm similar to that used with white noise. Throughout the first three months, when transitions from state II to state I on days of unobtrusive observation were compared to those with rhythmical rocking, the experimental intervention shortened the mean duration of transitions significantly. In a few of the infants who were tested beyond the third month, the effect lasted well into the fifth month. As in the case of white noise, rocking had a reliable effect only when it was continued for at least two minutes *after* the breathing pattern had shifted to the regular form. When rocking was stopped as soon as the respiration had changed, there was no significant effect. The induction of state I by rocking also required a certain time during which the component state variables were presumably integrated as dynamically stable ensembles.

As earlier tabulations indicate, the upper limits of spontaneous state I sleep are well defined. Except during the first two days after birth, or when infants have a fever, a period of state I sleep rarely exceeded twenty-four minutes before terminating spontaneously. To test the upper limits on the duration of state I sleep episodes under experimental conditions, I tested the effect on state I duration when the white noise was used to induce state I, and was then kept on for the duration of the sleep episode. The results indicated that monotonous sound significantly prolonged the duration of state I sleep in the first, second, and third months; there were distinct upper limits even to the artificially maintained state I. Under experimental conditions, it never exceeded 35 minutes, and the mean was 27 minutes. A frequency distribution histogram indicated that the primary effect of white noise was to eliminate relatively short periods of sleep lasting less than 10 minutes.

The same effect could be demonstrated by starting the white noise as soon as state I was established and keeping the white noise on throughout the state and for at least 3 minutes after the infant had shifted to state II. Again, the experimental manipulation reduced the relative frequency of short periods of state I lasting 10–12 minutes, and increased the number of episodes of state I sleep extending beyond the usual 21-minute period (i.e., episodes lasting from 25 to 35 minutes). Such findings are consistent with the assumption that continuous monotonous stimulation buffers the infant against the potentially disruptive effect of spontaneous startles or environmental perturbations, which when they provoke movement occasionally terminate state I sleep prematurely. Monotonous stimulation may facilitate the self-correcting properties of sleep by suppressing movements that would otherwise act as proximal causes for terminating state I sleep. However, this buffering effect never overrides the boundary conditions that limit the overall duration of state I sleep.

Brackbill et al. (1966), had reported that the soothing effect of monotonous stimuli can be enhanced when two or more monotonous or continuous modalities are presented simultaneously. To follow up this observation I therefore combined white noise, rocking, flashing lights, and pacifier sucking in various combinations to test their cumulative effect on the duration of state I sleep. The results

47

indicated that two or three concurrent sensory channels of stimulation were no more effective than a single channel.

The length of individual state II sleep episodes was much more variable from one day to the next, and from one infant to the next, and it was not possible to test by the same paradigm whether monotonous or rhythmic stimulation maintains or prolongs state II sleep, particularly since monotonous stimulation facilitates the shift to state I sleep.

The Experimental Disruption of Sleep

Parents who either try to keep their infants on a rigorous feeding schedule or change the baby's timetable in keeping with their daily routines, and investigators who try to terminate the infant's "natural cycle" of state sequences in order to carry out their clinical examination or experiment, know very well how hard it is to awaken an infant from state I sleep before it is ready to wake up spontaneously. Vigorous stimulation can interrupt ongoing sleep momentarily, but as soon as the stimulation stops, the infant usually returns to sleep or is at least unsuitable for reliable observations. Particularly state I sleep exhibits a powerful tendency for self-equilibration.

To examine the phenomenon systematically, I compared the perturbability of state I and state II sleep in response to various experimental manipulations. In a previous study on the interaction of sucking and tickling stimulation (Wolff and Simmons 1967), we had used a camel's-hair brush to tickle the face of the sleeping infant, and to test whether the sleeping infants' aversive motor responses to noxious stimuli could be modified by allowing them concurrently to suck on a pacifier. According to these observations a tickling of the inner and outer canthus of the eye or the nasolabial fold with a few hairs of the brush reliably produced localized and generalized motor responses of the limb, head, and trunk. The vigor of motor responses did not diminish significantly with repeated stimulation, and infants did not "habituate" to tickling. The sensation produced by light strokes with a cotton wisp or camel's-hair brush is apparently transmitted by the same nerve fibers that transmit superficial pain, which also does not fatigue or habituate. The observations also indicated that concurrent nonnutritive sucking significantly reduces the vigor of movements in response to the tickling. To compare the perturbability or self-equilibrating properties of state I and state II, I tested the effect of the same nociceptive tickling stimuli on the infant's motor responses across states. Sensitive regions of the facial skin were stroked with a camel's-hair brush lightly three times in succession across the inner or outer canthus of the left and right eye, the locus of stimulation being changed constantly. Five trial blocks, each consisting of three strokes and separated by two-second intervals after the infant stopped stirring, were used to determine whether sleep could be disrupted, how the infant responded, and whether the state, once the stimulation stopped, was self-correcting or terminated. State transitions were recorded by pneumotachography and behavioral observation. In addition I timed the duration of general movements in response to each trial. Experiments were always started after a particular state of sleep had been established for at least three minutes.

In almost every instance, tickling produced diffuse or generalized movements, and there was no decrement in motor responses. There were also no differences in the frequency or duration of movement responses between state I and state II. In 93 percent of trials during state I, and in 79 percent of trials in state II, tickling failed to induce any persistent state changes. In subsequent experiments I increased the number of trial block from five to twenty or more. Under these conditions there were some state-related differences in sensitivity to stimulation. State II was replaced by waking, fussing, or crying in 53 percent of instances, whereas the prolonged tickling experiments during state I induced transitions to state II in only 20 percent of instances. However the full schedule of twenty or more trial blocks took a considerable time, and in the case of state II it could not always be concluded without introducing the possibly confounding effect that state II might have terminated spontaneously.

I also tested whether white noise could modify or suppress generalized movements in response to tickling. Table 4 indicates that the frequency of responses to individual trials, as well as the duration of generalized movements in response to each tickling stimulation were substantially reduced by the simultaneous presentation of continuous monotonous noise. This effect persisted throughout the first three months, even though white noise was no longer effective in causing a shift from state II to state I sleep. The buffering effect of white noise was significant in both state I and state II. Similarly, when infants were sucking on a blind pacifier they responded less often and less vigorously to the tickling stimulus than in corresponding sleep states without pacifier. The buffering effect of nonnutritive sucking was again significant in both states. The results are essentially the same as those previously obtained. The observations suggest that monotonous stimulation or repetitive motor activity stabilizes sleep, and particularly state I sleep, whereas the effect of

49

Table 4: Effect of White Noise on Tickling in Sleep

	No. of Responses/5 Trials		
State	Without White Noise	With White Noise	p
I	4.4 (0.4)	2.1 (0.7)	**
II	4.8 (0.2)	2.2 (0.2)	**

	Mean Duration (Secs.) Movement/Trial		
State	Without White Noise	With White Noise	p
I	1.78 (0.4)	0.85 (0.3)	**
II	2.35 (0.5)	0.68 (0.3)	**

intermittent nociceptive stimuli which may cause a disruption of sleep, can to a large extent be buffered by the simultaneous presentation of monotonous stimuli.

Summary

The daytime observations of sleep in the natural setting of the home are generally consistent with objective polygraphic recordings of sleep patterns in the newborn infant, indicating that the sleep of the young infant can be characterized as two qualitatively distinct and mutually exclusive behavioral states that follow a predictable sequence of alternations. State I is characterized by its relative stability of duration that converges on a preferred frequency of 20–22 minutes and that rarely exceeds this length throughout the first six months. By contrast, no exact time boundaries can be specified for the duration of daytime state II sleep even at the end of the sixth month, whereas polygraphic studies on nighttime sleep suggest that state II gradually converges on a fixed periodicity of approximately forty minutes. If such discrepancies in the mean duration of day- and night-time state II sleep could be confirmed by objective measures, they would again suggest that state II sleep is influenced by environmental events to a much greater degree than state I.

The overall duration of daytime sleep diminished predictably from the first to the sixth month, as did the mean duration of uninterrupted daytime sleep. By contrast, the mean duration of single episodes of state I sleep did not change over that time, and state I sleep was also consistently more resistant to premature disruption by environmental disturbances than state II. In other words, it exhibited the tendency for self-organization to a much greater extent. Finally, the motor patterns characteristically observed in state I differed qualitatively from those commonly seen in state II. The startle pattern which is more common as a spontaneous phenomenon in state I can also be provoked experimentally by a sudden slight jar of the head, and the intensity of jarring required to elicit the modified "Moro reflex" is considerably less in state I than state II (see Wolff 1959, 1966). Similarly, facial grimaces, including "smiles," which occur spontaneously in state II but not in state I can be provoked by appropriate stimulus configurations in state II but not in state I.

Finally, the asymmetrical distribution of various movement patterns in state I and state II sleep also gives clues about their respective self-correcting tendencies in face of environmental perturbations. In state I, but not in state II, respirations are typically rhythmical or near periodic. Episodic sighing inspirations observed primarily in state I appear to reset the amplitude and rate of near periodic respirations, reestablishing their rhythmical character. Spontaneous mouthing in state I is typically organized as a more or less stable sequence of burst/rest alternations with a highly constant frequency of interresponse intervals within each burst of mouthing movements, whereas the spontaneous mouthing in state II is typically episodic, conforming to no stable spatial configuration or temporal order. By analogy, from observations on nonnutritive sucking on a pacifier as an activity that inhibits general motility, one could further speculate that the rhythmic organization of motor activity exercises a buffering function which suppresses the appearance of episodic and therefore potentially disruptive motor events. Similarly a comparison of phase interactions between breathing and sucking movements in state I as contrasted with state II suggests that the rhythmic motor actions are synchronized in a determinate pattern in state I but not state II. As the first approximation of a testable hypothesis one might therefore conclude that the temporal organization of state-related motor patterns and the possibility of their mutual entrainment confer on each state a variable degree of self-correcting potential. The greater the temporal stability of periodically repeating motor patterns, the greater is the likelihood of their mutual entrainment and stabilization in the face of environmental perturbations (Fentress 1976). Similarly, the more variable or episodic the state-related motor patterns, the less is the potential for mutual entrainment among concurrently active motor patterns, and the more vulnerable will the behavioral state be in face of disruptive environmental events.

Drowsiness

The boundaries which might mark the transition from waking to sleep or from sleep to waking can be easily specified by discrete behavioral criteria and are generally classified under transitions of indeterminate duration or composition. Although drowsiness exhibits none of the properties of a distinct behavioral state, the condition may be of more than trivial interest because the detailed description of drowsiness can disclose clues about mechanisms of state transitions.

Drowsiness was defined as that condition when the infants were motorically less active than in state II and more active than in state I, and when the rhythm of respiration was more variable than in state I but less variable than in state II. The eyes opened and closed intermittently, and when open they had a "dull glazed" appearance and were apparently unfocused. Just before the eyes closed, they frequently rolled upwards and backwards in their sockets as if the infant had an oculogyric crisis. At such moments the otherwise fairly regular respirations became intermittently tachypneic and at that time some infants also emitted an occasional high-pitched squeal. Drowsiness in the transition from waking to sleep could be distinguished categorically from drowsiness in the transition from sleep to waking. Shortly before infants shifted from waking to sleep, the eyelids began to droop, became heavy, and the sclera of the eyeballs became red. Brief spurts of writhing were rare while the infants were falling asleep. Drowsiness lacked the distinctive features of a unique ensemble of four distinct continuous variables, and therefore did not qualify as a behavioral state. The striking phenomenal differences between drowsiness during the transition from waking to sleep and from sleep to waking could initially be specified only in the context of their respective antecedent and consequent conditions.

All entries in the running record lasting three minutes or longer were scored as drowsiness when the infant had been awake for some time and the eyelids had begun to droop or to close and open intermittently until the infant eventually fell asleep. Similar criteria were set to define drowsiness in the transition from sleep to waking. Figure 3 indicates that drowsiness from waking to sleep was longer at all ages than drowsiness terminating a period of sleep. Although the latency of transitions to sleep decreased significantly over the first three months, it took infants longer to fall asleep (to state I) than to wake up from state I. Differences in the duration of transitions were significant for the entire group as well as for each infant separately.

The distribution of spontaneous-movement patterns during drowsiness, particularly during the transition from waking to sleep, was of theoretical interest as a possible clue to the origins or "causes" of spontaneous movements in sleep. Many of the motor patterns preferentially distributed either in state I or state II sleep were commonly present during drowsiness. Numeric accounts of these events in drowsiness are of only limited value because the precise boundary marking the end of waking and the onset of sleep remained ill defined throughout the observation. Spontaneous startles during the transition from waking to sleep commonly had the paradoxical effect that they delayed the onset of stable sleep because the startles themselves caused the drowsing infants to wake up again. A sequence of events such that drowsiness, drooping of the eyelids, and preparation of sleep predisposed the infant to being reawakened by startles was sometimes repeated four or five times before the infant finally settled into stable sleep. Such a phenomenon may be analogous to the myoclonic jerks reported by some adults at the moment when they fall asleep, moments when they report a sensation of "falling" (Oswald 1962). Many of the spontaneous-movement patterns including startles, facial grimaces, smiling, rhythmic mouthing, and general movements occurred within 3–5 seconds after the eyelids closed, as if lid closure itself and the elimination of visual stimulus input triggered or facilitated the appearance of the motor phenomena, in the way of a release mechanism. The temporal relations described here between eye closure and spontaneous movements were not sufficiently stable to warrant any direct causal association. Spontaneous startles, smiles and mouthing movements also occurred while the drooping eyelids were still open. Yet 80 percent of all self-initiated motor events recorded during the transition from waking to sleep occurred within 5 seconds after the eyelids had closed.

As a first approximation one might conclude that the transition from waking to sleep is accompanied by a major reorganization of component neurological systems that make up a well-defined behavioral state. This transition is accompanied by a number of motor "release" phenomena expressed in various outputs, some of which are characteristically activated during state I sleep, others during state II sleep. Both kinds of movements tend to be concentrated during the transitional period of drowsiness when they are apparently facilitated by eye closure or the elimination of nonspecific visual input. By contrast, drowsiness during the transition from sleep to waking was rarely associated with spontaneous movement patterns, except for generalized movements. The presumed neurological processes which effect a transition from waking to sleep may thus differ qualitatively from mechanisms required for the transition from sleep to waking.

Wakefulness

"Attentional processes" which enable the infant to respond to discrete stimulus events, have been investigated in considerable detail by experimental child psychology (Kessen et al. 1970; Kagan 1970; Sameroff 1979; Posner and Rothbart 1980). Like psychological studies on older children and adults, such investigations usually take wakefulness per se for granted and focus on attention as a self-evident quantity or entity even though it may be only a component of wakefulness as a self-maintaining behavioral state. Except for occasional normative studies on altered states of consciousness and state-dependent learning, and clinical observations on psychiatric and neurological patients, the effect of waking behavioral states on variations in perception, cognition and social adaptation has rarely been investigated. Instead, studies in experimental psychology generally assume that wakefulness is a homogeneous disposition.

According to the observations summarized here, wakefulness may be defined as that disposition when the infant practices and refines acquired sensorimotor patterns, discovers novelties in the environment, and invents new combinations among component elements that become the means for intellectual exploration and social communication. The development of wakefulness should therefore be one essential baseline for all experimental descriptions of psychological and behavioral development. Yet, relative to sleep states, we know remarkably little about the phenomenology of wakefulness in early infancy, or about the developmental processes that transform transient episodes of alerting susceptible to interference by organic disturbances and environmental events into stable dispositions that prevail during at least half of the twenty-four-hour day without interruption. They are the dynamic context in which humans carry out most of those activities which make them uniquely human. Most infants spend most of the twenty-four-hour day asleep, and waking periods are brief and easily disrupted by external interventions; adults, on the other hand, spend fourteen to eighteen hours of the twenty-four-hour day awake. Therefore, theoretical questions concerning sleep-waking cycles, and experiments designed to test these questions, have usually been stated in different terms for infants, on one hand, and for children and adults, on the other.

Sleep seems to be the "natural" condition of the infant, and research on infancy has usually focused on the question of what causes them to wake up and to stay awake. By contrast wakefulness is the "natural" condition for the adult, and research interest often focuses on the question of why we need to sleep at all, what purposes sleep serves physiologically or psychologically (e.g., dreaming, the restoration of mental capacity, physical rest, and the like), and what physiological conditions or chemical variables cause the organism to fall asleep. Obviously the distinction is semantic rather than substantive since both sets of questions address the same problem of rest-activity cycles that characterize the life of all complex organisms. Nevertheless this distinction serves to illustrate one reason why there may be relatively little systematic knowledge about wakefulness as a general condition or behavioral state, either in infants, where it is usually at first only a transient phenomenon, or in adults, in whom it is frequently taken for granted.

The taxonomy of sleep states proposed by Prechtl and his colleagues (Prechtl 1974; Prechtl and O'Brien 1982), and adopted here has proven very satisfactory for describing the behavioral organization not only in newborn infants but also in older infants and children. It is not clear however that the same classification of waking states is useful beyond the neonatal period (see, for example, Wolff 1984). At the risk of further confusing current nomenclature of behavioral states, I abandoned Prechtl's operational taxonomy of waking conditions and substituted the more phenomenological descriptive category of *alert inactivity, waking activity,* and *alert activity* as defined above, until such time as we have sufficient knowledge about their essential characteristics to construct an equally coherent classification of waking states for older infants, children, and adults.

Kleitman's (1963) global distinction between a wakefulness of "necessity" and of "choice" implies that there are qualitative changes in the organization of waking disposition during the early months after birth. One can disagree with details of the definition as well as with the observations on which the distinction was based, but the fact remains that Kleitman called attention to an issue that is critical for any developmental analysis of waking behavioral states. Wakefulness of necessity referred to those conditons when the infant is awakened by recurring physiological needs or discomforts such as hunger, bowel distention, changes of body temperature, and the like, such transitory periods of waking being terminated as soon as the discomfort has been relieved. Thus the proximal causes for wakefulness in the young infant were assumed to be essentially extrinsic to the wakeful condition itself. Kleitman further assumed that wakefulness of necessity is the only condition of waking in the early months after birth, and that infants sleep unless they are uncomfortable. By contrast wakefulness of choice was meant to indicate conditions of wakefulness emerging during later months of the first year which are not caused by organic discomforts. Wakefulness of choice was assumed to depend on maturation of the neocortex and the parallel development of sensorimotor and mental processes that enable the infant or child to take an active interest in the concrete physical or social environment. Finally, Kleitman assumed that the neural mechanisms allowing infants to engage the physical or social environment actively rather than respond simply to periodic physical discomfort do not reach a critical density for sustained wakefulness until the third or fourth month. The formulation is of immediate interest in the present context because it implies that wakefulness of choice is the emergent property of a sufficient density of interactive sensorimotor patterns, rather than a preformed condition of the organism switched on and off automatically by an autonomous clock of the central nervous system (Meier-Koll et al. 1978). The gradual increase in duration and stability of sustained wakefulness may then be attributed to an increase in the number of differentiated goal-directed activities. In this sense, wakefulness of choice becomes synonymous with the acquisition of novel and potentially interactive motor patterns.

The unobtrusive observation of infants in their homes afforded a unique opportunity to examine the early stages in this emergence of wakefulness of choice, to explore by what criteria the various waking condition of young infants could be classified and how the acquisition of novel sensory motor patterns might be associated with the maintenance, prolongation, and stabilization of alert waking states. In the descriptive account of wakefulness that follows I will again begin with a quantitative tabulation of developmental changes in the overall duration of wakefulness during an average day and with the mean duration of individual episodes of wakefulness. Next, the distribution of wakefulness in relation to other behavioral states and environmental conditions will be considered, as well as the "types" of wakefulness that can be recognized and the criteria by which such types might be described. Thereafter I will again report on experimental manipulations that were designed either to prolong or to terminate a period of wakefulness, manipulations that were used as an indirect measure of the extent to which wakefulness is self-organizing.

Cumulative Tabulations of Waking

All entries in the running record on days of unobtrusive observation that referred to waking for three minutes or longer, but excluding crying, fussing, drowsing, feeding, or other parental interventions, were tabulated as a percentage of total observation time per week (see figure 1). The first week after birth was again treated separately because the infants were awake and apparently alert for extended periods of time during the first twenty-four hours and thereafter showed a rapid decline of wakefulness which was not reversed until the second week at home.

The mean duration of sustained waking was considerably longer during the first twenty-four hours (mean, 46.8 minutes; range, 18–87 minutes), than during the remainder of the first week (mean, 17.8 minutes; range, 9–27 minutes; $p<.01$ by Wilcoxon signed-ranks test). By most behavioral criteria wakefulness during the first twenty-four hours was approximately the same as alert inactivity after the second week. Waking newborn infants were able to track a moving target briefly with their eyes both in the horizontal and vertical plane. However, they were not able to sustain such pursuit for more than 20 seconds at a time, and then usually abandoned the object although they could be made to resume the pursuit movements 30 to 60 seconds later. Pursuit movements during the first twenty-four hours rarely if ever involved a coordination of head and eye movements so that the range of pursuit was limited to an angle that could be spanned by eye movements alone. The "quality" of wakefulness was in this sense, different during the first twenty-four hours than after the second week.

The prolonged periods of wakefulness in the first twenty-four hours were observed across infants with very different obstetrical histories or levels of obstetrical medication, as well as across babies delivered by vaginal route and cesarean section, and appear to be a characteristic of behavioral states during the transition from an intrauterine to an extrauterine environment. It has been suggested, for example, that birth marks a radical shift in the environmental context, to which the newborn infant must adapt as it is rudely removed from a fluid, relatively weightless environment to an extrauterine context where gravity plays an important role. Moreover, the infant must now support its own respiratory movements and nutritional status, and it is no longer buffered against sudden changes in the ambient light, sound, and temperature environment. The behavioral patterns observed during the first twenty-four hours of the neonatal period may therefore reflect ontogenetic adaptations well suited for an intrauterine environment but not particularly adaptive for existence in an extrauterine world in which the infant must, for better or for worse, spend the rest of its life.

When the data on wakefulness during the first five days were excluded from the tabulation, the overall duration of waking showed a progressive increase during the daylight hours, from 24 percent of observation time during the second week to 64 percent of total observation time by the end of the third month (range, 53–70%). The increase in wakefulness was statistically significant when computed for each two-week interval (p<.01, by Friedman 2-way-analysis of variance). Although the increase was the approximate reciprocal of a decrease in daytime sleep, such a reciprocal relation is not self-evident since all conditions of the baby other than defined sleep and defined wakefulness were excluded from the tabulation. The results are generally consistent with the observation of sleep-waking cycles reported by others, whether carried out in the home or in a supportive institutional setting (Sander et al. 1970; Paul et al. 1973; Thoman 1975; Emde et al. 1975).

A longitudinal follow-up study of healthy infants carried out by Dittrichová and Lapačkova (1964), in a group home, is particularly instructive in this respect because the infants were observed unobtrusively, intensively (12 hours a day) and extensively (over the first six months), in an optimal but nevertheless controlled environment of a day-care nursery where they were not isolated from their "natural" social environment or perturbed by systematic experimental intervention. For these investigations wakefulness was defined as all conditions when the infants were not crying or being fed, when their eyes were opened, and when they were able to "respond selectively to a variety of environmental stimulations." As in my sample, the increase of wakefulness over the first twelve weeks followed a near linear course, although the rate of increase differed significantly between the two studies. By twelve weeks, home-reared infants were awake for 60 percent of daytime observation, whereas infants in the day-care nursery were awake for only 45 percent even at the end of twenty-four weeks (Wolff 1984). There is no reason to assume that being awake longer is necessarily better for intellectual or social development. Nevertheless the comparison is of interest by suggesting that normal variations in the physical and social environment can substantially influence the overall duration of wakefulness. In this respect, wakefulness as a behavioral state differs qualitatively from either state I or state II sleep.

Uninterrupted Waking Periods

Wakefulness computed as percentage of total observation time does not represent accurately the mean duration for which infants may be awake and alert without interruption. Data from the running record were, therefore, retabulated as an interval histogram for the duration of individual waking periods, which is summarized in figure 5. It indicates that the length of time for which babies could stay awake without interruption (of 3 minutes or more), increased rapidly from the second to the twelfth week, and more slowly thereafter. In the first week at home infants stayed awake for an average of only 7 minutes (range: 3–21 minutes) before shifting to another behavioral state, and the longest recorded period of sustained waking during this time was 21 minutes. By the end of the twelfth week, the average duration of uninterrupted waking was 64 minutes (range: 10–140 minutes), and the longest recorded period of sustained waking was 180 minutes.

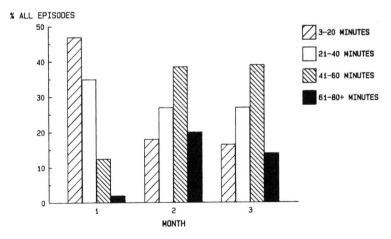

Figure 5: Duration of Sustained Waking Episodes

The mean increase in the sustained alertness over the first three months was significant when computed for each two-week interval (p<.01, by Friedman two-way analysis of variance). This increase was accounted for in part by the reduction of relatively short periods of waking, and in part by an increased number of extended alert periods. By the fifth or sixth months infants could stay awake and alert for as long as 200 to 210 minutes without any interruption. The mechanism that may have contributed to this extension will be explored below.

Behavioral States of Wakefulness

The data summarized so far pertain to waking as a global condition that obtains as long as the infant's eyes are open and scanning the environment and it is neither crying nor being cared for by the mother. This global definition does not reflect important variations in the organizational properties of alertness or different waking states that might have important effects on input-output relationships. As in the case of sleep states, the global condition of waking had to be reclassified to identify the more refined dispositions of wakefulness and to account for unexplained variations in spontaneous motor activity as well as in the infant's responses to environmental events. The taxonomy of behavioral states outlined earlier indicates that it is possible, even during the first week, to distinguish between periods when the infant is "alert" relatively immobile and capable of making discrete visual pursuit movements, and conditions when the infant is

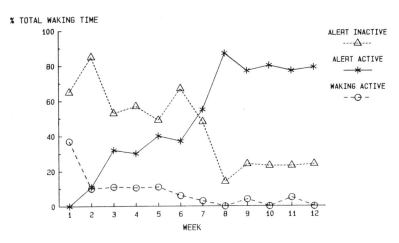

Figure 6. Distribution of Various Waking States

60

Table 5: Rank-Order Distribution of Waking Behavorial States

Week	Waking State
1	WA > AI > AA, n.s.
2–5	AI > AA > WA**
6–12	AA > AI > WA**

**p .01
WA=Waking Activity
AI=Alert Inactivity
AA=Alert Activity

motorically active but its responses to environmental events are relatively nonspecific.

A third condition of alertness, which I called *alert activity,* does not emerge clearly until the end of the first month, and its definitional properties as well as functional characteristics will be dealt with in some detail later. Based on the taxonomy of waking states outlined above, figure 6 illustrates the percentage of waking time that was spent by infants in each of the waking conditions in each week of the first three months. Until six weeks, the largest percentage of time was taken up by alert inactivity. Thereafter, there was a sharp increase in alert activity which was for obvious reasons the reciprocal of alert inactivity, because the defining criterion of the latter in comparison to the former was the combination of generalized movements and goal-directed actions. Alert activity increased progressively from the second to the sixth month; but at all ages, infants still spent a substantial part of the time quietly scanning the environment or in alert inactivity (table 5). The boundaries between alert inactive and alert active states were arbitrary and depended on subjective judgments about the level of generalized motor activity that was combined with goal-directed action; the shift from a condition of waking in which infants could do only "one thing at a time," so that either their motility stopped when they pursued a moving object or they ignored the target while moving, to a condition in which visual pursuit or other controlled-movement patterns were no longer incompatible with generalized movement was a consistent phenomenon across all babies. This consistency of findings suggests important shifts in behavioral organization of wakefulness at the end of the second month, but it may also have important implications for the capacity to carry out two goal-directed actions at the same time, and in this way to invent or discover new combinations among established action patterns that will open the way for the discovery of new goals (Piaget 1952). Because the shift from performing only one action at a time to the capacity for "dual task performance" may have important implications for intellectual development as well as for the organization of wakefulness as a self-maintaining state, the detailed behavioral observations illustrating such a shift are discussed in more detail below.

State Sequences of Wakefulness

In order to characterize the conditions that facilitated spontaneous wakefulness on the basis of unobtrusive observations, I selected all alert periods that listed five minutes or longer as reference points and tabulated which behavioral states or environmental conditions preceded and followed each of the reference points (see also figure 7, which uses feedings rather than alert periods, as the reference point, but obtains very similar results).

Until the sixth week, the condition most often preceding a period of alertness (alert inactivity or alert activity) was either a feeding or a feeding combined with a change of diapers (47 percent of all tabulated instances). In 21 percent of occasions, an alert period was preceded by drowsiness, such drowsiness frequently following a feeding before the infant became alert. The temporal link between feeding and alertness was more clearly expressed in bottle- than breast-fed babies. Particularly during the first two months, breast-fed

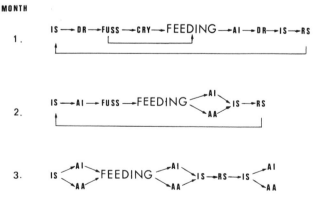

Figure 7. State Sequences in Relation to Feedings

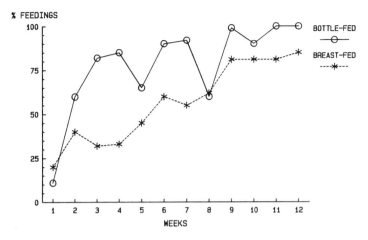

Figure 8. Relation of Alert Waking to Feedings

babies were more likely to fall asleep at the breast, and then to continue in a drowsy or sleep state, or to begin fussing when they were removed from the breast. Such protest-sounds usually motivated the mother to continue the feeding until the baby was in stable sleep. Bottle-feeding mothers often decided that the feeding should be terminated when the bottle was empty or the infant refused to take any more nourishment, whereas nursing mothers seemed to consider it important that their baby be asleep at the end of a feeding, perhaps, in part, because they had no independent information about the amount of nourishment their baby had taken. Group differences in the events preceding a period of alert inactivity were statistically significant between bottle- and breast-fed infants during the first and second months (chi^2 = 7.3; df 1; p<.01). However, by the third month, both groups were more often than not awake and alert after a feeding before they eventually fell asleep (see figure 8).

The state sequence in which waking alertness followed immediately after hunger satiation is not compatible with Kleitman's concept of wakefulness of necessity, and will therefore be examined in some detail below. Several mothers volunteered the information, and arranged their infant's daily routine on the assumption that the baby "needed" a period of crying before it could fall asleep. Because I was skeptical of the claim, I tried in various ways to prevent babies from crying once they were put into their crib after a feeding and waking period, by soothing or amusing them with various interventions, including the presentation of moving targets, attempting to elicit smiles, patting the back, and other maneuvers which at other times were successful for a particular baby. Such interventions did, in fact, usually arrest and inhibit crying as long as I kept up the interventions. More often than not, however, they started to cry again as soon as I stopped. The sequence could be repeated for up to a half hour at a time, and usually the infants did not fall asleep. By contrast, when I did not try to stop them from crying as, for example, on days of unobtrusive observation, they usually cried for 1 to 2 minutes and then fell asleep. The observation was consistent with the mother's hypothesis that infants did, in fact, fall asleep more quickly when allowed to cry for a brief period; but since the phenomenon was observed in only a few infants and then only during the first two months, the reason for this apparently idiosyncratic preparation for sleeping was not clarified.

Abrupt transitions from state I sleep to waking alertness without an intervening period of state II or drowsiness were very rare at any time during the first six months. Almost as rare were abrupt transitions from alertness to state II or I without a transient period of drowsiness and fussing (less than 5 percent of all recorded instances). Alert waking and state I sleep do not turn on and off automatically, but require some preparation for their induction and transition to another state.

Wakefulness of Necessity

Kleitman proposed that organic stimuli of discomfort such as hunger, cold, and bladder or bowel distention are the necessary and sufficient causes for waking during the first three months. From such a hypothesis it should follow that if organic discomforts could be maintained at subthreshold values, the infant would sleep throughout the twenty-four hour day. Behavioral technology has not advanced to the point where all offending organic discomforts can be readily controlled; there is at present also no critical test of the assumption that organic stimuli are the necessary and sufficient conditions of wakefulness in early infancy. In infants who are fed continuously by gastrostomy tube because of tracheo-esophageal fistulas, hunger contractions are presumably eliminated (see, for example, Wolff 1972a; Salzarulo et al. 1980). By itself, the fact that such infants were awake intermittently does not argue against the notion of "wakefulness of necessity" since they were constantly subjected to acute or chronic pain stimuli from their healing surgical incisions.

As an indirect test of the hypothesis that organic discomforts are a necessary condition for wakefulness during the early months, I compared periods during the day when the presumed organic causes were likely to be at a minimum with periods when the discomforts were likely to be more intense. Preceding sections indicated that infants are more likely to be awake and alert *after* than *before* the meal. Since most of the mothers in the study sample diapered their infants either before or in the middle of a feeding, after the infant had moved its bowels in response to the "gastrocolic reflex," at least one other source of organic discomfort had been relieved before the end of the meal. Yet that was the time when infants had their longest periods of waking alertness. To examine the relation between hunger and the duration of wakefulness directly, the cumulative data on waking were regrouped in relation to the time since last feeding or diapering. Figure 9 indicates that during the first, second, and third months the largest percentage of alert waking time occurred one hour after the meal. Among breast-fed infants this temporal relationship was not as clearly expressed as in bottle-fed infants until after the sixth week.

The relation of feeding to waking alertness was also examined by computing the percentage of all feedings that were followed within ten minutes by a period of sustained alertness lasting three minutes or more. Among bottle-fed infants 60 percent of the feedings were followed by a period of alertness during the second week, and by the ninth week almost 100 percent of the feeding episodes were followed

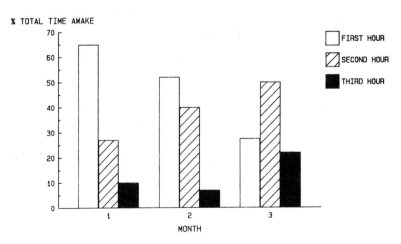

Figure 9. Sustained Alert Periods in Relation to Feedings

65

by a period of alertness (see figure 8). However, breast-fed babies were more likely to fall asleep or to fuss as soon as they were removed from the breast. In this subgroup only 35 percent of feedings were followed by sustained alertness in the first month. However, by the ninth week there were again no statistically significant differences between bottle- and breast-fed babies.

Such observations suggest that food deprivation or hunger is not a necessary condition for sustained wakefulness in the early weeks. On the contrary, the results indicate that the reduction of hunger seems to be a necessary precondition for sustained alertness. During the first month infants were awake for prolonged periods almost only during the first 30 to 60 minutes after a meal, and alert periods that followed by more than an hour after the meal compromised only 15 percent of all observations. By contrast, during the third month bottle-fed infants frequently stayed awake 45 minutes after a meal, then fell asleep for 1 to 1.5 hours, woke up again and stayed awake for 30 to 40 minutes before beginning to fuss or cry, or before the mother decided that it was time for another meal. Far from being the necessary condition for waking in young infants, organic distresses associated with food deprivation appeared to be incompatible with alert inactivity, so that one might characterize the development of wakeful behavioral states as showing an increased tolerance for hunger (latency of time since last feeding).

The observation on behavioral waking-state cycle is therefore most consistent with the hypothesis that full-term infants are equipped at birth with the theoretically undefined neural mechanisms for the organization of waking states as distinct dispositions. Waking is initially a fragile and easily disrupted condition; and the development of waking *states* is characterized by a progressive stabilization of motor mechanisms specific to wakefulness, as well as by the acquisition of "buffers" that protect wakefulness against the disruptive effects of hunger and other organic stimuli.

While hunger is probably the most common and certainly the most readily predicted organismic variable that might contribute to Kleitman's wakefulness of necessity, it is evidently not the only one. Sensations of wetness from diapers do not by themselves constitute a significant source of distress in infants, who can easily sleep through an episode of voiding (Wolff 1973; see also below). In contrast, sensations of coldness due to evaporation from wet diapers may constitute a disruptive variable. Another possible source of organic discomfort may be bowel and bladder distention. As indicated above, infants frequently responded to the feeding with a gastrocolic reflex and therefore with a bowel movement. The onset of bowel movements was readily recognized from the overt behavioral concomitants such as the total arrest of a feeding, facial flushing, and general suppression of generalized movements. The exact time of urination was much less apparent except by direct inspection, but bladder and bowel evacuation commonly occurred simultaneously. Thus, when all occasions of bowel movements were tabulated in relation to periods of sustained waking, 56 percent of them occurred during or immediately after a meal; 35 percent were unrelated to meals; and 31 percent of all occasions of bowel movements occurred while the infants were asleep (state II). Since only 13 percent of recorded episodes of stooling occurred towards the end of an extended period of wakefulness, it seems unlikely that either bowel or bladder distention played a significant contributory role to the maintenance of wakefulness in infants at any time during the first three months after birth.

The Experimental Manipulation of Wakefulness

During the first two weeks after birth, waking is a transient and relatively unstable phenomenon with few characteristics of a behavioral state but, as the preceding sections indicate, the duration and stability of waking alertness increases dramatically in all infants over the course of the first three months, despite considerable inter- and intra-individual variations in absolute duration of wakefulness. Therefore, it was of theoretical interest to determine what factors contribute to the stabilization of alert waking as a behavioral state and account for the marked individual and day-to-day variations in alertness. Intrinsic clocking mechanisms analogous to those hypothesized for the control of state I have also been proposed as possible constraints on the duration of wakefulness during the early weeks after birth (Meier-Koll et al. 1978; Emde et al. 1975), but such constraints are difficult to demonstrate because the manipulations of the environment required to test them empirically are very stringent and would probably distort the environmental context that favors wakefulness as a behavioral state (Sosteck and Anders, 1975).

To examine the question of mechanism, I explored various avenues for extending the usually expected duration of waking alertness and for terminating the usual duration prematurely. The length of time for which infants are likely to be awake in the absence of organic stimuli (wakefulness of choice) may be a function of the scheme of action at the infant's disposal for acting on or interacting with physical and social environmental events. To the extent that action in progress is an essential determinant of sustained wakefulness, it might also follow that the differentiation of sensorimotor schemes for intellectual adaptation is paralleled directly by the increased duration of waking alert periods. While such a relationship may hold globally, any simple correlations would be no test of the hypothesis because both variables might increase progressively over the same time-period without implying any causal association.

As a more direct test of the hypothesis that goal-directed transactions with the environment contribute to the maintenance of wakefulness, just as wakefulness is a precondition for their occurrence, I tested the influence of presenting infants with various "interesting spectacles" (Piaget, 1952) on the mean duration of alert waking periods. Because wakefulness, unlike state I sleep, conforms to no preferred duration and may be quite variable from one day to the next, it was first necessary to establish by some independent behavioral criterion when the waking infant was likely to fall asleep or begin to cry and fuss. The three behavioral markers that had a relatively consistent relationship to the onset of sleep after a period of waking, were yawning, reddening of the eye sclera, and drooping of the eyelids. Yawning was easily observable in the first day after birth. Whenever it occurred after a period of waking alertness, state II sleep usually followed within a mean period of 7 minutes (range: 5–21 minutes), but the frequency of yawns was relatively low; many episodes of sleeping began without a prior episode of yawning; and the latency between yawning and onset of sleep was quite variable. Reddening of the eye sclera was also readily apparent by direct observation, and it occurred more often before the onset of sleep than at other times (64 percent of occasions; range: 34–83 percent across babies) with a mean latency to sleep of 8 minutes (range: 2–14 minutes). Again, the latency between reddening of the sclera and onset of sleep was too variable to make it a satisfactory behavioral predictor for the termination of wakefulness and the onset of sleep. The third of the markers drooping of the eyelids, occurred almost invariably before infants fell asleep after a period of alertness. The latency between drooping of the eyelids and onset of sleep was short; and the predictive relation held across all of the infants observed. On days of unobtrusive observation, the running record indicated that drooping of the eyelids was observed in 80 percent of all transitions from alertness to sleep (range: 73–94 percent across babies); latency between the first time the eyelids drooped and the onset of irregular sleep was 180 seconds (range: 30–360 seconds). There were no significant developmental changes, either in the frequency or the latency of this association; and in 92 percent of all occasions when the eyelids did begin to droop, state II followed within three minutes. Drooping of the eyelids therefore seemed the best marker for testing whether environmental interventions could experimentally prolong the duration of alert states.

The adequate "interesting spectacle" used for maintaining the infant's interest during the first month was a large red pencil. The target was first oscillated back and forth rapidly in the baby's visual field. Once it had caught the baby's attention, it was moved slowly back and forth across the visual field in the horizontal and vertical planes to elicit visual pursuit movements that required a rotation of the head as well as conjugate eye movements. The red pencil was introduced into the visual field as soon as the infant's eyes began to droop, and it was moved back and forth continuously until the eyes closed and the infant was asleep. By the third month, infants were no longer interested in the movement of red pencils; a human face moving back and forth across the visual field was therefore substituted to maintain the infant's interest and to prolong alert states.

As a conservative estimate, I used six minutes or twice the mean latency between the time when the eyelids drooped and the eyes closed permanently to distinguish between spontaneous falling asleep and experimentally induced alertness. Visual pursuit movements were used as experimental variables because the visual stimulus was "nonperemptory" so that infants could easily close their eyes when they were ready to fall asleep. Intermittent pursuit movements for more than six minutes after the eyelids first drooped were used as the criterion that alert inactivity had been prolonged, whereas such an effect could not have been assumed if I had used a peremptory loud noise or a pain stimulus (tickling) to keep the baby awake.

During the first month, induced visual pursuit movements prolonged alert inactivity or alert activity for a mean of 23.8 minutes beyond the expected time (range: 6–63 minutes); and in 2–3 month infants the moving face prolonged alert inactivity or alert activity for a mean of 40 minutes beyond the expected time (range: 15–83 minutes). In each of the three months, this increase was statistically significant under the conditions described ($p < .01$ by Wilcoxon matched-pairs test; see also Wolff 1973).

The experimental induction of goal-directed activity such as visual pursuit movements can therefore prolong the time for which an infant will remain awake, significantly beyond the time when they would otherwise have fallen asleep. However, the environmental events that produced the effect changed systematically over the first three months, the differentiation of sensorimotor schemes determining whether "spectacles" were of sufficient interest to maintain the baby in a waking state by inducing coordinated motor action. The experimental interventions were not simply responses to arousing stimuli that provoked an orienting reflex (Sokolov 1963), since the effect depended critically on the infant's active participation to maintain itself in a state of wakefulness.

Alert Activity

Originally, the term was introduced to make sense of variations in spontaneous behavior and input-output relations in the waking two-to-three month-old infant and to designate a qualitatively new condition in which infants were apparently able to carry out two acquired motor patterns at the same time. Occasions when infants could make visual pursuit movements with the head and eyes without a simultaneous arrest of ongoing generalized limb movements were used as the operational criterion for distinguishing "alert activity" from alert inactive states. Since the waking alert infant is never completely immobile in its limbs and trunk when scanning the environment, the boundaries between the two waking dispositions could not be sharply defined but depended on some implicit judgment concerning the quantity of generalized or intermittent rhythmic activity. Such decisions would not have been materially improved by using a motility crib or by other objective measures on level of motility because the cut-off point would still have been arbitrary. Given these limitations on state-definition, which also pertained to the distinction between waking activity (state IV) and crying (state V), the observations indicated that there was a relatively sharp increase of alert activity sometime between six and eight weeks across all infants, and a comparable decrease of alert inactivity (see figure 6). The concept of behavioral states may and has been used in at least two connotations—as a convenient taxonomy for categorizing the variable distribution of behavior patterns, and as a window on human brain-behavior relations, or "as an explanation of brain mechanisms which modify the responsiveness of the infant" (Prechtl 1974). In the latter sense, alert activity exhibits a number of properties of theoretical interest for any biological account of human behavioral development. It marks the onset of a phase in development when infants become capable of carrying out two or more acquired activities concurrently. The capacity for dual task performance has long been an issue of central interest for cognitive psychology and neuropsychology as one possible experimental approach for measuring boundaries on human information processing, for determining hemispheric specialization of function in neurologically intact subjects, and for examining the process of automatization which transforms a newly acquired goal-directed action into a mean-behavior or a routine which no longer requires the subject's deliberate "attention" (Allport 1980). I proceeded on the assumption that detailed observations concerning the kinds of novel behavior patterns that occur at the same time without mutual contamination could serve as an early analogue of this critical dimension in psychological development. They also provide further clues about the transformation of waking from transient episodes which are readily disrupted by organic or environmental disturbances, to stable dispositions that have all the characteristics of a self-correcting state.

On days reserved for experimental manipulation I carried out informal studies to explore the early correlates of dual-task performance. Instead of starting with a priori presuppositions about what constituted dual-task performance at a point in development when voluntary activity could not be clearly defined, I have summarized a number of observations that may be relevant to the topic, leaving for later the question whether such observations help to define dual-task performance in early infancy.

In preceding sections I described the effect of visual pursuit on the overall level of activity and the duration of wakefulness, and proposed that the performance of goal-directed action is an essential variable in maintaining waking alertness. Korner and Grobstein (1966), Boismier (1977), and others have reported that changes of body posture and the attendant vestibular stimulation induce transient periods of alertness even during the first week. Similarly, polygraphic studies indicate that postural variables have a major effect on the infant's behavioral state (Prechtl et al. 1975; Casaer 1979). The direct observation of alert infants in their homes, as well as the experimental elicitation of coordinated motor actions, indicated that even within one behavioral state there may be a considerable waxing and waning of focal attention or the ability to persist in a newly acquired motor skill. However, without controlled experiments it is difficult to measure the presumed waxing and waning of attention, or to determine whether there are any significant developmental changes in the infant's capacity for focal attention. Using behavioral observations, I could, however, test the infant's ability to "work" continuously at a task of visual pursuit, examine developmental changes in the duration of continuous pursuit, and under different experimental conditions test whether the capacity for dual-task performance increases over time.

For this purpose, I subclassified pursuit movements into vertical and horizontal eye displacements, and scored whether pursuit movements involved conjugate eye movements alone or coordinated head and eye pursuits. A 5 cm red disc mounted on a white surface and attached to a stick was used as the target stimulus in each week of the first three months. Once the red disc caught the baby's interest, I moved it slowly across the visual field, making sure the infant could not see my face. The disc was moved in either the horizontal or vertical direction in a sufficiently wide arc so that the baby had to move its head and its eyes to keep the target within its visual field. Experimental stimulation was continued until the baby lost interest, could no longer be induced to make eye pursuits, fell asleep, or began to cry. The total duration of continuous pursuit without interruptions was timed, and the type of pursuit (horizontal vs. vertical; head and eye vs. eyes alone) was recorded. The tests were carried out only when infants were alert and either active or inactive at the start (see table 6).

Even during the first twelve hours after birth, all infants made distinct pursuit movements for brief periods, with a mean of four complete sweeps as the upper limit. Six of the twelve infants tested in the first twenty-four hours pursued the target with their eyes only and then abandoned the search. The other six infants made occasional coordinated head-eye movements, so that they were intermittent. All of the infants persisted longer at the task when the target was moved in the horizontal rather than in the vertical plane. The effect was particularly noticeable with respect to head and eye pursuit, suggesting that control of head movements in the vertical plane was considerably less well developed.

Forty-eight hours later, only two of the six infants were still able to make coordinated head-eye movements, and only eight of the twelve infants made proficient eye pursuit movements, as if there had been a regression or disorganization of coordinated visual pursuit during the first forty-eight hours. By the seventh day, all infants again occasionally tracked the target with their head and eyes for at least four and sometimes six full sweeps in the horizontal planes (for each plane: $chi^2 = 14.7$; $p<.01$ by Friedman two-way analysis of variance). By the fourth week, some infants could pursue for twenty-five full sweeps in the horizontal direction. Developmental changes in the infant's capacity to work at the task during the first month were significant when computed in terms of total number of complete sweeps ($p<.01$); number of conjugate eye movements across the midline ($p<.001$); total number of pursuit movements with coor-

Table 6: Visual Pursuit of Moving Targets

Week	Conjugate Eye Movements		Head and Eye Movements	
	Mean Duration of Search (Secs.)	*Maximum (Secs.)*	*Mean Duration of Search (Secs.)*	*Maximum (Secs.)*
1	20″ ↔	37″ ↔	3″ ↔	4″ ↔
2	39″ ↔	60″ ↔	27″ ↔	40″ ↔
3			44″ ↔	113″ ↔
4	60″ ↔	112″ ↔	32″ ↔	249″ ↔
5–8	10″	40″	118″ ✛	240″ ✛
9–12			213″ ✛	342″ ✛
13–16			180″ ✛	260″ ✛
17–20			113″ ✛	390″ ✛
21–24			150″ ✛	216″ ✛

dination of head rotation and conjugate eye movements (p<.05); and number of completed movements in the vertical plane (p<.01). The duration of sustained visual pursuit of a moving target increased significantly between the beginning and end of the third month, but decreased again thereafter (see table 5). After completing three or four complete sweeps of the target with their head and eyes in either the horizontal or vertical planes, the older infants lost interest, and turned either to other visual spectacles in the environment or to their prior activity. Apparently, they were now less "slaved" to the target, and an element of choice or self-selection became characteristic of their behavioral organization (Haith 1976). More generally, the development of wakefulness seems to involve a progressive release from obligatory responses to environmental stimuli. The coordinated motor patterns themselves were now at least as proficient as earlier, but their activation by environmental events no longer conformed to linear machine-like sequences. The development of alert active states therefore implies the differentiation and integration of novel sensorimotor patterns, as well as the potential for making practical choices among alternative action patterns.

Doing Two Things at the Same Time

To define and describe waking behavioral states from a different perspective, I adapted an experimental procedure that is commonly used in studies of dual-task performance in adults. Observations of infants, even under controlled conditions, will not adjudicate among various competing models on divided attention (Friedman and Polson 1981), but they identify how behavioral state contributes to the ontogenesis of dual-task performance, and bring into focus the importance of behavioral state as one parameter to be considered in all investigations of divided attention. Limits on dual-task performance were already implied above by the distinction between alert-inactive and alert-active states, and the observations that infants either carried out a discrete sensorimotor task such as a visual pursuit movement, reaching for a desired object, or else they smiled. When engaged in rhythmical limb motility they either did not or could not be induced to engage in visual tracking of moving objects, the practice of newly discovered hand-eye movements, or to respond specifically to appropriate social stimuli. When confronted with alternative modes of action, they either stopped moving their limbs to carry out the focal activity or continued to move and ignored the environmental events. However, incompatibility between concurrent activities was relative rather than absolute, even within the first month. For

74

example, infants sucked on a blind nipple while making visual pursuit movements (see, for example, Wolff and White 1965), and they could readily nurse while pursuing objects with their head and eyes.

The boundaries of what constitutes dual-task performance or the phenomenon of divided attention are therefore no less complex in young infants than in experimental adult subjects under controlled conditions (Allport 1980).

All humans, including newborns, must be able to carry out two or more anatomically discrete and functionally distinct motor patterns concurrently in order to survive. Peiper (1963), in reviewing the literature on the coordination of respiratory movements, sucking behavior, and swallowing in newborn infants, demonstrated that healthy, full-term infants have no difficulty carrying out all three periodic motor patterns at the same time and combining them into more complex temporal patterns. Such "relative coordinations" (von Holst 1935) are probably an essential strategy by which the organism controls the many independent degrees of freedom in the motor system (Bernstein 1967; Turvey et al. 1978), as well as problems of dual-task performance. From a practical perspective, the inherent tendency of the motor system to construct larger synergies from component tasks makes it more difficult in the young infant to distinguish between dual-task performance and the concurrent performance of two autonomous but unrelated motor tasks.

One could, of course, dismiss the hypothesis that the coordinated motor patterns of young infants are examples of dual-task performance (see for example Peiper 1963; Dreier et al. 1979), on the grounds that these are merely reflexes and therefore irrelevant to the issue of dual-task performance. Yet, it is far from self-evident what the concept of reflex should mean when applied to spontaneously goal-directed action; when, in other words, the term "reflex" is meant to connote the basic unit of behavioral organization rather than an artificially elicited response to an arbitrary stimulus.

The possibility that older infants, when compared to young infants, are better able to abandon one visual stimulus for another, so that "choices" enters into the definition of waking behavioral states, was explored by testing how infants respond to two moving visual stimuli when both are introduced into the visual field simultaneously. Two physically identical objects (pencils) were presented in the center of visual gaze while the experimenter was hidden behind a screen. One object was then moved slowly to one side of the field in a horizontal plane, while the other object was held in place until the infant tracked the moving object. The second object was then jiggled back and forth in place until it caught the infant's attention. As soon as the direction of gaze shifted, the second object was moved a short distance laterally, in the opposite direction, and when the infants began to track the second object, the first one, which had been kept in place, was jiggled and displaced further (see also Graefe 1963; Fantz 1966).

Until the fifth week, infants either ignored both objects, fixated on only one stimulus, or else made rapid oscillating movements between the objects at such a frequency that they were probably not focusing on either of the pencils. After the sixth or seventh week, infants moved their head and eyes deliberately back and forth, staring first at one pencil and then at the other for several seconds, and constructing an alternating pattern which differed qualitatively from the rapid oscillations observed earlier. The infant's gaze could now be "teased" back and forth across the visual field for up to fifteen times. Of course, one might argue that the infants were not at all emancipated from stimulus-boundness but "slaved" to look at two objects in alternation rather than at only one. After several more weeks, however, infants became more selective in their "choice," and could then only be distracted briefly by the pencil game before they returned to their own action in progress. A slow and deliberate alternation of gaze between two objects may represent one functional link between the obligatory motor responses that characterize the behavior of the one-month-old infant, and the spontaneous motor behavior of older infants and children from which we infer "voluntary action" or "choice."

After the second month, this game lost much of its appeal. Infants no longer seemed interested in tracking the red targets at all, just as they had previously lost interest in simply following a red pencil. Instead, it was necessary to introduce more complex stimulus configurations with richer internal features. To test gaze alternation in older infants I therefore used the face and voice of two adults sitting at the right and left sides of the baby, so that the infant could see neither of the persons without turning its head in the appropriate direction. The two persons (usually myself and the mother) began to talk to the baby, and as soon as the latter turned toward either source, the other person began to speak while the first stopped. Once the pattern of alternating gaze was established, both persons stopped speaking, and the infant's behavior was again recorded. By three months infants made slow, and apparently deliberate, head rotations to the alternating sound sources, and smiled or vocalized as soon as they made visual contact with either face. After both persons had stopped talking, they continued to look back and forth three or four times, as if looking for the place from where the voice would come next. By the fourth month, all fourteen infants performed such gaze alternations under the described experimental conditions, but there were considerable variations in the stability of such behavior from one day to the next. The mean frequency of successful trials with at least two slow head oscillations ranged from 20 to 50 percent of trials across the infants.

Under Piaget's formulation, these observations would imply that infants had acquired the first approximations of concepts of object permanence, physical space, physical time, and causality, since they returned to the place where they were last successful in reconstructing the visual spectacle. Under the formulation of behavioral states of wakefulness, the same observations would imply that infants had been liberated from their earlier stimulus boundness, and were now able to choose among alternative actions. The two accounts are not mutually exclusive but probably refer to different perspectives on the same phenomenon. The capacity for making choices follows logically from having access to a sufficient density of sensorimotor patterns and the consequent possibility of "negating" one action in order to select another. In some cases the choice was between two physical objects or things, rather than between alternative actions. In other cases, the choice was between two qualitatively different motor patterns.

For example, I examined the infant's capacity for dual-task performance of motor patterns that could be readily distinguished by their form and function but were not mutually incompatible, as might be the case in crying and sucking, or crying and smiling (Kahnemann 1973). The tasks were also chosen so that neither would be peremptory enough in its demands on "functional space" to block all other activities. At eight weeks and increasingly thereafter, infants were able to persist in one acquired sensorimotor pattern, like rythmically kicking their legs or waving their arms, while smiling or talking to another person at the same time, or vocalizing while playing with a favorite toy. Infants now also used both hands for specialized manual action such that one hand scratched the back of the head or held a foot while the other reached for objects in the near visual field. Many of these observations pertained to the development of social communication and will be discussed in more detail in the appropriate sections. In the context of the present discussion, they indicate that visual pursuit combined with generalized movements is one example of a general increase in capacity for dual-task performance. This marks a radical shift in the infant's behavioral organization, and the onset of a behavioral state that is probably essential for the discovery of new combinations among already acquired and practiced actions, the linking of means to ends behavior, and the construction of new ends realized by the novel combination of action patterns (Piaget 1952). Alert activity may then be characterized as that condition when the infant's behavioral repertory is less "slaved" to specific stimulus conditions, when an element of choice enters in the organization of the behavioral repertory, and when infants act, instead of simply reacting (Thomas 1973; Posner and Rothbart 1980). Emancipation from stimulus-boundness, as defined here, appears to be the necessary condition for carrying out two activities concurrently, such that the performance of one movement pattern no longer limits the performance of concurrent activities.

Perhaps more critical for the emergence of alert activity as a stable and self-maintaining behavioral state is the onset of "self-initiated" goal-directed actions. At the point when infants can act "spontaneously," rather than responding to a stimulus world, the length of time for which they are able to stay awake and alert comes, so to speak, under the infant's "control." If the hypothesis is correct that states of waking alertness are dependent, initially, on the performance and, later, on the possibility of goal-directed actions, wakefulness is initially dependent as well on the vicissitudes of a compliant environment that provides opportunities for action, as for example when I presented infants with a constantly moving visual target. By eight or ten weeks, however, infants seem to be less dependent on specific events in the environment (e.g. experimental stimuli). Now they initiate the action either by selecting events in the environment or by exercising motor patterns in the process of formation. At the same time their repertory of self-initiated actions expands, making them increasingly autonomous of environmental contingencies and extending the time during which they can stay awake and alert by their own activity.

Crying

Sustained crying is typically associated with physiological and behavioral changes other than vocalization itself. Visually it includes in addition the crying grimace, changes in overall level of motor activity, rate and amplitude of respirations, heart rate, blood pressure, skin vascularity, as well as the behavioral input-output relations which alter the infant's relation to the physical and social environment. To the extent that these features of crying constitute coherent ensembles within and across babies, they fulfill the essential criteria of a behavioral state and are usually treated as such in current state taxonomies. The inclusion of crying among the behavioral states also highlights conceptual problems inherent to any discussion of behavioral states but most clearly illustrated by crying. At the phenomenal level, crying always involves a dimension of intensity that has a direct effect on the parameter prescriptions of each state variable, and that presumably determines the degree to which the state is self-maintaining, the kinds of spontaneous behavior observed, as well as the infant's responsiveness to environmental events. Intensity of state I or state II sleep has no operational meaning in the sense that behavioral states were defined above, although alternative classification schemes based on electroencephalographic data speak about the "depth" of sleep; and observations summarized in preceding chapters suggest that stability or self-correcting tendencies of state I sleep may decrease systematically from the beginning to the end of any one epoch. Similarly, it has been proposed that the infant exhibits different degrees of alertness within a waking condition (Parmalee and Sigman, 1983). Again, it is unclear how such "degrees" of alertness should be measured independently of the events which engage the infant's attention. By contrast the intensity of crying can be measured by objective criteria such as, for example, the amplitude, pitch, and temporal organization of cry vocalization, the amounts and type of generalized movements, the changes in blood pressure and the like (Stark et al. 1978).

Another definitional problem arises from the fact that vocalizations are the single most important state criterion for distinguishing crying from all other behavioral states. Yet vocalizations are not unique to this state but are also a common correlate of alert states in the two-to-three-month-old infant. Therefore the *quality* of state criteria must be specified in keeping with the convention of defining behavioral states as mutually exclusive ensembles of behavior patterns and physiological concomitants. The distinction between cry and noncry vocalizations presents no problems, in the pure case. The hunger cry can easily be distinguished from vocalizations that occur during alert activity. Problems of definition arise when one tries to distinguish noncry vocalizations from fussy noises or early cry vocalizations. For this descriptive taxonomy I did not attempt to score intensities of crying on an ordinal or interval scale, but I did distinguish between crying as a behavioral state and fussiness as a state transition. Fussiness was defined as that condition when the infants made intermittent moaning or crylike sounds which conformed to no distinct temporal pattern and were separated by periods of silence lasting three seconds or more. During this time, the face could be contorted into a grimace of discontent or pouting, which was easily distinguished from the cry face. By contrast, crying referred to occasions when the infants vocalized repetitively in five or more distinct cycles and individual utterances were not separated by more than three seconds and were accompanied by the "typical" cry grimace and usually by vigorous limb activity. The acoustic features by which I distinguished fussing from cry vocalizations are described in more detail in the section on crying as an expression of emotion. This chapter summarizes primarily observations on the overall duration of crying, the duration of individual crying bouts, the conditions that preceded and followed the bout, and manipulations that induced or terminated a period of crying. Although I found it convenient to distinguish between crying as a behavioral state and fussiness as a transition, the boundaries could not always be sharply drawn. A number of previous reports by others have either not included fussing in their descriptions or combined it with crying proper.

Cumulative Tabulations

As in the case of other behavioral states, the total time spent by each baby crying or fussing as a percentage of observation time, and the mean duration of individual episodes of crying or fussing on days of unobtrusive observation, were extracted from the running record and computed as the mean for each month as well as related in time to other behavioral states. However, the results of these tabulations cannot be compared directly to parallel data on sleep or waking states because crying almost always provoked some social response from the mother which terminated crying before it had run its course. The quantitative data summarized here are therefore more closely related to the mother's child-rearing patterns than to the spontaneous onset and termination of crying as a behavioral state.

Figure 10a indicates that time spent crying and fussing as a percentage of total observation time, was surprisingly short even during the first month and decreased further during the second and third months. On many days of observation after the third month, there were no entries in the running record of any crying at all. Intra- and inter-individual variations in duration of crying were considerable and probably reflect differences in the mother's way of dealing with her child. Furthermore, each of the babies who was observed for at least three months had at least one and usually several days during that time when it was inconsolable because of a mild illness, a cold, or gastrointestinal distress. On such days it was extraordinarily difficult for mothers to pacify their infants either with food or by holding them, and the total duration of crying, despite parental intervention, was considerably longer than the mean for any other week of observation. Data on days when the infants were clearly uncomfortable are therefore not included in the summary tabulation.

The absolute duration of individual crying bouts, like the cu-

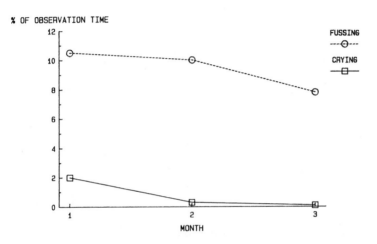

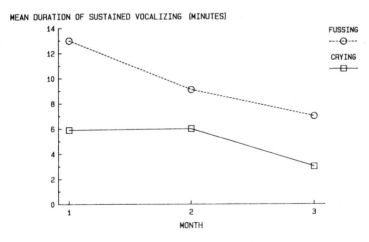

Figure 10. a. (above) Total Duration of Crying and Fussing

b. (below) Mean Duration of Cry and Fuss Episodes

mulative percentage of total crying, was unexpectedly short (see figure 10b). Periods of crying rarely exceeded six minutes during the first month, or three mimutes in the second or third months and thereafter. Such findings are not consistent with data by Brazelton (1962) and Bernal (1972), who both report that infants may cry from two to three hours a day in the first half-year of life. One reason for such discrepancies may be that my continued presence in the home caused mothers to respond more quickly to the cries of their babies than they would otherwise have. Yet the mothers' casual attitude toward my presence and their healthy skepticism about the advice of child-development experts makes such an explanation unlikely. Since the data reported by Brazelton and Bernal are based for the most part on parental reports, it is also possible that parents applied more liberal definition and included fussing with crying.

The mean duration of time spent *fussing* was considerably longer in each month than the time spent *crying* (figure 10ab). Similarly, the mean duration of individual fussing bouts was significantly greater than those of crying in each of the first three months. Fussing is clearly a less peremptory social signal. Many of the mothers were inclined to let their babies fuss without intervening, in the hope that the baby might go back to sleep. By contrast they usually abandoned this hope once the infant had actually started to cry. Thus the likelihood that a mother would pick up her infant to hold or feed it was significantly greater in response to crying than to fussing, in each of the first three months (p .001 by Mann Whitney U-Test). However, differences in maternal response to fussing and crying were not as categorical as the description might suggest. Mothers often picked up their babies for a feeding at the first fussy sound, when they thought the baby must be hungry or that the preceding feeding had not been sufficient. Similarly, they intervened early when they wanted to run an errand and did not want the baby to start crying while they were away. For similar reasons of convenience, they sometimes picked up the baby for a feeding even while it was alert or while it was still asleep.

State Sequences Relative to Crying

The organismic condition or environmental events that preceded and followed a bout of crying and lasted thirty seconds or longer, were so closely interwoven with the social context that spontaneous state sequences in relation to crying could be described only on rare occasions. Figure 7 indicates that fussing was the most common condition preceding a bout of crying. In other words, fussing was clearly an early response to the offending cause which, if left unattended, resulted in crying, but the sequence was by no means invariant. Among all instances of fussing where the mother did not intervene, the infants were as likely to stop again and fall asleep or to become alert (mean of 47 percent of all reported instances over the first three months) as they were to start crying. Next to fussiness, alert activity or alert inactivity were the behavioral states that most commonly preceded crying.

Maternal interventions were the events that most often followed after and terminated a bout of full-blown crying (73 percent), whether or not the infant had already been fed within the preceding hour. Sequences in which mothers picked up their crying baby to provide a feeding, even when the infants had been fed within the preceding hour, were particularly evident among breast-feeding mothers who during the first two months tended to feed their baby on the average of four to six times during any four-hour observation period, whereas bottle-feeding mothers usually offered one or at most two feedings during the same period. The events that followed after and terminated a period of fussiness were much more variable, and, as indicated, they depended as much on the mother's child-rearing practices as on the baby's own spontaneous state changes.

The relation between feeding (hunger) and crying was also examined by using feedings rather than crying bouts as the reference point for the description of behavioral state sequences. As might be concluded from the preceding discussion, crying was the event that most often preceded a feeding, and in many cases the mother seemed to be simply waiting for the appropriate signal in order to start the meal. In fact mothers often anticipated that babies would soon be hungry and began to heat the bottle or formula, but usually waited until the infant gave a vocal signal before actually offering a meal. As figure 7 indicates, feedings were most often preceded by either a period of fussiness or crying during the first and second months. However, by the third month and increasingly thereafter mothers often decided to feed the baby when it was still alert and happy, to maintain the baby on a predictable schedule conforming to the mothers' work habits or because they expected that the infant was probably hungry even if it was not crying.

Five mothers in the sample independently arrived at the conclusion that their baby "needed" a period of fussing or crying before it could go to sleep. Acting on this notion, they usually put the baby to bed once it had been properly fed and after they had reassured themselves that there was no specific cause for the fussing or crying. Because I was skeptical of such a "need" to cry, I carried out a number of experiments after the third week to "test" the mother's impression. The manipulations were limited to those infants whose mothers believed they had a need to cry themselves to sleep. On occasions when the baby had been fed, diapered, had played for at least ten minutes in the mother's presence and was then put to bed although it was still fussing, I carried out a series of maneuvers designed to stop the baby from crying. For example, I presented the baby with interesting visual spectacles, smiled to it, nodded my head, talked, rocked the crib, offered it a pacifier or gently stroked its back. Any one of these interventions briefly stopped the baby from fussing or crying and sometimes induced a condition of state II sleep. However, in most cases the infant began to fuss and cry again as soon as I stopped my intervention. Such sequences could continue for up to half an hour or more; each time when I stopped amusing the baby it started to cry again. Yet when I let the infants cry or fuss one to three minutes without interfering, they usually fell asleep on their own and then stayed asleep. The results lend some support to the mother's impression that their infants in fact needed a period of crying in order to fall asleep, as if this had become a part of their daily routine. There was, however, no evidence from the overall tabulation that babies as a group needed to cry a minimum of time each day or week, or that crying fulfills some essential function during the early months after birth, such that all infants will cry for a fixed, minimum amount of time on any one day or in any one week.

Motor Activity during Crying

The most striking feature of crying as a behavioral state, other than vocalization and cry grimaces, is evidently generalized movements of the limbs, which typically accompany most periods of full-fledged rhythmical crying. Direct observation permitted only rough estimates of the overall quantity of the movement types and motor coordination patterns in crying. A more detailed analysis of film or video sequences would be required to make a quantitative analysis of the overall amount of activity or of particular aspects of motor coordination during crying. Instead, I made rough estimates by tabulating on one day each week the frequency of common movement- patterns observed during sustained crying that lasted at least three minutes on one day a week. On the same day, I tabulated the amount of motility while the infants were fussy and while they were alert and active (see table 3).

One feature of limb movement during sustained crying was the apparent phase correlation between the discrete limb movements of the arms or legs and rhythmic cry vocalizations, such that one or more limbs moved in unison with each expiratory cry sound, but this phase correlation was not a consistent feature. Nor was it possible by direct observation to determine the temporal precision with which cry sounds and limb movements were, in fact, synchronized, since pattern perception tends to impose relationships which on objective measurement prove to be false. Nevertheless, there were periods when the coordination between vocalization and limb movements seemed more closely synchronized than at other times. During fussing, by contrast, a one-to-one correspondence between vocal patterns and leg movements was never noted. Similarly, when infants were allowed to cry for an extended period and their vocalization patterns gave the impression that they were "desperate" or "angry," the phase correlation between movement patterns and cry vocalizations broke down.

During the first two weeks after birth, 40 percent of entries on full-fledged crying also made reference to an approximate one-to-one correspondence with limb movements, such that one or more of the four limb movements began and stopped with each cry vocalization. In 30 percent of the entries no relationship between the two motor patterns was noted; and 30 percent of the entries did not indicate what the relationship might be. About the same distribution of one-to-one correspondences between crying and limb movement obtained for the last two weeks of the first month. During the second month, however, only 15 percent of entries refer to any approximate temporal relation between the two motor patterns, whereas 60 percent of entries indicated no such relation. By the third month, the sustained crying periods were so few and so short that the comparison could not be continued.

An additional feature of crying which distinguished it from other behavioral states was the kind of limb movements observed. To make the comparison, I tabulated the total number of various motor patterns within successive five-minute periods one day each week over the first six weeks, when the infants were alert and active (and ready to pursue a visual target or to smile), when they were fussy (as defined above), and when they were crying vigorously. The motor patterns scored were mouthing and tonguing, hand-face contacts, hand-mouth contacts, episodes of hand sucking, and kicking (either extension or flexion of the knee of either leg). The mean values of the various motor patterns over a five-minute period in each of the states, summarized in table 3, indicate that crying was most notably

85

associated with a sharp increase in frequency of kicking relative to both alert states and fussing; that mouthing and hand-mouth contacts were equally common in alert activity and fussing but rare when the infant was crying; and that hand sucking, which was more common during fussiness than during alert states, dropped precipitously where the infant was crying, as did hand-mouth contacts. The results were even more striking when hand sucking or hand-mouth contacts were computed as a percentage of hand-face contact; such proportions indicated a sharp decrease in the infant's "ability" to bring the hand to the mouth when it was vigorously active, as if the agitation associated with crying interfered with hand-mouth coordination.

Experimental Manipulation of Crying as a Behavioral State

The preceding sections illustrate the difficulty of separating crying as a behavioral state from crying as an expression of emotion, and of distinguishing between the natural duration of crying and its "experimental" manipulations, since most mothers made a concerted effort to comfort their infants as soon as the latter began to cry. The recorded duration of crying in the home was therefore not representative of its "natural" duration in the same sense as were the durations of sleep and waking alert states.

The experimental manipulations I used to terminate crying as a behavioral state were variations on interventions used by mothers to comfort their infants. Many of these involved changes in social context (mother coming or leaving, the presence of a stranger), and will be described in later sections on the expression of emotions. However, other experimental manipulations designed to induce or terminate crying provided clues about the mechanisms of "self-organization" that were less obvious from parallel observations on other states.

Medical routines in any modern newborn nurseries amply support the claim that acute physical pain automatically elicits sustained crying in young infants. The young of animal species with well-developed vocal repertoires also respond to physical pain with distinctive cries, but there are important differences in the temporal organization of cry vocalizations of infants and animal young which may help to clarify the distinction between crying as an experssion of emotions and as a behavioral state.

The crying of animal young in response to pain, hunger, or environmental threats, usually lasts only as long as the cause for the crying persists. By contrast, human infants frequently continue to cry in cyclical repetitions accompanied by rhythmic limb movements long after the offending pain stimulus has presumably stopped. Among the naturally occuring organismic and environmental events that reliably elicit human crying, hunger is probably the most common cause in Western cultures where the mother does not carry her infant all day long (Konner 1983). Hunger induces the same self-perpetuating cycle of crying and limb activity as physical pain; sometimes this cycle becomes so immune to external events that it is impossible to feed the infant until it has shifted to a different behavioral state. While it is difficult to tell in infants exactly when a physical pain stimulus stops "hurting," the same cyclical perpetuation of crying can be observed in older infants, children, and even hysterical adults, in response to panic, anxiety, and desertion, where no physical pain is involved. In all such cases, crying as a behavioral state will, under specifiable conditions, become self-equilibrating once the crying response to an adequate stimulus exceeds threshold intensities. Nothing similar has been described in the young of other animal species, whereas it is an important feature of human behavioral organization that clearly distinguishes crying as a behavioral state from crying as an expression of emotions.

From the perspective on behavioral states as collectives of interacting components, such observations are also of interest by emphasizing that the input-output relations between the initial trigger stimulus and the intensity and duration of cry vocalizations or motor activity are nonlinear. Once initiated by an external event, crying becomes a "spontaneous" condition of the organism which maintains itself in relative autonomy from the triggering cause (Fentress 1976).

Alternative Perspectives

The description of crying as a behavioral state supports the assumption that states cannot be defined independently of their motor constituents. The same point was raised earlier in discussions of state I sleep when I proposed that the self-maintaining characteristics of a state are causally related to the synchronizing potential of their near periodic motor patterns. It was implied again by the hypothesis that sustained wakefulness is determined in part by the density of potentially interactive motor schemata and postural adjustments. However, the concrete overlap between the organizational characteristics of a state and its motor constituents became clearest in the case of crying. As a state, crying is defined not only by its characteristic facial grimace and vocalization patterns but also by associated postural tonus, periodic limb movements and respiratory patterns, and presumably by variations in heart rate and other autonomic variables (Stark and Nathanson 1973).

Until now it was possible to ignore the dimension of quantity or intensity because it is neither a necessary nor a helpful criterion for distinguishing among sleep states of the newborn infant, except if quantity refers to the temporal characteristics of respiratory movements and other near periodic motor patterns. Nor was the quantitative dimension necessary for distinguishing between sleep, waking, and crying. The dimension of quantity can, however, not be overlooked when one characterizes the behavioral states of older infants, examines their input-output characteristics during crying and waking states, or tries to make specific comparisons between the behavior of infants who are whimpering continuously, crying rhythmically, or screaming in desperation. All three conditions would, under the established taxonomy, be scored as crying. Yet they differ significantly in their vocalization patterns, respiratory movements, limb activity, postural tonus, and input-output characteristics. The theoretically interesting question then becomes whether conditions of crying differ only along a continuum of intensity and quantity, or changes of "intensity" within one state eventually produce qualitative shifts in the organizational properties of component elements even when the infant remains in the "same" state. A dialectic shift from quantity to quality was suggested, for example, by the extent to which crying maintained itself, or could be disrupted by exteroceptive stimulation. The hysterically crying (or laughing) infant was less susceptible to environmental interference than the same infant when whimpering or smiling. Rhythmic crying seemed considerably more stable as a self-equilibrating condition than either whimpering or screaming. Analogous comparisons can be made with respect to wakefulness, although in this case the appropriate measure of "intensity" remains problematic.

When behavioral states are defined as ensembles of interactive motor patterns, the scaling up or down on any one major state-criterion should be associated with qualitative shifts in the internal organization of motor components, as well as with changes in organism-environment interactions—not because such state differences are causally related to some linear executive agency like hunger, arousal, or instinct, but because the mutual interaction among motor components induces different self-organizing conditions and radically alters the internal state dynamics and the infant's responsiveness to environmental events or perturbations.

Experimental interventions during state I suggested that subtle variations in the self-organizing potential and sensitivity to environmental events may obtain even within one continuous twenty-one-minute period of stable sleep; and that such differences may be associated with gradual shifts in the temporal organization of breathing movements until, at a critical point, a discontinuous break to another state occurs. Presumably, such gradual shifts also occur in other states (for example, fatigue or boredom during waking states) and alter patterns of spontaneous movement, emotional expression, and the infant's responsiveness to environmental events. At what point a quantitative continuous change on one or more variables induces a qualitative change in the dynamic interaction of the motor ensemble may therefore be an important topic for future empirical observations.

To study the effect of quantitative changes along some dimension on behavioral state characteristics, I used hunger as the most convenient independent variable, even though it is a factor that is probably extrinsic to state organization itself. Hunger, or time since last feeding, has been used extensively as an independent variable for experiments in drive-motivated learning, and as an analogy to the instinctual drives in psychoanalysis. Hunger recurs periodically and predictably in the everyday life of the infant, and it can be estimated approximately without instrumental manipulation. The choice of hunger as the independent variable was also consistent with Kleitman's formulation of wakefulness of necessity which implies that the cycle of hunger-hunger satiation may be the physiological basis for rest-activity cycles in the young infant (Kleitman 1963). Similarly, Piaget used hunger as the prototype for organic conditions of discomfort in the young infant that may contribute to the earliest differentiation among sensorimotor schemata, by increasing the infant's ability to discriminate among alternative sucking objects in terms of the motor patterns they produce (for example, nipples that do or do not elicit a swallowing reflex [Piaget 1952]).

In one informal experiment I examined how infants respond to the *interruption* of feeding at various points during the meal, i.e., when they had taken at most two or three swallows from the bottle, in the middle of a feeding, and close to the end while they were still awake and alert. These experiments were carried out routinely during at least one feeding each week. Hunger contributed significantly to the vigor with which infants protested when their meal was interrupted. Near the end of a meal, almost none of the infants at any age protested. However, at the beginning of a meal, infants below one month of age frequently responded to the interruption with vigorous crying, whereas three-month-old infants rarely if ever did. These results suggest that the observable influence of hunger on behavioral state was considerably greater in one-month than three-month-old infants, and considerably greater at the beginning than near the end of a meal.

Along similar lines I examined the influence of hunger on the infant's anticipatory behavior before being placed in the feeding posture ("Trinklage"), before they actually saw or received the bottle. For technical reasons, breast-fed babies were not examined in this way. The outcome measures were spontaneous mouthing, tonguing, mouth searching or rooting, and hand-mouth contact, and these were scored just before and just after the mother had positioned her baby for a feeding; or before and after she had interrupted the feeding and was ready to resume the meal. Responses were recorded only when the infants were alert and not crying. In order to distinguish responses to postural changes (being placed into the "Trinklage") from those presumably triggered by the sight of the bottle, I sometimes asked mothers to show their baby the bottle before changing its position, and at other times to change the baby's position without letting it see the bottle. During the first week after birth neither the feeding position nor the sight of the bottle produced any measurable increase in mouthing behavior. By the end of the second week, the feeding position without seeing the bottle produced a significant increase of mouthing, tonguing, spontaneous rooting, and hand-mouth contacts, relative to a comparable period immediately before, when the infant was still in a fully reclining or upright position. The effect of position on the amount of oral activity was significantly greater at the beginning than in the middle of a feeding, but had no behavioral effect near the end of a meal, even when infants were still fully alert.

Until six or eight weeks, the sight of the bottle alone had no measurable effect on mouthing activity. Apparently infants of less than eight weeks responded to positional attitude as the clue that the feeding was about to start or resume, but this effect was limited to periods when the infants were hungry. By the end of the second month the sight of the bottle alone triggered increased mouthing and mouth searching, but only during the *middle* and not at the start or near the end of a meal. Apparently, the sight of the bottle triggered oral activity only when the infants had been sucking during the preceding one to two minutes, as if the preceding motor activity reminded them of the bottle's functional significance. By four or five months, infants occasionally made deliberate mouthing movements even when I showed them the bottle between two meals while they were alert; but the response was unpredictable and could not be clearly distinguished from random mouthing movements.

Another coordinated motor pattern that is functionally related to hunger satiation is the "rooting" or directed head-turning response to the place where the skin of the mouth is stimulated. The rooting response is fully operational within a few minutes after birth. Gentle stroking of the right or left corners of the mouth elicit directed head rotations in the appropriate direction, while contact with the upper or lower lip elicit head movements in the up or down direction. As the head rotates, the mouth may open and the lips stretch in the direction of stimulation, as if the mouth were preparing itself to receive an adequate sucking object. The vigor and precision of rooting is generally less in the vertical than horizontal direction, possibly because the head control is relatively better in lateral than in vertical movements.

Sainte-Anne Dargassies (1977) identified four "cardinal points" at the two corners of the mouth and the upper and lower lips that were particularly responsive to stimulation. Prechtl (1958) refined the method of stimulation by also testing the facial region at some distance from the lip, to determine the radius of sensory area sensitive to tactile stimulation. More important, he compared rooting responses while infants were awake and when they were asleep, and noted that adequate stimulation typically elicits head rotation *towards* the site of stimulation when the infant is awake, but *away* from the site of stimulation when infants are asleep (state II), whereas stimulation has no predictable effect when infants are in state I sleep.

All infants of the longitudinal sample were tested at least once every two weeks over the first three months, for rooting behavior in the hour immediately after a meal and three hours after a meal. Rooting was tested while they were awake, while they were fussy, and during state II sleep. Points of stimulation were the four "cardinal points," as well as four sites 2 cm peripheral to these points. Before testing, infants were always placed in the supine position, with the head readjusted to the midline after each trial. The response was elicited by stroking a latex nipple gently back and forth across each point three times, keeping the nipple in the same place relative to the infant's head but lifting it from the skin after stimulation, so that the distance between the nipple and the center of the mouth after head rotation could be used as the reference point for estimating "accuracy of rooting." To control for random head rotations, only responses accompanied by opening of the mouth or lip pursing were scored as rooting responses; and the latency between onset of stimulation and onset of rooting was measured by stopwatch.

At each time of testing from the second to the eighth week, the frequency of rooting responses during wakefulness was significantly greater before than after a meal ($p<.05$ for each month). The radius of skin sensitive to stimulation was also greater before than after a meal. After the meal, waking infants usually rooted only when the *lateral* corners of the mouth were stimulated, whereas the upper and lower lips, and all four sites 2 cm removed from the lips were insensitive. Before a meal, the frequency of responses was the same for vertical and horizontal movements to stimulation at the mucocutaneous junction, but greater in the horizontal than vertical direction when sites 2 cm removed from the lips were stimulated. Thus hunger had a graded effect on rooting, relative to the area of facial skin that was sensitive to adequate stimulation.

By the end of the second month the overall frequency of rooting responses had diminished considerably, regardless of hunger state. Infants were readily distracted by other events in the environment. Visual pursuit of moving objects as well as visual search for the source of stimulation frequently preempted rooting behavior so that the effect of hunger could no longer be demonstrated quantitatively. *Age* therefore had only a general effect on rooting.

During state I sleep, infants made no directed head-turning movements towards or away from the stimulus, and either ignored it or stirred briefly. In state II, they occasionally turned their heads away from the site of stimulation, but they did so far less often than one would have anticipated from Prechtl's descriptions of full-term infants. When fussing or crying in the hour *before* a meal, infants usually rooted after a brief latency, making a vigorous head rotation that frequently overshot the mark. However, when fussing or crying in the hour *after* a meal, they either rooted rapidly and accurately, or else failed to respond altogether. When only trials resulting in active rooting behavior were counted, accuracy was greater *after* than *before* the meal because of a tendency to overshoot the mark before they were fed. By contrast, accuracy was greater before than after a meal when infants were alert. The latency of rooting was always significantly shorter before than after a meal whether the infants were alert, or fussing and crying. In sum, hunger influenced the probability, vigor, and latency of responding to an adequate stimulus within one behavioral state (waking alertness) as well as the radius of skin surface that would elicit the appropriate rooting response. At the same time, behavioral state influenced rooting behavior as an independent variable.

The observations so far refer only to the effect of food deprivation on dependent measures of motor activity which were in each case functionally related to hunger satiation. They do not indicate whether hunger and other organic needs might also have a more general "organizing" or disorganizing effect on motor patterns which are not functionally related to the independent variable. In previous studies, I had demonstrated that *nonnutritive* sucking does not interfere with visual pursuit, but rather facilitates sustained visual tracking (Wolff and White 1965; see also Bruner 1968). For the present study I examined how *nutritive* sucking might interact with visual pursuit at different points in a feeding. As the visual target, I again used a large red disk mounted on a white cardboard which was moved slowly either in the horizontal or vertical direction across the infant's visual field during the bottle feeding. Mothers were always asked to hold their babies so they would have no difficulty continuing to suck if they pursued the target. Pursuit was scored as eye movements alone or as coordinated head-eye movements. Pursuit was scored at three times during the bottle feeding—shortly after the start of the feeding, when the infant had consumed half of the usual amount of milk, and toward the end of the feeding when the infant was still sucking actively and was still alert. Observations were discontinued whenever the infants fell asleep at any point during the meal.

The original purpose of the observations had been to test developmental changes in dual-task performance, but the infants defeated this aim by resorting to strategies I had not anticipated. For example, older infants frequently abandoned the sucking nipple altogether to continue pursuit movements before returning to it, so that "dual-task performance" could not be measured. Moreover, since all infants could suck and pursue concurrently within the first week after birth, the effect of age on dual-task performance could also not be tested.

The primary outcome measures were (a) sucking without visual pursuit; (b) sucking *and* visual pursuit; (c) pursuit without sucking; or (d) temporarily abandoning the nipple in order to pursue the object. They were scored at the beginning, in the middle, and the end of each feeding to control for the degrees of hunger satiation. Experiments were performed once a week during the first, second, or third months after birth, and restricted to bottle-fed infants. For various reasons, the full testing schedule could be completed in only ten infants. The results summarized in figure 11a indicate that, even during the first month, most infants pursued the moving target with their eyes alone, or sometimes by partial movements of the head, all the while continuing to suck, although the bottle in the mouth obviously limited their range of head movements. Hunger did, however, have some effect on dual-task performance during the first month (see fig.

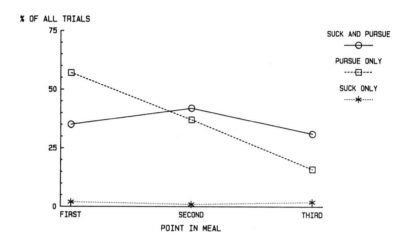

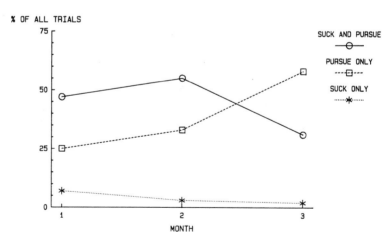

Figure 11. a. (above) Nutritive Sucking and Visual Pursuit within Meal

b. (below) Nutritive Sucking and Visual Pursuit over Time

11a). At the beginning of a feeding the most common response was combined sucking and eye pursuit. By the middle or near the end of a meal, even one-month-old infants temporarily abandoned the bottle to pursue the target with their head and eyes, where three-month-old infants often stopped sucking even at the beginning of the meal to pursue the target with their head and eyes, and only then started the meal, after they had satisfied their curiosity (see fig. 11b). The interaction between two potentially competitive and mutually exclusive coordinated motor patterns therefore differed in part as a function of continuous variables such as hunger.

By themselves, such observations make no persuasive case for introducing the quantitative dimension as an essential defining criterion for the behavioral states. For one thing, the observations pertained only to (inferred) hunger and most of the outcome measures were consumatory motor patterns directly relating to hunger. If used as the logical basis for changing current criteria for classifying behavioral state, the change of strategy would raise the troublesome question of how many other similar extrinsic variables must be considered. Should hunger-specific variations in state organization be distinguished from variations of state due to wet diapers, thirst, or distress after an unpleasant experience?

One possible alternative solution to the problem of state classification that arises from the finding that quantitative variations within state can induce radical changes in organism-environment interaction, is to keep the concept of behavioral state as proposed but to assume that the essential state criteria must be readjusted to age or developmental differentiation. Different sets of essential state criteria would then have to be specified for each discontinuous developmental shift or "stage" until we arrived at a comprehensive taxonomy for adults. This is hardly a satisfactory solution, because it leaves us with a long list of pragmatically derived state criteria that may or may not be developmentally related and therefore preclude any longitudinal analysis of behavioral states. Furthermore, since there are no self-evident decision rules for determining the point in development when new state criteria must be specified, one would in effect be formulating a new taxonomy of arbitrarily defined behavioral *stages* in terms of behavioral states.

Another alternative implied by earlier discussions defines behavioral states not by specific criteria but in terms of a functional principle that classifies state according to the actual number of mutually exclusive ensembles of interactive motor patterns which can be shown to exhibit the property of self-organization. The empirical task for a developmental analysis of states then becomes the formulation of methods to determine under what conditions interacting motor patterns meet the criteria of self-organizing condition, and by which units of measurement such self-organizing conditions can be described or quantified. Although methods for investigating mutually interactive motor patterns as "coordinative structures" (Turvey et al. 1978) have not been applied systematically to the study of young infants, there is preliminary evidence to suggest that such methods are applicable (Thelen 1985), and that they can contribute to our understanding about the development of waking behavioral states.

Summary

The definition of behavioral states as a finite set of mutually exclusive ensembles that can be described exhaustively in terms of a small number of variables has proven invaluable for empirical studies and clinical comparisons of newborn infants. The fact that such ensembles and their predictable sequences are observed in all healthy infants throughout the early months after birth, suggests that the behavioral state concept refers to more than a convenient classification scheme, and also implies something about the underlying physiological processes that modulate input-output relationships in nonlinear fashion. In this second sense, the essential state criteria are only surface markers of presumed underlying physiological processes. By themselves, they are not sufficient for investigating the physiological mechanisms that confer dynamic stability and self-organization on behavioral states, since other continuous or episodic variables may contribute in important ways to the internal dynamics of state organization. The distinction between state criteria and the dynamics of interaction among the component variables of a state becomes particularly important when we investigate the developmental differentiation of waking states.

To highlight this distinction, I propose a general redefinition of behavioral states that examines the *coherence* among sets of variables as the metric for a developmental analysis of states, rather than listing age-appropriate criterion variables at different points during development. Such a redefinition can serve as a point of departure for empirical studies to determine the parameter settings on variables that facilitate the interaction or synchronization among concurrently active motor patterns; to examine the minimum density of synchronized motor patterns operating "relative coordinations" that is needed to induce dynamic stability within a state (von Holst 1937; Katchalsky et al. 1974); to measure how this stability is preserved under conditions of experimental perturbation; and to explore how experimentally produced parameter changes on any one state variable influence the overall stability of that state (Kugler et al. 1982; Kelso and Tuller 1983). Since the redefinition should, in principle, be applicable throughout development, it would eliminate the need to specify new criteria for waking behavioral states in each discontinuous stage in development; and it would shift the focus of empirical studies from a selection of age-appropriate, mutually exclusive state criteria, to an analysis of the ways in which developmentally changing patterns of behavior interact dynamically.

At present, the proposal has the obvious disadvantage that "rules of coherence" among ensembles of repetitive motor actions in the young infant remain to a large extent undefined. On the other hand, there are a number of relevant experimental and clinical findings on children and adults that could eventually serve as the basis for defining such rules of coherence in young infants. For example, the mechanisms by which distinct motor patterns are coupled into synergies, thereby stabilizing the motor system and inducing new coordinated patterns, have been studied extensively in adults (Kelso et al. 1981), and should be ideally suited for the study of motor development in young infants.

Most directly, the model provides a metaphor for studies on the temporal regulation of individual movement patterns as stable rhythms which are self-corrective when temporarily disrupted by environmental intrusions (for example, in the case of respirations or nonnutritive sucking). Further, the model implies that the interaction among individual movement patterns are the means by which behavioral states become self-organizing or self-maintaining to different degrees during early infancy. Within limits, the model proposed here is susceptible to experimental investigations by examining, for example, how changes in any one constituent state variable alerts the resistance of that state to disruption by experimental interventions, as illustrated by the tickling experiments in state I and state II. Because the alleged synchronization or relative coordination among periodically repeating motor variables never achieves perfect equilibrium or synchronization, the model also provides a means for examining how the dissociation among rhythmic patterns as they reach critical parameter variables spontaneously will result in the transition from one state to another (as in the case of rhythmical respirations during state I). Monotonous or rhythmic external stimulation and rhythmical mouthing movements produced by a pacifier, for example, may have a stabilizing effect on behavioral states, beyond the time when they would otherwise terminate, by facilitating the synchronization among two or more rhythmic motor patterns whereas intermittent disruptive environmental stimuli may accelerate their uncoupling (Pavlidis 1973).

The temporal coherence among motor variables during wakefulness was not tested directly, although it is amenable to experimental investigation even in infants (Thelen 1985). Experimental manipulations to prolong wakefulness may produce an effect either by activating or reactivating oscillating sensorimotor systems (oculomotor movements) which confer greater stability on wakefulness as a self-organizing state. As the infant acquires new sensorimotor actions, new postural controls, and the like, and as these sensorimotor patterns become "voluntary" or self-initiated, in other words when acquired motor patterns no longer depend on environmental stimulation and become mutually interactive, they also confer increased internal stability on wakefulness, transforming it from transient episodes to self-equilibrating dispositions.

Finally, the proposed alternative may help to resolve apparent contradictions between the use of quantitative and qualitative criteria for defining behavioral states. When the interaction of motor patterns is defined quantitatively in terms of parameter prescriptions on continuous variables of rate, temporal order (rhythm), density, and spatial displacement (intensity), these prescriptions become synonymous with the definition of behavioral state itself. Any critical scaling up or down on a single state-variable will alter the potential of that variable for interacting with other motor variables, and change the dynamic stability of the corresponding behavioral state. Thus, when any *quantitative* change on a continuous variable reaches a critical point, it will induce *qualitative* breaks or discontinuous transitions from one state to another.

3

The Development of
Emotional Expressions

Long ago, Descartes concluded that "In the writings of the ancients there is nothing in which the defective nature of the sciences is shown more clearly than in what they have written on the passions" (Hillman 1964). In 1958, English and English concluded in their dictionary of psychiatric terms that "emotion is virtually impossible to define . . . except in terms of conflicting theories." Similarly, the twelfth edition of the *Encyclopaedia Britannica* concludes that "our knowledge of the topic of emotions is less complete than our knowledge of any other topic in the field of psychology."

A brief survey of the contemporary literature in clinical, experimental, developmental, and comparative psychology suggests that our understanding of the emotions has not advanced materially since the time of Descartes' bleak assessment. The same definitional confusions remain, as we ask whether the term "emotion" should refer to observable motor expressions, unconscious affects, autonomic arousal, feelings, social structures, energies, values, moods, "organizers of experience," or all of the above. We all think *we* know what we mean by emotion, and are convinced that the term refers to something at the core of the human condition. Yet, when asked to be specific, we are hard put to give a concise definition, and our attempts are so discordant that the hope for adjudication among conflicting views seems remote.

Given the lack of any discernible scientific progress in the field, one might reasonably expect contemporary scientific psychology to abandon the effort to study emotion altogether, until the various competing terms and the theoretical formulations subsumed under each had first been decomposed into operationally defined units of observation and measurement.

Yet the recent psychological literature suggests that emotions have enjoyed a remarkable renaissance over the past fifteen years,

99

motivated to a large extent by increased interest in the socialization of young infants, their emotional development, "bonding," and the mother-child interaction. The third edition of *Carmichael's Manual of Child Psychology* (Mussen 1970), for example, makes only passing reference to the emotions, but the fourth edition (Mussen's *Handbook*, 1983) devotes one of its longest chapters to the topic of social emotional development; and most of the empirical studies cited in that chapter refer to young infants. Similarly Campos et al. (1983) conclude in their review chapter that there has been a dramatic reevaluation ("upwards") of the importance of emotions and their consequences for adaptation from infancy to old age.

One enduring problem for all contemporary studies on emotions is the question of embodiment: whether the emotions are entities that have a specific locus in the organism, the environment, or at the interface between organism and environment. Some investigators assume that emotions are discrete entities, energies, or essences, controlled by genetic programs that can be located in specific regions, for example, of the central nervous system (such as the hypothalamus), or recognized by particular patterns of physiological arousal. Further, they assume that these loci act as autonomous agents for the induction of the specific organismic experiences and behavior patterns we equate with emotion. Others assume that emotions cannot be reduced to biological essences but are the counterpart or by-products of cognitive functions as the latter undergo developmental transformations. Still others attribute emotions to the social reinforcing conditions of the environment and treat them as a subset of all learned phenomena. Finally, some commentators assume that emotions are always the product of a social context or a situation and can therefore not be located either in the organism or in the environment. Whichever among these and other conflicting views about emotions is adopted for any empirical studies, the choice clearly determines the level of discourse at which the relevant phenomena are investigated and analyzed. Hillman's extensive review of the major philosophical commentaries on human emotions (1964) illustrated how closely contemporary disputes about the emotions in empirical psychology still parallel traditional disputes in philosophy and phenomenological psychology.

An observational descriptive study during the first six months can hardly hope to clarify theoretical issues that have resisted resolution for a thousand years. It can, however, point to partial answers for some of the relevant questions, to the extent that the status of emotions in the naive organism, and the process of the differentiation during the early months, set the stage for many conflicting theories of emotion. Studies on early infancy have, for example, resurrected the enduring question of whether one can identify a fixed number of "basic" emotions that are either preprogrammed in the genome or are the derivatives of cognition and developmental transformation. On the assumption that emotions can actually be defined, and that a specifiable number of emotions can be identified, investigations on human development have attempted to specify the number of basic emotions in the newborn infant and how they can be recognized by objective criteria.

Within philosophy, St. Augustine and Spinoza identified *desire* as the common substrate that gives rise to, but differs qualitatively, from all true emotions, whereas Kierkegaard traced all emotions back to a basic source of anxiety. In empirical psychology, Bridges (1931) identified excitement as the source for all later true emotions, whereas psychoanalysis has variously identified either one or two roots for all the emotions, equating these with desire and anxiety.

A very different approach to the study of emotions is implied by the assumption that there is a finite set of a priori emotion units, distinct entities, programs, substances, or forces, each of which has its own nature and its own way of acting, so that they cannot be reduced to more basic determinants. Descartes identified six basic emotions and St. Thomas Aquinas proposed eleven. Watson (1919) named four, Cobb (1950) eight. Sroufe (1982) proposed three, and De Rivera (1977) forty-eight. From infant studies, Izard (1977) identified one, three, or four basic emotions, while Campos et al. (1983) lists the five which are most frequently mentioned in various taxonomies: joy, anger, fear, sadness, and interest. No persuasive reasons beyond intuition are given for adopting any one taxonomy in preference to others, or for assuming that emotions are in fact discrete entities with definable boundaries, whose essences can be discovered by introspection or empirical observation and classification.

Studies on human infants have thus redirected our attention to the need for objective descriptions of emotional expressions, and particularly of the context in which they occur, because infants cannot be relied upon to give subjective reports about their feelings. The studies also point out the importance of distinguishing between those expressions of emotion that are presumed to be modified or elaborated by cultural influences and local preferences (Leach 1972), and those expressions which are universally present in all young infants and therefore presumed to represent the biologically given structures of emotion. Yet the boundary conditions that distinguish one emo-

101

tion from another in terms of behavioral or physiological variables remain ambiguous. Psychophysiological patterns of autonomic activation or brain electrical activity are imprecise. No discrete ensemble of physiological response patterns was found to correspond precisely to any specific emotion (Schachter and Singer 1962). Neurophysiological investigation on emotional expression in animals further indicated that the neural circuits for expression are widely distributed across the central and peripheral nervous system, so that localizing any particular emotion in a specific structure of the central nervous system is probably an impossible task.

More promising have been attempts by numerous investigators to localize expressions of emotions in the human face, equating emotions with their expression as distinctive patterns of facial motor coordination, although this restricted definition clearly does not satisfy the demands of cognitive, clinical, interpersonal, or most comprehensive psychological theories of emotions. Darwin (1873) was among the first to provide detailed objective descriptions of emotional expressions in animals and humans.

The detailed description of facial movement patterns as possible clues to human emotions has in recent years been greatly expanded by Blurton-Jones (1972), Ekman and Friesen (1978), Oster and Ekman (1978), Izard and Dougherty (1982), and others, each proposing an "emotionally neutral" taxonomy of facial expressions to describe the finer details of variation in human emotion within and across cultures (see, for example, Rinn [1984] for a recent review). On the assumption that the communication of emotions is a critical factor in early social experience, and that it may be at the core of the social process generally (Hamburg 1963), some investigators have speculated that the social communicative function of emotions may also have shaped the evolution of human facial muscles for the purpose of expressive behavior. A number of ethologically informed investigators of human emotions have therefore examined the universality of basic facial expressions as the evolutionary means of transmitting socially relevant information across a wide, diverse group of cultures (Eibl-Eibesfeldt 1970; Ekman 1979). The expression of emotions, and in some cases the emotions themselves, are conceived as residing entirely in the movements and postures of the facial muscles, because they are probably the source of "maximally discriminating" information of human emotional expression (Izard 1977). However, the facial muscles are by no means the only motor systems involved in the process of expression (Campos et al. 1983).

Exclusive attention to facial movements may therefore define the problem and function of emotion too narrowly.

Like others, I started with an ethological orientation, taking my cues from Darwin's evolutionary perspective, but extending the domain of observations to include ensembles of facial movements, vocalizations, discrete limb gestures, and general movement patterns that could be observed repeatedly in the same infant over time, as well as across infants. I made no a priori assumptions about the ontological status of "basic" emotions, or about the intrinsic functions of emotions as social communicative signals or organizing principles, and the descriptions given here do not aspire to any exhaustive classification of all possible emotional expressions in the young infants. Nor do they exclude the possibility that new expressions of emotion emerge during the course of the first six months.

Because there is near universal agreement that smiling and crying are legitimate categories of emotional expression, even during the neonatal period, and because they are culturally invariant, I initially focused on these to examine the development of emotional expressions under unstimulated conditions. Thereafter, I attempted to identify the necessary and sufficient stimulus conditions, the social context, and the behavioral state under which such expressions could be observed and elicited reliably, and how the relation between expressive patterns and their causal conditions might change over the first six months. Using this strategy, I hoped to provide observational data for a more general ontogenetic account of emotional expressions, one that would permit provisional inferences about the functional significance of particular emotional expressions and thereby perhaps provide clues about the ways in which expressive motor coordination patterns might acquire "meaning" through usage and differentiation within particular social contexts. Further, I hoped to describe how the motor patterns of emotional expression as well as the necessary and sufficient conditions for their instigation changed over time and how such changes in turn might provide further clues about the enduring question of whether and how emotions develop.

As in descriptions on the development of behavioral states, descriptions on the development of emotional expressions in the chapters to follow will include a section on free field observations combined with ad hoc experiments intended to specify the boundaries within which particular emotional expressions were stable phenomena, how changes either of environmental context or behavioral state altered the expression of emotions, and how ontogenetic changes influence the interaction between organismic state and social context and the expression of emotions.

Procedures

In principle, I followed the same two-pronged approach for the developmental analysis of emotional expressions as previously for the development of behavioral states: four days each week were committed to nonobtrusive observations concerning the form, frequency, and social context of emotional expressions as they occurred in the home, with particular emphasis on smiling, laughing, crying, and their possible subtypes. Such observations, particularly on the context in which emotional expressions occurred, served as the basis for experimental manipulations on the fifth day of observation each week. On these days, I examined the contextual boundaries within which particular expressive behavior patterns were stable, and tested the effect of going outside these boundaries on behavioral state and the quality of emotional expression. These experiments were designed to determine the necessary and sufficient stimulus conditions for eliciting particular expressions of emotion, examining the interaction between expressions of emotion and behavioral state, and inferring the "meanings" that might be associated with expressions of emotion, from the context of their occurrence.

Spontaneous expressions of emotion in the waking infant in its natural environment necessarily refer to motor events occurring in a set of surroundings where the stimulus events could not be controlled, when they were not experimentally provoked, and when there was no direct evidence that accidental stimuli were causally related. By contrast, the experimental provocation of emotional responses refers to instances when particular expressive motor patterns could be repeatedly elicited by specific environmental events, as long as the behavioral state variable remained constant. On days of experimental manipulation I usually closed the door to the room where the infant and I spent the day, so we would not be disrupted by other children, pets, or unforeseen "perturbations." Whenever there were unforeseen stimuli that might have obscured the response, the results were not included in the final tabulations. Given the vicissitudes of the home environment, the distinction between spontaneous and experimentally induced expressions of emotion was never categorical, although such distinctions could usually be made with reasonable confidence. Each of the sections to follow deals with a particular expression of emotion, and the observations are presented according to the distinctions made above. Observations on emotional expression occurring in the free field conditions of the home are always presented first; and experimental manipulations based on these observations follow.

Smiling

Among universal expressions of human emotions, smiling has probably received the greatest attention by investigators of early behavioral and emotional development. It is a nonperemptory social signal which demands no specific response from the social partner but is pleasing to both parents and investigators and is generally considered to be an essential aspect of socialization of the young infant. Smiling is a reliable component of the behavioral repertoire in healthy infants by at least the end of the first month; its global configuration remains an essential component of nonverbal social communication throughout the life cycle, although the finer details of its configurational morphology as well as of the underlying "emotions" communicated to the social partner undergo extensive developmental transformations. While analogues of the smile have been described in other mammalian species (especially higher primates and perhaps dogs) (Darwin 1873; van Hooff 1972), only humans exhibit the progressive differentiations of the smile pattern itself and of the context in which it is used as an instrumentality. Far from being a stereotypic "fixed action pattern," the smile of the child and of the adult may be used to signal fear, aggression, doubt, contempt, or defiance as well as pleasure, amusement, or contentment. Most of the subtle variations in smiling as an expression of emotion are not evident during the early months after birth and are acquired during the course of ontogenesis and could become increasingly culture-specific. If taken literally, the claim that the smile is a species-typical social releaser mechanism would foreclose systematic investigations of changes in the form-function relation of smiling which young infants in all cultures clearly exhibit. By extrapolation, it would short-circuit attempts to investigate emotional development altogether, giving the erroneous impression that the problem had been solved by genetics and preformationist assumptions. Detailed observations of changes in smiling behavior in young infants over the first six months may be particularly well suited for purposes of developmental investigation because the changes in form and function are rapid and distinct.

The Earliest Smiles of the Full-Term Infant

The motor configuration of smiling will be defined initially as the bilateral sideward, upward drawing of the corners of the mouth into a partial U-shaped configuration that is achieved by contraction of the major zygomatic muscles. The lips may be closed or partially open as they will be in later months when smiling first shifts to "open-mouth grin" then to laughter. The more mature forms of smiling include the lifting of the upper lips, producing an elevation of the cheeks and a wrinkling of the eyes. Essential criteria for scoring smiling during the neonatal period, however, will be the bilateral sideward, upward displacement of the corners of the mouth. Later recruitment of other facial muscles for broad smiles, laughter, and the like will be described in detail in the appropriate section. Although usually not classified as a "social" event by conventional usage, expressive movements resembling a smile can be observed reliably during the neonatal period while the infant is asleep, particularly in state II. There have been extensive discussions about spontaneous smiling in sleep as a morphological or perhaps functional "precursor" of social smiling. These discussions touch directly on the question of basic emotions and their evolutionary antecedents. The section to follow will describe in some detail the spontaneous and elicited smiling behaviors observed during sleep.

In full-term infants smiling was rarely observed during waking states but was commonly observed in state II sleep and almost never in state I. Fetal smiling has not been reported but methods of observation by ultrasound imaging techniques may not be sufficiently refined to identify whether subtle changes in facial expression do occur during late periods of gestation. By contrast, premature infants as young as twenty-six weeks of gestational age frequently demonstrate facial grimaces which have all the requisite morphological characteristics of a smile (see figure 12). To examine the generality of this observation, twenty healthy premature infants ranging in age from twenty-four to thirty-four weeks gestational age at the time of delivery were observed weekly for a one-hour period between feedings until they went home from the hospital; facial movements were scored by a running record. All of the infants exhibited "smiling behavior" as defined above but there were no clear developmental trends in frequency of spontaneous smiles. Until thirty weeks gestational age smiling was not reliably associated with any particular behavioral state or general waking condition, and smiling could not be reliably elicited by environmental sounds or tactile stimulation.

Although behavioral states of premature infants are difficult at best to classify when one relies exclusively on behavioral criteria, the overall frequency of spontaneous smiles did not appear to differ between conditions when the infant's eyes were open and when they were closed. However, spontaneous smiles were never observed as long as infants were motorically active, and general motor inactivity seemed to be a necessary precondition for smiling in the premature infant. At the same time it should be noted that smiling was only one in an array of facial grimaces observed in the premature infant. That array also included expressions analogous to "frowning," pouting, sneering, looks of surprise or disgust. The various facial expressions of the preterm infant appeared to succeed one another in random fashion and seemed to be nonspecific motoric activations unrelated to specific organismic or environmental conditions. In this respect they did not differ in principle from sporadic limb movements and twitches of the arms and legs, commonly observed in premature infants. The most that could be said about the functional significance of smiling and other facial grimaces during the preterm period was that the superficial facial muscles tended to be coactivated as coherent ensembles formally resembling emotional expressions in older infants rather than as random twitches, and that such facial expressions were present in all healthy premature infants. Because such ensembles of movement patterns are present in the preterm infant, and probably in the fetus, long before they have any functional significance for the expression of emotions or nonverbal communication with the social partner, a central task for any systematic developmental analysis of human emotional expressions is therefore the description, and eventual explanation of, how particular expressions are linked to particular internal states from which we later infer meaning or feeling.

In the full-term, healthy, newborn infant, by contrast, spontaneous smiles and other grimaces occur primarily during state II sleep or while the infant is drowsy in the transition from waking to sleep, but not from sleep to waking. Such spontaneous smiles during sleep follow no obvious temporal pattern and may, as previous sections have suggested, be one specific variant of spontaneous, nonrhythmical mouthing. Similar smiles without apparent provocation may occur while the infant is drowsy during the transition from waking to sleep; and it is the spontaneous smiles during drowsiness which can provide indirect clues about possible mechanisms because they usually occur in close temporal contiguity to eyelid drooping and eye closure. In full-term infants, 96 percent of all spontaneous

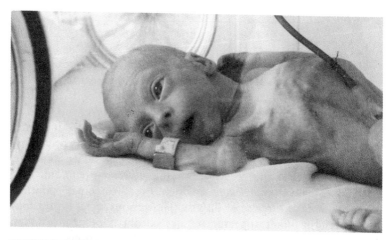

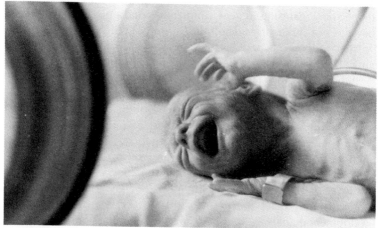

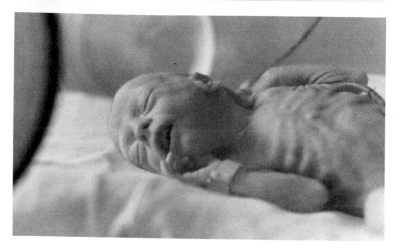

smiles during drowsiness occurred within two seconds or less after the infant whose eyes were already drooping had closed its eyes. Assuming that eye closure eliminates a source of nonspecific perceptual input, the close temporal relation between eye closure and smiling or startles and diffuse mouthing (see above) raises the possibility that smiles and other spontaneous-movement patterns constitute "motor release phenomena," which are more likely to occur when sensory input to the system which might otherwise serve as a buffer against

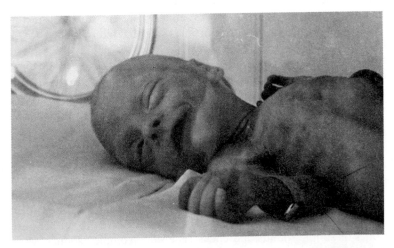

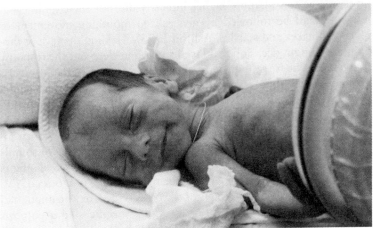

Figure 12. Emotional Expressions in Sleeping Premature Infants (Postconceptional Age, Twenty-six to Thirty-four Weeks)

"spontaneous motor discharge" is suddenly removed. From such speculations, it would follow that "spontaneous" smiling is more likely to occur during sleep than while the infant is awake and exposed to a continuous input of nonspecific visual and probably other sensory stimuli; that the physiological basis as well as the form-function relation for spontaneous smiling and sleep differs qualitatively from that observed several weeks later when the infant is awake and alert. Therefore one could conclude that spontaneous smiling during sleep has little, if any, functional significance as an expression of emotion beyond indicating that the ensemble of movement patterns necessary for the expression of a smile is present long before the movement pattern is used for purposes of social interaction.

Quantitative aspects of sleep smiles. Among full-term infants the frequency of spontaneous smiles in sleep (state II) increased significantly from the first to the fourth week but then decreased again, although smiles were still a common event in sleep among six-month-old infants.

Like other sleep-related spontaneous movement patterns of the face and limbs (startles, mouthing), smiling and sleep could also be produced experimentally by presenting infants with appropriate stimuli at low intensity but with sudden onset while the infant was in state II and motorically inactive. Acoustically complex sounds presented at a low intensity were usually more effective than either pure tones or simple sounds and clicks. The same complex sounds when presented at considerably higher intensity did not elicit smiling but might instead be followed by generalized mouthing movement or precry grimaces and startles (Ashton 1973). Tickling the face or tapping the chin on occasion produced smiling in sleep but the response frequency to these stimuli was so low that responses could not be distinguished from spontaneous motor events. Experimental provocation of smiling and sleep was therefore limited to sound stimuli. A high-pitched brass bell, an Audubon bird whistle, and my high-pitched (male) voice had, on previous observations of newborn infants, been found to be generally effective. The same array of sounds was used with older infants during state II, state I, and while infants were drowsy, the individual stimuli being presented in blocks of five trials for each sound at intervals of thirty seconds after the infant had stopped responding to the previous trial. Specific sound patterns were always presented in a counterbalance design. In addition to bilateral smiling, I scored mouthing, diffuse limb movements, startles, changes of respiration, other facial grimaces, and changes of state.

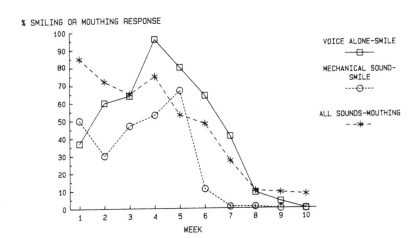

Figure 13. Facial Expressions to Sounds in State II

Responses to a trial block were scored as positive when at least one of the five stimuli elicited a particular response. In addition the percentage of all trials producing one particular motor response was computed. As figure 13 indicates, the frequency of smiling responses to sound increased from the beginning to the end of the first month, paralleling the instance of spontaneous smiles, but then gradually diminished. However, unlike spontaneous smiles in sleep which continued at a lower frequency until the end of the sixth month, sleep smiles to auditory stimuli had essentially disappeared by the end of the second month. No smiling to sound stimuli was ever observed in state I sleep. This distribution paralleled that of spontaneous smiling in sleep.

In state II, the bell was consistently less effective in producing a smile than the Audubon bird whistle, which in turn was less effective than my high-pitched voice, while my natural (low-pitched) speaking voice was almost totally ineffective. Since infants are generally more responsive to complex than to simple sounds or pure tones (Eisenberg 1976), the apparent preference for the human voice was probably a function of its acoustic complexity rather than of its social meaning for the infant (see, however, section on Down Syndrome). Yet the pitch range or quality of the human voice was a major determinant of the likelihood that the sleeping infant would smile.

Drowsiness is a transitional condition of short duration whose boundaries are at best difficult to define. Furthermore the infant's spontaneous facial expressions and responses to sound were quite variable and therefore difficult to assess quantitatively. Given these limitations, the results of direct observation and experimental stimulation indicated that the various sounds were relatively more effective in producing smiling responses during drowsiness than in state II sleep (smiling $p < .01$, mouthing $p < .01$, other grimaces $p < .05$) in every week from the second to the sixth, as if the response threshold to acoustic stimuli was relatively low during drowsiness. This conclusion is consistent with previous observations indicating that spontaneous smiling and startles occurred at a higher frequency during drowsiness than in sleep states. The experimental provocation of facial expressions in drowsiness was successful only during the transition from waking to sleep and not in the transition from sleep to waking.

During the first six weeks, spontaneous and sound-elicited smiling were common events in state II sleep and drowsiness, and they appear to be nonspecific motor events that do not differ in kind from other spontaneous facial grimaces or nonspecific limb movements commonly seen in state II. Therefore their detailed description probably does not contribute very much to our understanding of the development of "social" smiling, other than to indicate that the configuration of the smile face is already organized in a coordinated motor pattern at birth (see figure 13). The nature of the stimulus determined in part which among the various spontaneous or elicited motor events will occur during state I or state II sleep, but the behavioral-state variable was of overriding importance. Startles and rhythmic mouthing, for example, occurred primarily in state I, while facial grimaces, generalized movements and the like are more common in state II; the same asymmetrical distribution of motor patterns held for responses to adequate environmental stimuli. In state I sleep, a slight jar to the crib wall elicited a motor jerk (Moro reflex) quite similar in form to the spontaneous startles observed primarily in state I. However, in state II, where spontaneous startles were rare, the same jar to the crib elicited either no response, or a slight stir, or a facial grimace.

The transitional condition of drowsiness may be of particular interest in this respect, because spontaneous movements and elicited responses, which during sleep characteristically occur either in state I or state II, are both commonly seen in drowsiness during the transition from waking to sleep. The preparation for sleep may therefore represent an unstable reorganization of state variables when the threshold for all spontaneous motor discharges is relatively low. At the same time, the infant is particularly sensitive to a variety of sub-threshold stimuli capable of triggering the same motor patterns.

Natural History of Wakeful Smiling

During the first week after birth, waking infants as a group did not smile reliably to the human or nonhuman sounds, visual stimuli, tactile stroking of the face, bouncing, or the like. Only four of the newborn infants smiled occasionally when awake and presumably alert. For example, two hours after birth, K. A. smiles while alert, upon hearing the voice of a nearby nurse whose face she cannot see. Three times during the subsequent days in the hospital, she smiles while awake when a nearby nurse is talking. The latency between the nurse's voice and the onset of smiling in each case is between four and six seconds. Similarly, D. F. smiles while his eyes are open and the nursery nurse speaks softly to him, although he cannot see her face; the latency between the nurse's speech and the onset of smile is between four and seven seconds. At three days and again at four and six days, T. W. smiles broadly while her eyes are open, six to seven seconds after she hears her mother's voice, even though she cannot see the mother's face.

By the end of the second week, nearly half of the sample smiled regularly to the human voice when they were alert inactive; and occasionally they smiled immediately after they heard the Audubon bird whistle or the bell. By contrast, visual stimuli such as a silent, nodding head, a stationary head, a smiling face, or a two-dimensional model of the face produced no smiling, although the infants made visual pursuit movements to the face with the eyes alone or the head and eyes, and were clearly responding to the visual stimulus. On rare occasions, tapping the chin, stroking the cheek, or tickling the face with the blunt end of the finger also provoked a smile in the waking infant, but the apparent link was so unreliable that it could not be distinguished from chance occurrence. Again, there was independent evidence that infants were responsive to the tactile stimuli, since appropriate touching in the regions of the mouth elicited rooting responses, mouthing, or tonguing movements reliably.

During the third week, sixteen of the twenty-two infants, and by the fourth week, twenty of the infants smiled consistently to both human and nonhuman sounds. By appropriate manipulations of the environment, it was possible to demonstrate that the voice was the critical stimulus variable, and that visual stimulation by itself had no effect. The latency between voice-stimulus onset and smiling decreased from the second to the fourth week (see below for quantitative descriptions).

By the fourth week, the human voice was more effective than mechanical sounds (bell, Audubon bird whistle), and sounds generally were more effective than the silent, nodding head or a stationary, smiling face.

By five weeks all waking infants smiled reliably to the human voice while they were alert but the overall frequency of smiling to voices diminished and the infants now seemed more selective in their choice of responding or less "stimulus bound." By contrast the frequency of smiling to the silent nodding or stationary face had increased; and the combination of voice and face was consistently more effective than either of the socially adequate stimuli alone.

By eight weeks the disembodied voice provoked head and eye rotations as if the infants were searching for the source of the sound; frequently they smiled only after making visual face contact. Consequently the latency between voice onset and smile was considerably prolonged. At the same time smiling was transformed from a "simple reflex" to a complex greeting behavior as implied by the anticipation of seeing a face when hearing a voice. This "cognitive" factor had not been evident until at least the sixth week. The face and voice did not have to "match," and babies smiled as often when they saw my face after hearing the mother's voice as they did when seeing their mother's face and hearing my voice. In adultomorphic terms the infant did not know "the person" but only an organic link between voice and face. The lack of need to match voice with face was made evident on days of unobtrusive observation whenever I sat near the baby but out of its visual field. When the mother spoke to her infant or to other children from the other side of the room, and the infant searched for an appropriate face and saw me instead of the mother, visual contact alone was sufficient to trigger a smile. Conversely when I spoke and the infant searched and found the mother's face instead of mine, it also smiled consistently. By eight weeks infants responded selectively to different speech sounds. For example, my high-pitched (male) voice was considerably more effective than my natural speaking voice, and the mother's baby talk and natural voice were consistently more effective than my high-pitched voice. Such observations first noted in the free field condition were subsequently confirmed by experimental manipulation. Until at least the eleventh or twelfth week, the infant's ability to discriminate among voices had no equivalent in visual discrimination among faces. All familiar faces were equally effective in producing a smile, and any familiar face when combined with a familiar voice was more effective than either the face alone or the voice alone. However, the experimental introduction of strange persons or familiar persons wearing a facial mask results in a significant decrease of smiling frequency, suggesting that some visual discrimination among individual faces occurred between the second and third month.

The "Nonsocial" Uses of Smiling

The descriptions so far refer exclusively to expressions that are responses to "social" encounters. However, by the second and third month infants were clearly smiling to events that served no obvious social function. Sroufe and Waters (1976) described a variety of experimental manipulations that elicited smiling in infants but could not be construed as social contacts by conventional definition, for example, after the infant had "solved" an unfamiliar sensory motor problem (see also Piaget 1952), or after infants had presumably "mastered" an unfamiliar nonsocial experience (Kagan 1974; Watson 1972; Zelazo 1972). Such observations are commonly interpreted within a cognitive frame of reference, but the emergence of the smile is attributed to a reduction of "tension" at the moment when the cognitive problem has been solved. The investigators in question do not indicate what constitutes such tensions or energies that are discharged once the problem is solved. The observations themselves are of interest by indicating that smiling serves functions other than social communication or bonding; that it cannot, in other words, be categorically defined as an innate releaser mechanism. Because smiling can reliably serve as instrumental function during the early months, it would be reasonable to expect that with developmental transformations the form-function relations between adequate stimulus conditions and smiling responses will be further elaborated.

A number of circumstances encountered during unobtrusive home observations brought further support for the assumption that the smile may serve "multiple masters," even if these are not either of a cognitive or a social emotional type. For example, when alert infants have been staring for some time at a complex geometrical pattern, such as the cover of a radiator, a figured curtain, or other geometric shape they frequently smiled exactly at the moment when they stopped their inspection. A reliable means for inducing nonsocial smiling in waking infants was noted by chance during experiments in visual pursuit when infants had to alternate their gaze between two identical physical objects such as two red pencils. During the period when infants were trying to alternately pursue one and the other of two pencils as these moved further to the periphery of the visual field and the pencils were suddenly brought back together into the center of the visual field and then crossed, the infants frequently broke out into a broad smile. Some infants responded with smiling under these conditions after the objects were crossed in the midline, whereas others were more likely to smile at the moment when a novel visual stimulus other than the competing pencils was suddenly introduced to the visual field, as if a factor of mild "surprise" was the determinant of nonsocial smiling.

Emde and Koenig (1969) reported that low-intensity tickling or kinesthetic stimulation were reliably effective in eliciting smiling behavior during the first three weeks after birth, and they identified tactile stimuli as the earliest sufficient conditions for eliciting a social smile. Similarly, Sroufe and Wunsch (1972) considered intense kinesthetic stimulation to be a major cause of laughter in older infants. My observations indicated that during the first month infants rarely responded by smiling to a gentle stroking or jiggling. However, two of the mothers independently introduced me to a procedure that induced smiling and later on laughter with remarkable consistency. The game of "pat-a-cake" (Wolff 1963) was of particular interest because it could elicit both smiling and laughter persistently across a large number of trials in all infants, did not require face contact or vocal stimulation, seemed to depend directly on the physical manipulation of the limbs, and was relatively immune to habituation or response detriment. Within a developmental context the procedure of playing pat-a-cake also demonstrated the relationship between smiling and laughter and provided some clues about how these two expressions of emotion might not simply be quantitative variations of intensity but qualitatively different emotional expressions. The game of pat-a-cake may have been a vigorous analogue of proprioceptive stimulation referred to by Sroufe and Waters; it became a highly efficient means for eliciting smiling behavior in infants of four and five weeks and for eliciting laughter in infants after the eighth week. The version of the game that seemed most effective for demonstrating this effect required that the infant's hands be held in the experimenter's own and then banged together within the fists of the experimenter repeatedly in bursts of three to five movements while the observer was silent and did not show his face. Until the third week the game provoked no reliable expression of emotion. Thereafter it became a potent method for eliciting smiling or laughter even after prolonged sequences of stimulation. By eight weeks infants responded with an open-mouthed broad smile and frequently produced chortling sounds which, when tape-recorded and played back to independent judges who did not see the infants, were generally identified as laughter.

Quantitative Comparisons of Smiling Behavior

The preceding sections served as a global road map of the common developmental transformation in smiling behavior of waking infants and it summarizes later changes in the necessary and sufficient conditions of smiling as inferred from nonobtrusive observation. However, anecdotal observations, particularly of emotional expressions, are susceptible to many errors of observer bias and a tendency to adultomorphize the significance of the facial movement patterns in order to identify the onset of social integration of the infant as early in development as possible.

The following account summarizes observations resulting from experimental manipulation that could be replicated reliably within one infant over several weeks and across the majority of infants. The stimulus configurations which included low- and high-pitched human voice, artificial sounds, silent nodding or stationary face, combinations of these as well as the game of pat-a-cake, etc. were tested according to a protocol one day each week in the various behavioral states. In addition I used tape-recorded samples of adults speaking, of babies crying or lalling; latex "Frankenstein" and "Jimmy Durante" masks, a clear plastic mask which was translucent to the essential features of the human face but gave the face a fixed appearance, a pink latex head-covering that obscured the hairline; various kinds of sunglasses, eye patches, and the like. These models were used to identify the essential components of more complex social stimuli that were necessary and sufficient for inducing smiling behavior. In addition I used repetitive tactile or kinesthetic stimulus configurations as well as various "cognitive" sensorimotor problems as means for eliciting smiling behavior. Intermittently I introduced the babies to men and women whom they had never seen before in order to test their "stranger anxiety." Within the time constraints of behavioral state durations the experiments were always presented in a "counterbalanced" design. The full array of presentations could not always be completed in all infants in each week within a state so that the total number of subjects tested by one set of stimulus patterns was variable.

For these experiments the emotional expressions of primary in-

117

terest were smiling and laughter, and some effort was made to distinguish among the different forms of smiling, i.e., a gentle smile (mouth closed), "broad" smile with the mouth open and the eyes wrinkled, involvement of other motor systems accompanying vocalizations and the like, with particular emphasis on the corrugator muscles of the eyes recruited during smiling. The classification of smile types was based only on direct observation and fell far short in precision of the refined kinesic analyses possible by off-line viewing of videotape and the neutral coding system proposed by Ekman and his colleagues (1978, 1979). The descriptions of response to smile-adequate stimuli was not limited to facial gestures but included also associated movement patterns, vocalizations, visual search, and behavioral state changes. Motor responses which were not initially classified as expressions of emotion, although they were the direct response to the smile-adequate stimuli, were recorded and will be reported here since it was not evident to me from the start which motor activities to socially adequate stimuli should qualify as "basic emotions" and which ones might constitute other forms of adaptive behavior, "interest," or goal-directed action. For the quantitative account of stimulus-produced smiling the number of trial blocks in which at least one of five trials elicited a defined social response as well as the percentage of all trials across blocks that produced either a smile or another emotional expression were reported. When any set of five trials elicited more than one kind of emotional expression, both types are reported. When the infants responded consistently with one or another facial expression to a stimulus array, experiments were later carried out to determine the stability of the response and the rate of "habituation." Behavioral state was always recorded as background information but will be explicitly indicated here only when the emotional expressions were elicited while the infant was not alert and awake.

Responses to Vocalization and Faces. As the preceding descriptions indicate, infants smiled consistently to the voice alone in the first several weeks after birth, but by six weeks they frequently turned toward the source of the voice before smiling. To distinguish between vocal and visual social stimuli as adequate elicitors of smiling, I structured the experimental conditions so that the relative effectiveness of each component of the social stimulus (voice or face) could be compared separately and in combination. Figure 14 summarizes the developmental changes in smiling to the voice alone to the silent nodding head alone, over the first twelve weeks in terms of percentage of

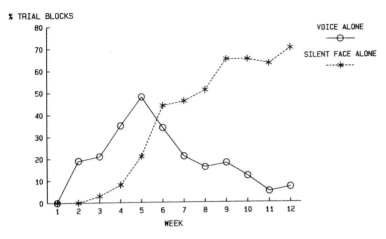

Figure 14. Smiling to Voice and Silent Face

trial blocks in which at least one of five trials is followed by smiling (see also table 7). The developmental increase of smiling frequency to voice alone was significant from the second to third and fourth weeks and from the fourth to fifth weeks ($p < .05$, $p < .01$, Wilcoxon unmatched-pairs comparison). Until the fourth week the voice alone was reliably more effective than the face ($p < .05$, $p < .01$), but by the sixth week this order effect was reversed and by the eighth week the silent face was consistently more effective than the voice ($p < .01$, $p < .001$). After the fifth week and until at least the tenth, the combination of voice and face was more effective than the voice alone or the face alone ($p < .05$). Reductions in the frequency of smiling to the voice alone when computed as overall frequency cannot be adduced as evidence for developmental regression or ontogenetic adaptation in the sense that smiling to the voice had served its adaptive purpose of social bonding and had now been replaced by a more direct link between visual stimulation and smiling as the infants progressively recognized faces among various visual stimulus configurations. On the contrary, this decline in gross frequency probably reflected the infant's growing capacity to discriminate among the acoustic properties of different voice patterns and a dissolution of the mechanical link between any human voice and an obligatory smiling response.

Figure 15 compares the frequency of smiling responses to the mother's voice alone talking to her infant and to my high-pitched

Table 7: Social Responses to Voice and Face

Month	Expression	Voice vs. Face	x^2	Face and Voice vs. Voice Alone	x^2	Voice and Face vs. Face Alone	x^2
						Comparisons	
1	Smiling	Voice > Face	8.6**	Face + Voice > Voice	2.1	Voice + Face > Face	7.9**
	Vocalizing	Voice > Face	6.5*	Voice > Face + Voice	0.7	Voice + Face > Face	5.2*
2	Smiling	Face > Voice	10.3**	Face + Voice > Voice	14.7**	Voice + Face > Face	0.9
	Vocalizing	Face > Voice	5.4*	Face + Voice > Voice	12.1**	Voice + Face > Face	7.6**
3	Smiling	Face > Voice	10.7**	Face + Voice > Voice	11.3**	Voice + Face = Face	—
	Vocalizing	Voice > Face	6.9**	Face + Voice = Voice	—	Voice + Face > Face	12.3**
4	Smiling	Face > Voice	8.9**	Face + Voice > Voice	7.3**	Voice + Face > Face	3.3
	Vocalizing	Voice > Face	2.4	Face + Voice > Voice	10.8**	Voice + Face > Voice	10.1**
5–6	Smiling	Face > Voice	Not enough data	Face + Voice > Voice	Not enough data	Voice + Face ≧ Face	Not enough data
	Vocalizing	Voice > Face		Face + Voice > Voice		Voice + Face ≧ Face	

* p .05
** p .01

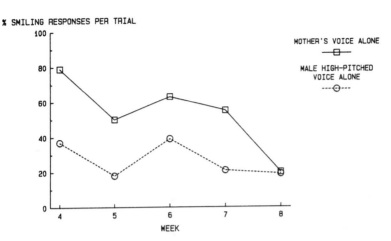

Figure 15. Smiling to Mother's Voice and High-pitched Male Voice

voice. From the sixth to twelfth weeks (in other words during the period when the overall frequency of smiling to the voice was declining) the mother's voice produced reliably more smiling responses than did my high-pitched voice ($p < .01$, $p < .05$). Similarly, my high-pitched voice was consistently more effective than my natural voice. Similar results were obtained when I compared the mother's voice combined with my nodding head, and my high-pitched voice combined with her nodding head. Between seven and twelve weeks the combination of my face and the mother's voice was consistently more effective in producing a smile than the combination of my voice and the mother's face ($p < .01$); and the mother's voice combined with her face was no more effective than her voice combined with my face. These results suggest that the voice was the essential clue by which the infants were discriminafing between persons, whereas the precise configuration of the face was still of relatively little consequence. This conclusion could be confirmed by comparing the mother's voice with the nodding head of a woman whom the infant had never seen before. After two minutes of familiarization with the stranger, during which smiling was not tested, the nodding face of the stranger matched with the mother's voice was as effective in producing smiling as was the mother's voice combined with her own face.

The infant's ability to discriminate among socially adequate stimulus variables was also tested while mothers were feeding their infants. However, under these conditions the confounding effects of visual and tactile proprioceptive stimuli could be excluded only by limiting the observations to bottle-fed and "propped" infants. When the infant was "prop-fed" while lying on its side on the kitchen table with the bottle supported by a pillow, the mother's voice alone interrupted a feeding and produced a transient smile with greater frequency than did my high-pitched voice, although the baby could see neither of the persons associated with that voice. By contrast, there were, at this time, no differences in smiling response to visual stimulation by my face or the mother's alone. By eight weeks, bottle-fed infants stopped sucking, even at the beginning of a feeding, in order to look or to look and smile at the face before they resumed their meal as soon as they heard the mother's voice, but they paid little attention and usually continued to suck when they heard my voice with or without the mother's nodding head. Again, it was the voice which was the essential variable for discriminating among human individuals.

On the basis of such observations alone it would be premature to conclude that two-month-old infants make sharp distinctions between the sound patterns of different human voices. Attempts to imitate a high-pitched voice may have distorted the acoustical features of the sound pattern, although my high-pitched voice produced more smiling than my low-pitched voice. The pitch pattern of the voice itself may therefore be one critical variable that influences smiling responses during the early months.

Aside from the increased precision of voice recognition implied by these observations, the infant's growing requirements for an integrated social response may have contributed to the general decline of smiling frequency at seven to eight weeks.

By seven or eight weeks, infants commonly responded to the voice (alone) with vocalization (alone); or when they smiled to the voice, the latency was substantially prolonged by a search for the sound source before smiling. As table 7 indicates, by the end of two months infants most commonly answered to the face or face and voice either by smiling alone or by a combination of smiling and vocalizing. This differentiation in the two kinds of social responses to two social stimuli remained relatively stable until the end of the third month. By five months the repertory of greeting behaviors available to the infant had become sufficiently context-dependent and complex so that the frequency counts alone no longer captured the pattern of social communication. Search for the source of the voice, the combination of smiling and speaking, a fleeting smile before returning to ongoing activity, or reaching for the familiar face had by this time all become variants of the infant's greeting behavior and, in many instances, the infant no longer "bothered" to respond to a casual social encounter. In other words, smiling and vocalizing were no longer obligatory responses to appropriate social stimulation.

The presumed associations between vocal *stimuli* and vocal *responses* were tested more objectively by using the five-minute tape-recorded samples of the mother's speech talking to her baby in random intervals of ten to twenty-five seconds, and tape-recorded samples of my high-pitched voice that had been prepared in the same way. These were played to the alert infant either when it could not see any face, even after a search, or while one or another person's face nodded to the infant and smiled. The total number of smiling responses, noncry vocalizations, other expressions of emotions, searching behavior, and the like were scored for each five-minute period of tape-recorded speech, for comparable five-minute control periods during which the infant neither heard nor saw any person, and for five-minute periods during which the familiar face only nodded and smiled silently. Over the period from six to twelve weeks, vocal responses to the taped voice alone increased in frequency while the number of smiles diminished gradually. During the early weeks (six to eight) the voice alone frequently produced both smiling and noncry vocalization, but by eleven or twelve weeks vocalization without smiling had become by far the preferred response (see table 7).

The frequency of social responses to the silent nodding face, and of either smiling alone or smiling and vocalizing, remained relatively stable.

Tape-recorded voice samples elicited more vocalizing and smiling than comparable control periods without any social stimulation in each comparison for the six to twelve weeks ($p < .01$). The voice presented alone or in combination with the face produced more vocal responses than the silent nodding head ($p < .05$); the silent face alone produced more smiling than the voice alone ($p < .01$), but the combined voice and face produced more smiles and vocal responses than either the silent nodding head ($p < .05$) or the voice alone. The mother's voice in isolation or matched with either my face or the mother's face evoked more vocal utterances and more smiles than my high-pitched voice presented alone or matched with my face in the seventh, ninth, tenth, and twelfth weeks.

As already suggested, the five-minute samples of adult tape-recorded speech could obviously not be synchronized temporally with the baby's own sequence of vocal utterances. Sometimes the taped speech overlapped with the infant's sounds or smiles, at other times the taped speech came when the infant was motorically active and unlikely to respond at all. Therefore I also compared five-minute periods during which I spoke in a high-pitched voice but coordinated my sounds with the infant's silences and my judgment that the infant was "ready" to respond, all the time staying out of its visual field. Under these conditions, the infants produced substantially more vocal utterances as well as a greater variety than in response to tape-recorded speech samples. The differences were statistically significant ($p < .01$), each at six, seven, nine, eleven, and twelve weeks). While the taped voice may have degraded the acoustic quality of speech sounds, the tape recorder had high fidelity (Ampex 6000) and was evidently sufficient to elicit smiling and vocalizations at a greater than chance frequency. A more likely explanation for the significant differences was that the voice stimulus was precisely timed to what I thought was the infant's "readiness" to respond so that the infant's vocalizations were time-linked to the natural voice, whereas no such "dialogue" was possible in response to tape-recorded voice samples. What exactly constitutes the optimal timing relations between voice stimulus and vocal response that can maintain an active dialogue probably exceeds in complexity any linear contingencies, and requires a careful assessment of the infant's preceding activity and overall disposition; but in these observations, the details of the timing relationships were not further explored.

The increased range of possible greeting behaviors as well as the infant's apparent release from "stimulus-boundness" accounted in part for the reduced overall frequency of smiling to the voice during the second month. It probably also accounted for the unanticipated finding that the latency between the time of social stimulation and the onset of emotional expression changed during the first three months. For each stimulus configuration, the latency to smiling was timed by stopwatch on each day of experimental manipulation. Such measurements are no substitute for objective recording or time-lapse analysis of videotapes, but they provided important clues about possible mechanisms contributing to the development of emotional expression. Developmental changes in mean latency to smiling were biphasic, decreasing significantly between the first and second months but then increasing again. A more detailed analysis of the latencies by interval histograms indicated that the total number of relatively short latencies for smiling to the voice (one to four seconds) remained relatively constant across the first three months. In addition, many prolonged latencies lasting from nine to twelve seconds

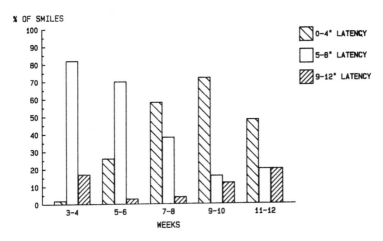

Figure 16. Smiling Latencies in Alert Infants

before the onset of smiling, emerged in the third month. The increase in long latency from the first to the third month was statistically significant (see figure 16). Long smiling-latencies could be related directly to the infant's increased range of emotional greeting responses. For example, by seven or eight weeks, when first hearing the disembodied voice, infants frequently searched for the source; and the smiling response was delayed until they had established visual contact with the social partner or for that matter with any face they encountered during the search. A comparison of smiling latencies to the voice that were and were not preceded by a period of search, indicated that the search itself materially increased mean latency to smiling from a baseline value of 4.4 seconds (SD ± 1.7), to 9.4 seconds (SD ± 3.8). The effect was significant at each week during the second month (p < .01, by Mann Whitney U-test). This search for the source of the disembodied voice illustrates not only the increasing complexity of the appropriate emotional expression at the infant's disposal but also changes in the infant's concept of permanence as it pertains to persons. Finally, the finding emphasizes the limitation of any extreme prefunctionalist account of emotional expressions as preprogrammed obligatory responses to fixed sign stimuli.

Smiling and Behavioral State

As would be expected, infants never smiled while they were crying. Even when they were only fussing, I never observed a phenomenon which seems to be quite common in older children and adults, namely, that unhappy individuals "smile through their tears." When the voice alone, or the combination of voice and nodding head elicited smiling in the infant who was fussing or crying softly, the sequence was usually that cry vocalizations stopped, the face relaxed to an attitude of repose, and then the infant smiled. Under such conditions the infant could be provoked to smile repeatedly, as long as the behavioral state remained favorable.

The effect of the voice on the fussing infants provides further evidence about the infant's ability to distinguish between the mother's and my voice, and about the importance of behavioral state as a codeterminant of emotional expression. For example, between seven and twelve weeks fussing infants occasionally responded to the mother's voice by an arrest of fussing, an active search for the source of the sound, and a gentle or broad smile as soon as they made face contact with the mother. My high-pitched voice rarely had this effect, and the frequency of smiling to my voice under such conditions was significantly less than to the mother's voice ($\chi^2 = 8.5$ p $<$ .01 mean for six to twelve weeks). When my voice did elicit a search and transient arrest of fussing, face contact almost never produced a smile, but sometimes actually increased fussing or crying.

The finding that the infants were more sensitive and responsive to their own mother's than to my voice when they were fussy, whereas such differences were not statistically significant during alert states, was a first indication that the behavioral state may in fact be one important determinant of social expressive behavior during early infancy. The findings also suggest that "meaning" of the social encounter (to the extent that meaning can be inferred) was determined in part by the infant's behavioral state, and that the latter provides a context of "cognitive" dimensions to the expression of emotions.

Smiling to Distorted Faces

A number of investigators, including Ahrens (1954), Spitz (1950), and Sroufe and Waters (1976), starting from different theoretical orientations, have tested the effect of experimentally distorting the visual configuration of the face on the smiling response. For the most part the investigators have used two-dimensional models or white cardboard ovals with eye spots, mouth, nose, and other features indicated in black ink, whereas Spitz used three-dimensional masks that covered the face of the observer and were presented to the infant either full face or from the side. Presentation of cardboard models has the advantage that the component parts can be experimentally modified to identify the minimum stimulus configurations necessary for provoking smiling responses or other expressions of emotion at successive stages during early development. They have the disadvantage of being flat, static, and two-dimensional stimuli. Even when experiments with such models are successful in producing smiling reliably, we may overlook the infant's sensitivity to subtle features of the human face that play an essential role in face recognition during later stages of development but may already be significant during the first three months.

In earlier sections, I indicated that one reason for the increase of smiling latency to voices alone might be the time infants need to search for a face that goes with the disembodied voice. The infant's search of the inner contours of the silent stationary face, before smiling, may be another factor contributing to increased smiling latencies. When confronted with a silent staring face, two-month-old infants frequently inspected the salient topographic features of the face first, then "zeroed in" on the eyes, and finally smiled. A comparison of the smiling responses indicated that their latencies were significantly longer when they were preceded by a search (mean, 11.5 sec; S.D. 3.9), than smiling without a search (mean, 3.9; S.D. 1.4); these differences were significant in every week from eight to fourteen.

There were no consistent differences in overall frequency of smiling to my face and the mother's, whereas differences in response to my voice and the mother's were clear by the second month. However, the smiling latencies were significantly shorter to the mother's than to my face in the second and third months. On questioning, mothers also reported that they rarely noticed their infants scanning their faces before smiling unless they altered their facial appearance. Strangers of both sexes, introduced when the infants were eight and twelve weeks old, were asked to approach the baby slowly and then stare into the face without making any sound. The frequency of smiling responses was substantially less to the stranger than to me or the mother, but the latency of smiling, when it did occur, was shorter to the stranger's than to my face, and of about the same duration as to the mother's. One possible reason for this counterintuitive result might be that the faces of strangers were sufficiently different from those the infant was accustomed to seeing, so that there was less hesitation and inspection before the onset of smiling. My familiar face in an unfamiliar presentation may have created doubt and required a period for reconciling discrepancies before the release of smiling. Subsequent experiments, in which the familiar face was distorted in various ways, are at least consistent with this post hoc explanation.

The infant's smiling responses to faces were also compared when either the mother or I kept our heads stationary while staring into the baby's eyes, and when we nodded our heads four or five times, focusing on the face but avoiding the eyes. There were no differences in overall smiling frequency between the two conditions, but from eight to twelve weeks smiling latencies were significantly longer to the stationary staring face (mean, 3.8 secs.; S.D. 9.8) than to the nodding head (mean, 8.7 secs.; S.D. 2.4). When the experimenter's head was held still, infants scanned the face "deliberately" before making eye-contact and then smiling. Apparently the nodding head did not afford the same opportunity for deliberate scanning of the face, and the infants smiled after a shorter latency. However, by the fifth or sixth month, they no longer scanned the face but instead smiled immediately on seeing the immobile face.

Another factor that may have contributed to the prolonged smiling latencies in older infants was the relatively greater complexity of their greeting behavior on seeing a familiar person. Older, when compared to younger, infants frequently smiled *and* vocalized during a greeting, rather than smiling *or* vocalizing. Therefore I compared the smiling latencies to a smiling, talking face when infants smiled only, when they talked only, and when they smiled and talked. In the last case, they usually smiled before vocalizing (60–75 percent of trials), or else smiled and talked at the same time (10–15 percent of trials). In other words, talking before smiling was not an important confounding factor contributing to the prolonged smiling latencies in older infants. The comparison indicated that smiling latencies were significantly longer when followed or accompanied by vocalization than when smiling occurred in isolation (p < .01, at six and twelve weeks).

To identify the features of the silent face that might specifically produce smiling in infants at different ages, I varied one component feature of the face while keeping the rest constant. Ahrens (1954) and Kagan et al. (1966) for example had scrambled two-dimensional representations of the human face in order to identify at an abstract level which isolated components of the human face were sufficient to provoke smiling in infants at different ages. By contrast, I began with a "normal" three-dimensional face and systematically eliminated or distorted one or another of its salient features. This was accomplished, for example, by wearing ordinary sunglasses, mirror surface or "cheater" sunglasses, skin-colored patches to cover the mouth or eyes, and a skin-colored latex cap to cover the hairline. In addition, I tested the effect of latex Halloween masks representing a Frankenstein monster and a Jimmy Durante face with a very prominent red nose, and a translucent plastic mask that transmitted the basic features of the face, its color, and so on, and distorted primarily the mobility of the individual parts of the face. During the first five weeks, there were no significant effects on smiling frequency, smiling latency, or other emotional expressions, by any of the distortions. The detailed experiments using these distortions were therefore not begun until the sixth week. Responses to the various distortions were tested after a control period during which it had been demonstrated that the infants smiled reliably to the natural face. The effects were tested by comparing emotional response to the artificial distortions and to natural faces, and behavioral state was monitored throughout. When there was a change of behavioral state before a presentation, the results were discarded and the experiment temporarily discontinued.

As table 8 indicates, the frequency of trial *blocks* in which the infants exhibited smiling and noncry vocalizations did not differ significantly between the natural face and the face wearing ordinary

Table 8: Smiling and Noncry Vocalization to Distorted Familiar Faces (N = 11)

Weeks	Comparison	Smiling x^2	Vocalization x^2
6	Nodding Face > Mirror Glasses	11.3***	10.6**
	Nodding Face = Ordinary Sunglasses	—	—
	Nodding Face > Clear Mask	10.1**	13.7**
7	Nodding Face = Ordinary Glasses	—	—
	Nodding Face > Mirror Glasses	9.6**	19.5***
	Nodding Face > Clear Mask	14.3***	8.7*
8	Nodding Face > Clear Mask	7.0**	6.3*
11	Nodding Face > Mirror Glasses	8.9**	7.0*
	Nodding Face > Clear Mask	8.0**	8.0**

*p .05
**p .01
***p .001

sunglasses or the colored latex masks (Frankenstein monster, Jimmy Durante), although the total number of smiles and noncry vocalizations was greater to the natural face than to similar distortions in most of the weeks from six to twelve. By the second month infants were more sensitive to the internal features of the facial configuration, as measured by the smiling or vocalizing. Since sunglasses enhance the contrast boundaries of the eyes, one might have expected them to increase the smiling responses of young infants, assuming that the eye parts themselves were the essential variable of face recognition (Ahrens 1954). For the same reasons the eye patches, which obscured the contrast boundaries of the eye parts, should have reduced the overall frequency of smiling. Instead, both distortions markedly reduced the overall frequency of smiling responses and increased the smiling latency.

The opaque mask displayed the eye-holes prominently, left a space for the wearer's eyes, but grossly distorted the color and configuration of the "natural" face, without obliterating or accentuating the contrast boundaries of the eyes. The latex masks also reduced the overall frequency of smiling from 64 percent of positive responses to the natural face, to 30 percent of responses to both latex masks. There were no consistent differences in smiling frequency to the Frankenstein and Jimmy Durante masks although they differed considerably in their salient features. The reduced frequency of smiling to the latex masks was statistically significant on each experimental day from seven to eleven weeks.

A pink patch placed over the mouth so that the patch blended approximately with the skin coloration of the cheeks and eliminated the mouth outline had no effect on smiling frequency, whereas the pink latex skullcap that obscured the hairline had a distinct effect. Between six and eleven weeks, the smiling frequency was significantly reduced when either I or the mother wore the skullcap ($p < .01$); and the smiling latency in successful trials was significantly longer ($p < .01$). Especially during the early weeks (six to eight), presentation of the immobile face without a distinct hairline caused infants to stare silently, search the face, and fixate on the forehead as if looking for the hairline, before they eventually zeroed in on the eyes and then sometimes smiled. Since none of the fathers in the sample and none of the strangers whom I introduced were bald, it was not possible to distinguish whether removal of a salient cue in the familiar person or the absence of a hairline itself was the critical factor.

A further variation in the infant's emotional expressions to distorted faces was the response to mirror sunglasses, which reflected light and confronted the infant with a face that clearly differed from that with the homogeneous and static black holes of ordinary sunglasses. Mirror glasses drastically reduced smiling frequency, when compared to ordinary sunglasses (mean for weeks 6–12, $p < .01$), significantly increased the smiling latency in successful trials, and frequently provoked the infant to stare at the face without motor activity (75–80 percent of all trials).

As a contrast condition, I used a clear plastic mask shaped to fit the contours of the human face while leaving openings for the eyes and the mouth and not covering the hairline. The mask transmitted the general coloration of the face and differed from the normal face primarily in that it obscured the finer aspects of skin texture, and fine movements of the eyes and mouth, the superficial facial muscles, and three-dimensional details of the face. In preliminary trials, when I wore this mask and suddenly turned to unsuspecting adults, almost all responded with an initial hesitation, staring, and a sensation of "disgust" in the pits of their stomachs before they either showed mild amusement or turned away from the mask altogether. On questioning, almost all of the victims reported an initial sensation of discomfort and eeriness which took some time to overcome. A number of the adults were in fact not amused at all, even after they had overcome their initial discomfort, and considered the prank a bad joke. When I presented myself to the baby while wearing the same clear plastic mask, there was a dramatic decrease in smiling frequency, a total arrest of noncry vocalizations, and an arrest of movement patterns, in every week from the seventh to the twenty-third ($p < .01$ for smiling reduction; $p < .001$ for the reduction in frequency of noncry vocalizations). Despite repeated exposures to this clear mask, even infants observed for six months never got used to this distortion. When they did smile, the latency was increased dramatically over the smiling latency to the natural face ($p < .001$), as well as to the latex mask, the ordinary sunglasses, the rubber skullcap, or combinations among these distortions. During the latency, which sometimes lasted over twenty seconds, the infants commonly stared, sometimes with their mouth partially open, or frowned, while all limb activity stopped. Emotional responses to the mask differed across babies and as a function of state, but the range of expression suggests that the infants were at the very least surprised. Sometimes they seemed frightened and frowned, contracting the corrugator supercilii, depressor supercilii, and the depressor globeli muscles. Rarely they cried (see figure 17).

131

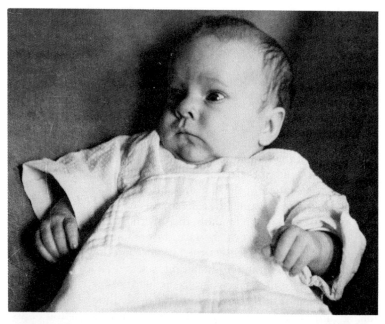

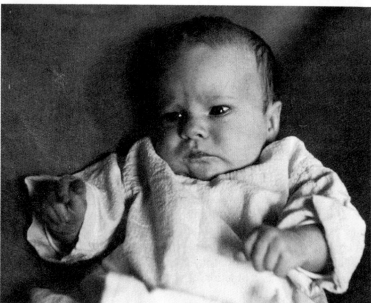

Figure 17. Emotional Responses to Clear Plastic Mask

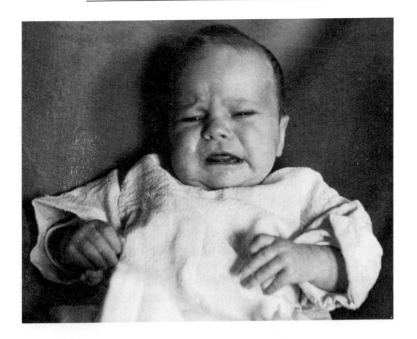

Since the clear mask did not eliminate eye contrast, hairline, or mouth parts, the dramatic aversive response was probably due to a general change in the texture and mobility of the face. In a technical sense, the clear mask was closer in appearance to the natural face than any of the other distortions, but its effect on smiling was dramatically different from that of other artificial modifications. Apparently, some as yet unspecified properties of the global configuration of the whole face are an essential element in reliably producing smiling responses among infants from two to three months, whereas isolated components of that configuration either are not sufficient by themselves or produce significantly fewer smiles. The crucial feature of the clear plastic mask that apparently produced such a dramatic aversive response may have been exactly the fact that it was nearly like the "natural" face, that all of the parts were present and in their proper relation, but that there was something definitely different about the mask that could not be immediately identified. Thus, subtle discrepancies, rather than gross distortions of the face to which the infant is accustomed, may be the distressing variable.

I also used the plastic mask to test the interaction between behavioral state and emotional expression. As indicated earlier, in the fussy infant, the smiling response to a nodding face speaking did not differ in kind from the response of the same infant when it was alert, although the overall frequency of smiling was considerably diminished. The clear mask not only reduced smiling frequency drastically but also provoked fussing or crying on rare occasions. On the other hand, when the infant was already fussy before it was presented with a clear plastic mask, the intensity of fussing increased considerably, and there was frequently a transition to full-blown crying, which was never observed as a response to the natural face, even when that was the face of a stranger.

The effects of the two opaque latex masks and of sunglasses on the quality of emotional expression during fussy periods was in the same direction, but much less dramatic. As a group the findings are consistent with the more general proposition that the behavioral state of the infant influences not only the frequency or probability of emotional expressions to reliable social stimuli but also the quality of the expressive pattern and therefore, by inference, the "meaning" which the infant presumably confers on social encounters.

The Development of Smiling in Down Syndrome

One finding from the preceding section that was stable across both infants and social context was the developmental invariance of adequate stimulus arrays for the production of smiling in the alert infant. Discrete sound stimuli, particularly the human voice, always preceded the silent visual presentation of the face as sufficient condition for eliciting smiling during the first three months. This section, by examining the natural history of smiling in mentally retarded children, outlines the boundaries within which such an invariance holds.

One global theoretical perspective on mental development in mental retardation holds that rates of development may be substantially delayed but patterns of progression in developmental sequences are essentially the same as those observed in normal children (Cicchetti and Sroufe 1978). The major competing hypothesis insists that mental retardation is by definition indicative of defect or deficit; therefore it predicts that at the appropriate level of analysis the patterns and sequences of behavioral development in organically caused mental retardation will be categorically different from those observed in normal children. Dr. Sadako Imamura and I used the natural history of smiling in mental retardation to examine these competing formulations of developmental variance or invariance by following a group of fifteen mentally retarded infants and children who were living in an institution and ranged in age from four to

% SUCCESSFULLY ELICITED SMILES

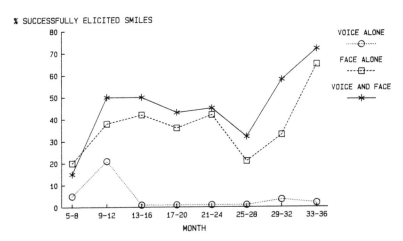

Figure 18. Smiling in Children with Down Syndrome

twenty-four months at the time of first testing. The potentially confounding effect of differences in social experience and organic etiology were controlled by limiting the sample to Down syndrome
children with a cytologically demonstrated trisomy-21, and to children who had all been institutionalized since they were two to four
months old. They were examined six times at two-month intervals by
a protocol similar in kind to the one used with normal infants to
elicit smiling behavior. Data on individual Down syndrome children,
who differed considerably in chronological age, were combined for
times of testing when they were of equivalent chronological age. We
predicted that the clinical sample would follow the same developmental sequences of smiling behavior as in normal children but that
the time scale would be significantly stretched out.

When computed either as successful trial blocks or as the mean
percentage of all stimuli producing a smile (see above), the results
indicated that Down syndrome children below one year smiled with
greater consistency to sounds than to silent faces (figure 18) and that
among the sound stimuli the voice was more effective than mechan-
ically produced sound, although smiling responses to the bell and
Audubon whistle remained statistically significant throughout the
first and well into the third year. Even four-month-old infants smiled
to the silent face so that the chronological age when Down syndrome
children first begin to smile to the human face was not established
within this sample.

From thirteen to twenty-four months the voice alone was significantly less effective in producing a smile than it had been during the first year, while the silent face produced smiling with greater consistency than during the first year, and with relatively greater frequency than the voice alone. Individual children followed sequentially from four to six months to sixteen to eighteen months showed essentially the same developmental sequence with a gradual increase of smiling to the face and a decrease in response to the voice. Between four and twelve months children almost never responded to the voice or face by vocalizing with or without smiling. From twenty-six to thirty-six months infants responded reliably to the voice alone with vocal answers, but their sounds were ambiguous and less well articulated than the spontaneous or elicited noncry vocalizations of the three-month-old healthy infants. However, blind judges could not distinguish between the spectrographs of vocalizations in healthy infants and Down syndrome children without hearing the tape recordings at the same time.

As in the case of normal infants the game of pat-a-cake was the most reliable and least readily habituated stimulus for the elicitation of smiling throughout the period of testing.

A search for the source on hearing a disembodied voice did not become a reliable response until the second year (eighteen to twenty-four months). Similarly, the smiling latencies to the voice alone were quite variable within and across subjects but generally longer than in normal two-month-old infants, although neither group searched for the sound source. By contrast, smiling latencies to the smiling face in two-to-three-year-old Down syndrome children remained relatively short and stable over the twelve months of observation; and they rarely inspected the internal details of the face of a familiar person or a stranger before breaking into a smile. Experiments using various masks or other alterations of the face were not tested.

Except for the considerably extended time scale, the sequence of adequate social stimuli for eliciting a smile was therefore quite similar to that reported earlier for normal infants, but there were some exceptions. For example, Down syndrome children continued to smile to the brass bell and Audubon bird whistle even at the age of thirty to thirty-six months although their preferred response to the voice was now a vocal answer and the preferred smiling stimulus was the silent face (figure 19). Thus stereotypic smiling response to socially neutral sound stimuli persisted longer in Down syndrome, even relative to the expanded time scale. A second difference was that even by three years of age the clinical sample rarely vocalized during the game of pat-a-cake although they smiled readily; and the sounds

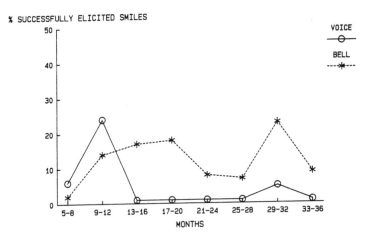

Figure 19. Smiling to Bell and Voice in Down Syndrome

they did make during the game were never identified as laughter by independent judges listening to the tape-recorded samples.

Individual differences in overall smiling frequency were considerably greater among Down syndrome children than in normal infants. These differences were consistent over the stimulus modalities, as well as over repeated observations, and they were apparently a characteristic of the individual child. However the etiology of such differences was not evident from the experimental observations alone. By casual observation, the child-care staff of the institution seemed to have distinct favorites among the children; with some they spent much more time than with the more unresponsive, lethargic infants who were physically the least attractive, showing more pronounced dysgenic features, drooling, repeatedly regurgitating their food, etc. Thus the staff may have inadvertently avoided the unattractive children, giving them less opportunity to "practice" their social responses. Alternatively, the lack of social responsiveness in the unattractive children may have been one manifestation of a more severe phenotypic expression of Down syndrome itself, discouraging the child-care staff from playing with infants who provided no feedback.

The sample was therefore rank ordered according to overall social responsiveness, and the three least expressive children were selected for special experimental "enrichment." An undergraduate college student was hired to spend two hours three times a week to play with the unresponsive infants, amusing them in order to encourage their smiling. After one month all children of the sample were retested and rank orders of social responsiveness were recomputed. The effect of one month of additional social stimulation was surprising. The three children who had initially been the least expressive were now in the top third of the sample by smiling frequency to "age-appropriate" stimulus configurations. The sample size of this pilot study was obviously too small to draw any firm conclusion, but the results suggest that the social responsiveness of institutionalized children depends critically on the level of social interaction to which they are exposed. In fact, the child-care staff now spent more time with the experimentally stimulated children; as a consequence the effect was stabilized.

From the results on mentally retarded children living in a socially impoverished environment, one cannot conclude that the mere quantity of social stimulation determines the level of social responsiveness of normal infants who grow up in a lively "average expectable" social environment. The more conservative conclusion from these pilot studies is that sequences in the natural history of smiling are probably invariant across children regardless of their overall intellectual potential.

Laughter

Phenomenological philosophy has traditionally conferred a privileged status on laughter, considering it to be qualitatively distinct among the repertory of universal human emotions. In contrast, empirical psychology has typically identified laughter as a more intense form of smiling and as an emotion that does not differ in kind from that associated with smiling.

Bergson (1928), Sartre (1948), and Buytendijk (1950), for example, stressed the uniquely social nature of laughter, as an emotion that always depends on the presence of another person, that has a powerful infectious quality, and that may in a social context become explosive or uncontrolled (see Hillman 1964). McDougall (1926) emphasized that laughter, in contrast to smiling, is not invariably a response to feelings of pleasure or exuberance but may become the uncontrolled reaction to a sense of desperation, hysterical panic, or acute fear. The ambivalent character of laughter is also mentioned by Ambrose (1963) and Bronson (1965), who emphasize that the social context strongly determines whether the same stimulus configuration will induce either laughter or signs of distress and crying. Bronson explained the apparently paradoxical link between emotional responses of laughter and crying to the same environmental events, by a cognitive hypothesis that all expressions of emotion, and particularly laughter, ultimately depend on the way in which the subject perceives and interprets the stimulus in its environmental context. In humans, expressions of emotion are therefore never mechanical "reflex" responses or innate releases to a specific sign stimulus. Within the natural sciences, Darwin was one of the first to locate laughter on a continuum with smiling, and to assume that laughter was simply a more intense expression of smiling: "Laughter seems primarily to be the expression of pure joy or happiness. . . . the man smiles, and smiling, as we see, graduates into laughter" (1873). The same perspective still characterizes most empirical studies in clinical and developmental psychology as well as in comparative animal studies. Freud's essay on wit (1905), for example, stresses both the quantitative aspects and ambivalent character of laughter and smiling as "discharge" phenomena of tension; but in contrast to many contemporary cognitive interpretations he gives a detailed theoretical account of the kinds of quantities that are presumably discharged either in laughter or in other expressions of emotion. Kagan (1974), Zelazo (1972), and Sroufe (1982), although they adopt an essentially cognitive interpretation of emotional expression, also attribute a "discharge" function to smiling and laughter that occurs at the moment when the infant or child has solved a cognitively difficult problem. All, however, fail to specify what energies are being discharged on such occasions. Similarly Berlyne's arousal jag (1960) implies that emotions are behavioral responses to manageable tensions when the individual is exposed to cognitive dissonance.

Within developmental psychology, Sroufe and Wunsch (1977) have given a detailed description for the causes of laughter in normal infants (see also Rothbart 1973). After examining 180 infants in a cross-sequential design they conclude there is an orderly developmental progression in the sufficient stimulus conditions that will produce laughter across the ages from four to eight months. Initially passively received but physically intense stimuli that require no cognitive processing were thought to be the most effective means for the provocation of laughter of young infants. Thereafter, more complex cognitive processes become the necessary conditions for laughter. The same authors note that conditions which sometimes produce laughter may at other times produce crying, but they do not indicate what variables determine the decision point. From the available developmental data it would appear that certain stimulus configurations typically elicit laughter rather than smiling, and that these remain as sufficient causes of laughter long after the infant or child has presumably mastered the cognitive dissonance of the event in question. Laughter rather than smiling, for example, appears to be an almost obligatory response to tickling throughout the growth years. Laughter also differs qualitatively from smiling in terms of the motor components recruited during the production of the emotional expression. At least by surface observation smiling can be defined exhaustively in terms of the activity of facial muscles. By contrast laughter always involves not only a facial expression of "open-mouthed" laughter, but a vigorous preparation and activation of the respiratory musculature, as well as distinctive vocalization patterns which require a complex control and release of subglottal pressure to give laughter its explosive character. Uncontrollable laughter will recruit not only the trunk musculature but also the upper limbs and may be associated with lacrimation and loss of bladder control. From a phenomenological and social perspective, as well as in terms of their physiological and functional characteristics, smiling and laughter therefore appear to be qualitatively different phenomena. As the observations reported by Sroufe and Wunsch indicate, laughter also differs categorically from smiling in terms of its developmental history, proximal causes, and effect on the social environment.

Laughter is probably unique to the human species. Some other mammalian species are said to emit various "pleasure calls" that might be considered as analogues to laughter (van Hoof 1972), but they are not associated with any specific facial grimace or smiling, whereas human laughter is typically defined as a combination of vocalization patterns that have an explosive character and may share some features with crying, and a particular facial grimace which is morphologically similar to smiling.

For this report, I made no a priori assumptions as to whether laughter is continuous with smiling, but provisionally treated laughter as an expression of emotion that differs qualitatively from smiling, with respect to its social and physical stimulus determinants, as well as its meanings for the laughing individual and the social partner.

Qualitative Descriptions and Quantitative Accounts

For the observations to be summarized here, I specified that an expression of emotion would be classified as laughter if, and only if, facial expressions resembling an open-mouthed smile or grin were accompanied by vocalization; but I did not insist that vocalization should be of the explosive type associated with laughter in children and adults. This "operational" definition left certain emotional responses ambiguous because, during the second and third months, the adequate social stimulation that elicited primarily smiling in earlier weeks at later times produced vocal replies or combinations of smiling and vocalization that were at the boundaries between smiling and laughter as defined above.

As a spontaneous phenomenon under free field conditions, laughter occurred so rarely that it could not be counted as part of the infant's repertory during the first six months. Laughter was almost always the response to a vigorous physical social interchange between infant and partner. The stimuli that reliably evoked laughter in infants included vigorous physical stimulation such as kissing the stomach, loud repetitions of familiar sounds, and jiggling the baby by bouncing it on the knees. Infants are also reported to laugh in response to subtler stimulus conditions with cognitive overtones but these were never observed during the first half-year. The account is therefore limited in scope, emphasizing primarily physically vigorous and intrusive stimuli. At best, it provides an account of the early onset of laughter, and is not a coherent description of the natural history of laughter in young children (see, for example, Sroufe and Wunsch, 1977). On days of experimental intervention, the conditions by which I attempted to elicit laughter were analogous to conditions used most commonly by mothers to elicit laughter on days of unobtrusive observation. These included the game of pat-a-cake as described above or its analogs of bouncing the child on the knees, etc., and tickling. In addition, there were occasions of laughter in response to other stimulus conditions during the first six months which will be summarized and described when they occurred with some regularity in more than one infant.

Pat-A-Cake. The method of playing the game and its remarkably robust effect in producing smiles have been described in earlier sections (see figure 20). Between four and six weeks but not before, the sequence of five silent pat-a-cake movements when the infant could not see either the experimenter or the mother produced smiling but not laughter, without any significant reduction in response intensity or "habituation," even after fifteen trials in all babies, and for up to forty trials in some infants. Nearly all trials were administered at five-to-ten second intervals to allow time for the baby to return to a baseline alert state. Within the first six weeks, nearly all trials of pat-a-cake produced a smile or a "grin," grin being defined here as a more intense smile with the lips widely parted. By six weeks, the repeated testing of the pat-a-cake game procedure with intervals no longer than ten seconds was usually associated with a mounting excitement on the baby's part, a progressive decrease in latency between onset of a pat-a-cake game and onset of grinning, and accompanying vocalization which, at first, did not resemble explosive laughter described in older infants. Over the next several weeks until about fourteen weeks, the associated vocal patterns increasingly resembled laughing sounds, and these could now be clearly distinguished from noncry vocalizations, for example, in response to the disembodied voice. Early on, vocalizations accompanying such grins resembled "ga-ga" sounds or deep-throated gurgles. Tape-recorded samples of such vocalizations played to blind judges led to the

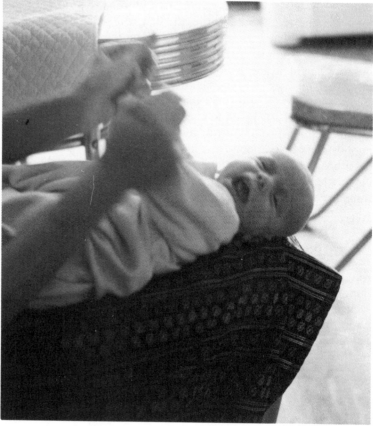

Figure 20. "Pat-a-Cake"

uniform conclusion that the sounds were not laughter. However, in older infants, vocalizations took on some of the explosive sound features associated with laughter; and tape-recorded samples of such vocalizations played to independent judges were typically labeled as expressions of pleasure, but not yet of laughter. By the age of twelve weeks, tape-recorded samples of vocalization in response to the pat-a-cake game were consistently classified as laughter by the judges. Some infants also responded to the game with high-pitched inspiratory squeals that were not heard under other conditions and had something of a hysterical quality. The sound spectrograms of noncry vocalizations to the pat-a-cake game in three-month infants were similar in form to vocalization patterns of eight-month-old infants who, by behavioral criteria, were unequivocally judged as laughing. The developmental sequence of vocalization patterns suggests a gradual transition from open-mouthed smiling or grinning associated with vocalizations at the back of the throat to wide-mouthed grinning, with explosive vocalizations taking on most of the characteristics of true laughter.

The game of pat-a-cake involved complex combinations of sensory stimuli in various modalities, although I made no sounds during experimental trials, and always made an effort to exclude visual stimulus input by holding the infant's hands from the sides. One obvious candidate for the necessary and sufficient stimulus conditions was the "bouncing" character of repeatedly opposing the hands against each other with some force at the moment of contact. Partial support for the assumption came from other games a number of mothers played, in which they placed their babies on both knees, making a lap, while rhythmically moving their lower legs up and down using the foot as a fulcrum and repeating a nursery rhyme which, in local jargon, was "Trot, trot to Boston, trot, trot to Lynn," in rhythm to the movements of the legs. During the last phrase of the rhyme, they spread their legs, holding onto the baby with its hands, and letting it partially fall between the legs. By no means all of the mothers tried this game spontaneously. In such cases, I occasionally interfered by asking mothers to try the game if they were willing to play it. The more daring of the mothers in the sample began playing the game gently when infants were still six to eight weeks old; others did not begin until the age of three months. During the first two months, infants were not amused by being dropped between the legs, and usually looked sober, surprised, or "worried." They did, however, smile consistently while they were being gently bounced on the knees. I also introduced a variation by asking mothers to bounce the babies without speaking, and by this procedure was able to confirm that the bouncing action itself rather than the combination of voicing and bouncing elicited broad smiling and grinning with a gradual increase in vocalization as the game progressed over several repetitions. By three and a half to four months, the game produced high-pitched squeals, usually during the inspiratory phase of respiration, at the moment when the infants were dropped between the legs, but they only laughed after they had been "primed" during the preceding trials and were already excited. By contrast, the first two or three occasions of being "dropped" between the knees usually caused surprise, dismay, or displeasure in three-to-four-month-old infants, even when they had been delighted with the game on previous days. A few of the infants actually began to cry when they were "dropped" for the first time on a day; and mothers usually abandoned the game rapidly or limited it to bouncing the babies on the knees, which always seemed a source of pleasure as long as infants were alert. Apparently the critical variables were the infant's age, how gently or vigorously it was usually handled under other circumstances, and the presence or absence of priming in the period immediately preceding trial. Until three months, infants who enjoyed the game laughed only at the moment when they were actually dropped between the knees. By six months, however, infants who were familiar with the game anticipated being dropped from the rhythm of the game and the accompanying rhyme, and laughed even beforehand. Under the circumstances of observation, it was, however, difficult to conclude that this was true anticipation and not the result of a general increase in pleasurable excitement.

A number of parents, almost exclusively fathers, occasionally amused themselves and, one hopes, their children by repeatedly throwing them into the air and then catching them. Two-month-olds were not at all amused. Sometimes they began to fuss or cry; more often they merely looked somber and worried. When fathers nevertheless persisted with the game, the infants gradually became accustomed to the procedure, were less afraid, and eventually smiled, then grinned and finally shrieked or laughed with what sounded like pleasure. Even after they had become familiar with the game, however, each new encounter required a warming-up period, before the infants would participate with any indication of pleasure. The initial priming period needed before infants willingly participated with being thrown in the air, was in marked contrast to the game of pat-a-cake, which was usually successful from the start, provided the infant was in a favorable state. However, after the fourth month, the need for an initial priming period also dropped out with respect to the game of being thrown up and caught; but unlike the bouncing or pat-a-cake games, it was very much state-dependent. When infants were mildly distressed, the procedure resulted in decidedly negative reactions, and sometimes crying.

Tickling. The sensation of tickling is thought to be transmitted by simple cutaneous nerve endings (pain fibers?), but the physical and neurophysiological mechanisms of impulse transmission which elicit the sensation of tickling are poorly understood (Bishop 1946). In everyday usage the term "tickling" has at least two connotations. The sensation that is produced when a fly wanders across the nose, or when the lip is stroked gently with a camel's-hair brush, is usually perceived as noxious, and does not depend on a specific social context. It depends entirely on the physical characteristics of the stimulus. The usual response is a wiping movement or diffuse motility, but the tickling does not induce uncontrollable laughter, although it may elicit some amusement when there is an understanding between the person tickling and the one being tickled. The other connotation of tickling involves complex maneuvers usually of the hands of one social partner moving in unpredictable ways over the skin surface of the other, and this form of tickling can elicit uncontrollable laughter, especially in persons who are particularly sensitive to tickling.

Some regions of the body are more ticklish than others. Rubbing fingers with pressure over the axilla, the lateral rib cage, the iliac crest, and so on, in slow, continuous movement and a variable pattern usually elicits squirming and laughter in most young adults, but the variables of pressure and relative rate of movement appear to be essential for obtaining reliable results. Gently stroking the same regions is either not experienced as tickling, or else as tickling of the first kind. Unpredictability in the direction of movement may also be essential, since repeatedly going back and forth over the same region is less effective than exploring continuously new regions in the same general skin area. Most essential, however, appears to be that the tickling stimulus be applied by another person. As Darwin (1873) already pointed out, "From the fact that the child can hardly tickle itself or in a much less degree than when tickled by another person, it seems that the precise point to be touched must not be known [by the individual who laughs]. Something unexpected or novel, or an incongruous idea which breaks through a habitual train of thought appears to be a strong element in the ludicruous [that elicits laughter]." Therefore, one would conclude that laughter in response to tickling always depends on a social context, and cannot be adequately characterized in terms of the physical parameters of stimulation alone. Although the laughter produced by tickling suggests that the sensation is experienced as pleasurable, ticklish individuals frequently make squirming efforts to escape from continued stimulation, and act decidedly annoyed if the social partner persists.

Because tickling of this second type seems well suited to elicit laughter at least during the early phases of an encounter, I also used it as a stimulus "modality" for examining the development of laughter in young infants, starting in the first week at home, and testing the infants periodically over the first six months.

The stimuli were always presented by running my fingertips up and down or in rotation across a circumscribed skin surface, applying moderate pressure, and making sure that the direction of finger movements was variable. As preferred sites of tickling, I used the axilla, lateral rib cage and supra-iliac skin region, but also tried the soles of the feet and the umbilical region, although I made no effort to map out in greater detail what might be the most sensitive regions for tickling or what were precisely the physical parameters of stimulation that would or would not produce laughter in young infants. In order to preserve the element of "surprise," I made no effort to "standardize" a schedule of tickling or a mode of stimulus presentation. Where quantitative results are summarized below, they typically refer to tickling trials lasting two or three seconds, interrupted by five-to-seven-second periods, and then repeated until infants either began to laugh or made it clear that they were not going to respond. The babies were tickled both when they could and could not see my face, to control for visual social contact as a precondition for the production of laughter. Once a particular stimulus configuration reliably produced laughter when the baby could see me making an approach, I performed the same gesture as if intending to tickle again but made no physical contact. In this way I proposed to test whether the infants could anticipate that they would be tickled, and whether such anticipation was sufficient to induce laughter. The infants' varied responses to tickling and simulated tickling were scored as indifference, squirming, smiling, grinning, laughter (grinning with an explosive vocalization), frowning, fussing, and crying. In all cases, the infant's behavioral state was carefully noted before the start of the trial; but, except when otherwise indicated, the results refer to testing trials when infants were in an optimal state of alert inactivity or alert activity. Preliminary trials on older infants and children had demonstrated the obvious result that it is impossible to produce laughter by tickling the subject during sleep, and very difficult to elicit anything resembling laughter or responses other than aversive turning away when the infants are drowsy or crying.

Until the fourth week, it was not possible to elicit any consistent squirming responses with an open-mouthed smile or vocalizations resembling laughter in the waking alert infant. As with responses to pat-a-cake, the sounds produced during open-mouthed smiling were tape-recorded and judged by individuals who could not see the baby's face. The judges were unable to reach consensus on the nature of the sounds produced to tickling during the second and third months; however, during the fifth and sixth months sounds were typically classified by listeners as laughter. By the fifth month (mean age: 154 days; range 113–60 days), all seven infants tested systematically responded to tickling of the armpits and lateral rib cage with vocalizations independently classified as laughter (see figure 21a,b). At the same time, they showed the "wide-mouthed" grin with a clear crinkling of the eyelids. Initially, such laughter could only be provoked by actual tickling of the axilla or lateral rib cage. Other skin surfaces, e.g., the back, buttocks, dorsal surface of the legs, arms, and face, were relatively insensitive to tickling. However, once laughter had been provoked by tickling a more sensitive region, the tickling of less sensitive skin-surfaces now occasionally provoked laughter, although the priming effects waned quickly unless infants were again primed by tickling the more sensitive region.

The same priming effect could also be demonstrated by the following procedure. Once infants had started to laugh in response to physical contact, the same gesture was made in a quasi-threatening fashion, so that the infant could observe the approach, but there was no physical contact. This maneuver could trigger another gale of anticipatory laughter, but it rapidly lost its effect when there was no further physical contact. Thereafter, physical contact had to be renewed to provoke laughter. In three-to-four-month-old infants, tickling gestures without physical contact could, after the initial priming stimulus, readily provoke laughter for repeated trials, physical contact being needed only to initiate the sequence during a five- or ten-minute experiment.

To test whether laughter to tickling depended on visual contact with another person, I also tickled infants when they could not see me. The results indicated that by five months, physical contact alone had become a sufficient condition to provoke real laughter. However, by this age it was no longer possible to exclude social learning effects. Parallel observations on the development of object permanence (see below), for example, indicated that by this age, infants

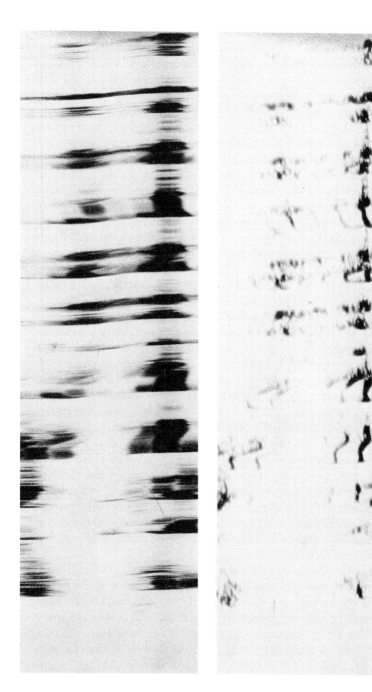

Figure 21: a. (above) Laughter to Tickling in Four-month-old (Broad-band Spectrograph)

actively searched for the disappearing human figure, and inanimate objects, and that they clearly responded with vocal protest on seeing their mother leave the visual field. At a much earlier age, they searched for a visual image on hearing the disembodied voice. Thus, recognition of the social partner no longer depended exclusively on seeing the visual configuration; instead the infants had acquired a "schema" of the social partner, such that one component element might suggest to them the other essential features; and physical tickling might imply the face of another.

During its early stages, the laughter of infants in response to tickling apparently depended more on the social context than on the physical parameters of the stimulus or the locus of skin surface to which the stimulus was applied. Once the expression of emotion we call laughter was well established, however, the same gestures could elicit in infants who expected to be tickled an anticipatory response which was sufficient to induce full-blown laughter. Such observations apparently remain a constant feature throughout the life of ticklish adults. They suggest that laughter is not, or need not be, the purely mechanical response to a particular stimulus configuration. Yet, in young infants, the social context alone was not adequate to define the sufficient conditions for the induction of laughter. Instead, the spatiotemporal features of tactile and pressure stimulus-sensations, as well as the region of skin being stimulated, were critical variables, particularly during the "priming" phase of inducing a level of excitation sufficient to provoke laughter.

To examine the importance of social context as a precondition for tickling, I also tested Darwin's conclusion that it is difficult to tickle oneself, and that tickling necessarily involves another person. I obviously could not ask the babies to tickle themselves; and therefore could also not test Darwin's conclusions critically. Instead, I used the infants' own hands as an instrument for passively tickling them by guiding their hands with mine across the appropriate skin surfaces with some pressure. By this procedure, it was occasionally possible to provoke laughter in five-to-six-month-old infants, although the laughter was generally weak and of short duration, infants becoming totally indifferent to trials after several attempts. A quantitative comparison between my hand alone and my hand guiding the baby's hands to tickle itself indicated that my hand alone was always significantly more effective, at each week during the fifth and sixth months ($p < .05$; $p < .01$). Nevertheless, laughing responses to being passively tickled with the infant's own hand were real and could be demonstrated repeatedly on the same day, on separate occasions, and in successive weeks. Tape-recorded samples of such vocalizations were again scored as "laughter" by independent judges.

Because infants seem able to tickle "themselves," I carried out exploratory studies with school-age children from six to twelve years, and with a few adults who identified themselves as ticklish. First they were tickled by the usual procedure to demonstrate that they were, in fact, ticklish. Then they were asked to tickle themselves repeatedly in various sensitive areas and to report their experience of the stimulation. Finally I took their hands, asked them to let the hands hang loose, and tickled them in the same sensitive areas. Because the experiment was bizarre, I could not rely on laughter as the outcome criterion, and had to rely instead on their personal reports. There was remarkable consensus across children and adults, all of whom reported that being passively tickled with their own hand, while I controlled the movement, produced mild sensations of tickling, which were more intense than when they tickled themselves. However, both sensations were less intense than when *I* tickled them with *my* hand.

The physiological basis for such differences remains unclear. One possible explanation may be that the tactile feedback from the hand itself diminishes the excitatory effect of tickling, but not sufficiently to block the sensation altogether. On the other hand, the combined effect of tactile and proprioceptive feedback, when subjects control their own movements, is sufficient to block the tickling sensation, perhaps by eliminating the element of surprise altogether that is presumably critical for experiencing tickling, and for laughing in response to it.

Crying

In the section in chapter 2 on crying as a behavioral state, I reported the overall duration of crying as proportion of total observation time, the mean duration of individual cry bouts, and the temporal sequences of crying and other behavioral states. Further, I suggested ways in which crying might be construed as a behavioral state analogous to sleep and to waking dispositions. In this section I am focusing on crying as an expression of an emotion; its morphological characteristics as manifested in facial expressions and vocal utterances; the organismic and environmental conditions that either produce or terminate crying at different points during the first six months. Although observations relating to behavioral states necessarily overlap with observations of crying as emotion, this redundancy serves the purpose of illustrating that states cannot be conceived as entities in their own right or as distinct from the ensembles of behavior patterns and physiological correlates by which the state concept is defined.

The developmental analysis of crying highlights some features of the development of emotional expression generally which may not be as clearly demonstrated in the account of other expressions. For one thing, crying is the most peremptory expressive behavior at the infant's disposal; it is competent at birth, and by most accounts its global manifestations change relatively little during the first year. Unlike smiling, the prefunctional organization and communicative value of this motor pattern is not disputed on theoretical grounds. Unlike smiling, crying is clearly a coordinated motor pattern that involves not only cry vocalizations and facial grimaces but also a collective of skeletal motor patterns and autonomic responses that presumably contribute essentially to crying both as an expression of emotion and as a behavioral state. Similar postural adjustments and autonomic responses may accompany smiling and other expressions of emotion, but they are not clearly manifested as in crying.

In contrast to their form, the proximal causes of crying and cry termination, and by inference the meaning or cognitive implications of crying as an expression of emotion, change dramatically during the first six months. Relatively little is known about these developmental changes although the information is critical for resolving the theoretical question of whether emotions are distinct entities or global dispositions at birth; and of whether emotional expressions are fixed species-typical action patterns invariably linked to underlying emotions, or prefunctional motor coordinations that go through extensive developmental transformations as a consequence of "maturation," experience, and cognitive development. The major emphasis of this section is on changes over time in the form-function relation, on the proximal causes of crying, and on the environmental context that predictably terminates a bout of crying. As a point of departure, the description will however focus on behavioral structures of crying during the neonatal period that have already been examined in detail by others. Darwin's original description emphasized facial movements, or cry grimaces, as the most distinctive features of this emotional expression; this line of investigation was further elaborated in recent years by objective "kinesic" analysis.

However, the major emphasis of contemporary research is on vocalization during infancy and on the objectively measurable acoustic properties of vocal utterances (Ostwall and Murry 1985; Murray

1979; Golub and Corwin 1985; Wasz-Höckert et al. 1985) as a direct parallel to comparative studies of vocalizations in animal young in which crying may or may not be associated with distinct changes of facial expression (Marler and Hamilton, 1967). As the section on behavioral states already indicates, crying is associated with a complex behavior pattern which extends far beyond the face and voice. The generalized motor activity, autonomic changes, and the rest may not have a strong signaling function but they are nevertheless integral features of the coordinated motor patterns associated with this expression of emotion that have a direct or indirect effect on patterns of cry vocalization as well as on the way in which adequate stimulus conditions will initiate or terminate crying (Stark and Nathanson 1973).

Darwin (1873), Ekman (1979), and Oster and Ekman (1978) have described in detail the movements and configurations of the facial muscles that produce the universally recognized cry grimace. Darwin (1873) used Duchenne's anatomical taxonomy of facial muscles to describe the movements of the young infant during full-blown crying or screaming: "The eyebrows are pulled down and turned inwards towards the nose by a contraction of the corrugator supercilii, resulting in the appearance of vertical furrows and disappearance of the transverse folds of the forehead. The superficial circular muscles around the eyes contract and produce a crinkling of the skin folds around the eye orbit; the pyramidal muscles of the nose contract pulling the eyebrows down further and producing transverse wrinkles around the base of the nose. The upper lips are raised and accentuate the nasal labial folds. The eyelids are tightly closed [once vocalization starts]." Ekman and his colleagues (Ekman and Freisen 1978; Oster and Ekman 1978), among others, used this account to establish a psychologically neutral coding scheme for detecting subtle variations in the face of the frightened, anxious disturbed, pouting, or crying infant.

The young of other animal species, including birds, kittens, and primates are equipped with a limited repertory of distinctive vocal expressions which are predictably produced by specific social conditions of isolation, hunger, distress, or threat. By spectrographic techniques these sounds can be distinguished relatively easily one from the other; they are characteristically observed in all members of the species although the question of individual differences within species has rarely been addressed. Taking cues from such comparative animal studies, a number of clinical and experimental investigators of human infants have also used acoustic and spectrographic analysis to classify the sound patterns of human cries according to their morphological acoustic features and their causal antecedents. Exclusive reliance on findings from comparative animal psychology may be misleading because the cry patterns of human infants differ qualitatively from those of animals along several important dimensions. For example, considerable controversy remains whether human cry patterns in fact represent distinct and cause-specific physical "types," or are simply quantitative variations along a continuum of one global morphological pattern whose intensity depends on a background of behavioral state variables, increased muscle tonus, and the like (Izard 1977). More concretely, the birth cry appears to be unique to the human species although the question has not been examined in sufficient detail to draw any firm conclusion. Further, when human infants and children cry as the appropriate response to an offending cause, this may set up a self-perpetuating cry cycle which persists long after the offending cause has presumably worn off. Abnormal full-term infants and prematures do not easily maintain a bout of crying for any extended period (Wolff 1970). In response to a pain stimulus, or spontaneously, they may begin to cry after one or two "cry attempts" but then stop vocalizing. The cry pattern therefore never accelerates sufficiently to maintain itself as the continuous rhythmic pattern characteristic of full-term infants. Physical weakness of the respiratory system may account for the abortive character of cry attempts in young premature infants or abnormal full-term infants; however, even when crying reaches a sufficient pitch to become repetitive, the repetition never achieves the stability of rhythm that is characteristic of sustained crying in healthy full-term infants (R. Ferber and P. H. Wolff, unpublished observations).

The Morphology of Cry Vocalizations

Most published taxonomies of cry types in young infants have arrived at three to five kinds of sound patterns which characterize the vocalization of the full-term infant as well as more or less type-specific etiologic conditions and communicative functions associated with these types (Truby and Lind 1965; Wasz-Höckert et al. 1985; Golub and Corwin 1985). However, some investigators have concluded that the typologies are artifacts of pattern perception which in fact represent quantitative changes along a continuum of distress or anguish and that the alleged cry types reflect scaling along a single dimension of distress (Izard 1977). The provisional classification of cry types which I proposed earlier (1969) includes the following categories.

153

The "basic" or "hunger" cry. Despite its name the term implies no direct causal link to food deprivation. The basic cry is the most common form of sustained crying in the young infant to a variety of organic conditions or environmental circumstances, and it is the form to which most infants will eventually revert from other cry types if they cry for a long enough period. Its most distinctive acoustic feature is the periodically repeating sequence of expiratory sounds lasting about 0.6 seconds, starting at 330–400 Hz (fundamental frequency), rising as a smooth curve to 550–660 Hz, and then reverting to the starting frequency before stopping, until the cycle is repeated in a typical rise-fall pattern (figure 22a). Each cry vocalization is usually followed by a short pause lasting 0.1 seconds, an inspiratory "whistle" (0.2–0.3 seconds) that has no distinctive fundamental frequency, and another pause (0.1 seconds) before the next clearly defined expiratory cry occurs. Once crying is turned into a rhythmic pattern, the individual components of this temporal sequence remain fairly constant throughout a cry bout within any one infant across different bouts and across healthy infants of the same age (see Wolff 1969).

Much greater variability of the component vocal elements was noted near the beginning of a crying bout when the individual expirations were typically longer, and towards the end of a crying bout, when voicing signal became intermittent. Data concerning the temporal stability of cry vocalizations were therefore computed on samples of crying recorded in the middle of an extended cry episode after infants had been crying for at least five seconds but were not yet prepared to stop. When measured within these constraints, the temporal sequence of basic cry patterns did not change significantly during the first six months. However, the overall duration of crying decreased rapidly during the first three months, and by the fourth month sustained crying was so rare that its temporal patterns could no longer be measured reliably. Rhythmic cry samples recorded shortly after birth, at two, four, six, eight, and twelve weeks, revealed no significant developmental changes of temporal organization, indicating that the physiologic mechanisms for rhythmic cry production are well established at birth.

By far the most common cry heard throughout the first six months was the rise-fall pattern in the fundamental frequency (see figure 22a), which was generated by an early increase and a late fall in subglottal air pressure within one expiration. Between two and three months, infants had apparently gained control over the mouth articulators, so that they were now able to either maintain a constant fundamental frequency throughout an expiration or generate a terminal rise in pitch. At that point, the sound patterns of cry and noncry vocalization were no longer under exclusive control of respiratory mechanisms (Lieberman 1984).

"Mad" cry. A variant of the basic cry was interpreted by some mothers as indicating that their infants were angry, in a rage or in despair. By sound spectrograph these mad cries could be distinguished from the basic cry pattern by the amount of turbulence or "paraphonation" superimposed on the signal. Such turbulence, associated with a rough, rasping quality of the audible signal (figure 22b), is presumably caused by a very rapid change in subglottal air pressure or by forcing more air through the vocal chords than can be accommodated (Truby and Lind 1965). On the average, the mad cries showed the same temporal organization as basic cries, but the variability of individual components within a sequence was greater. The overall frequency of mad cries diminished rapidly from the first to the third month in parallel with the overall decrease of crying, so that it was not possible to examine the stability of temporal relations in this cry type after the first month. Infants were either achieving relatively greater control over the subglottal air pressure, or they were less likely to give way to uncontrolled crying, or mothers consistently intervened at a point before the infants became desperate. When the mad cry was allowed to persist, its temporal patterns became disorganized and eventually shifted over into "screaming" which no longer had any distinctive temporal features. If the angry cry is, in fact, a distinct variant of the basic cry, the differences appear to be quantitative variations of the intensity of crying, and of the length of time for which the infant is left unattended.

"Pain cry." To sharp physical pain of sudden onset, such as a heel prick for obtaining a blood sample, nearly all of the infants responded with a vocalization pattern that differed qualitatively from the temporal organization of other cries and was consistent across the group. Such differences were determined, in part, by the fact that infants made a sudden shift from a condition of silence or nonvocalization altogether to intense crying, rather than the more gradual transition from silence to fussing to cry vocalizations in which fussing might be considered as an introductory phase. On the other hand, the shock of acute pain may contribute distinctive features to the pain cry. After a sharp-pain stimulus, the initial full cry was usually of much longer duration (4–5 seconds) than the usual expiratory

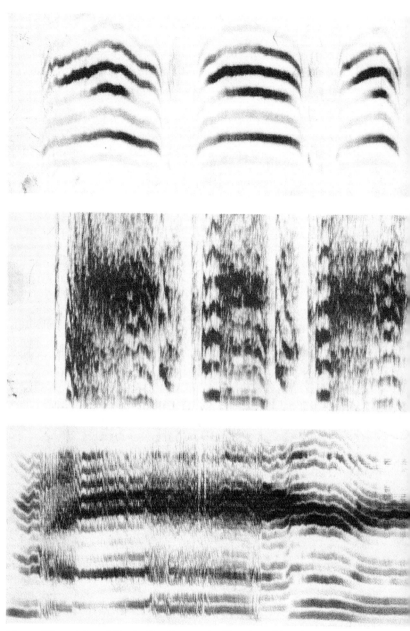

Figure 22: a. (above) Basic Cry Pattern in Five-day-old Infant (Reproduced
at Twice Real Time)
b. (middle) "Mad" Cry in Four-day-old Infant
c. (below) Pain Cry (Reproduced in Real Time; Followed by Six
Seconds of Silence)

156

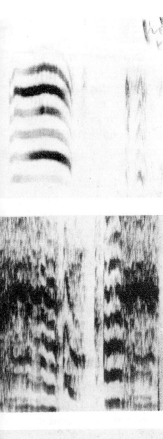

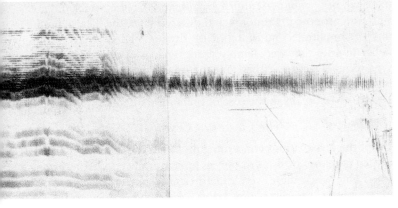

phase of the basic cry, and the rise time of the fundamental frequency was considerably slower, not reaching a peak until two or three seconds after the start. The long expiratory phase of crying was followed by a prolonged silence lasting from three to seven seconds as if the infant was holding its breath (figure 22c). This pause was followed by a much louder inspiratory gasp, and then by a series of transitional cries which gradually reverted to the usual rhythmic pattern, described above as the basic cry. Not all infants of the sample were recorded at a time when blood samples were being taken by heel prick. A cross-sectional study was therefore performed in a pediatrician's office during which we recorded the crying response to immunization shots among infants ranging in age from four weeks to fourteen months. The temporal pattern of the pain cry was essentially the same as that described above, and the pattern was relatively stable from four weeks to fourteen months. Sometimes infants started with two or three brief whimpers or "cry attempts" while their face manifested an expression of shock or surprise which gradually gave way to the extended howl. However, in all recorded samples, a prolonged cry was followed by a gradual transition to the rhythmic patterns of the basic cry. Latencies between pain stimulus and onset of cry varied from three to twelve seconds; during this time infants sometimes lay immobile with a staring or distressed face, as if overcome by the surprise and therefore unable to respond immediately.

The three cry patterns described above refer to "ideal" types. A substantial number of cry vocalizations consisted of transitions, groans, whines, whimpers, abortive cries, and the like, which did not fit into the proposed taxonomy and differed from the ideal types in terms of amplitude and stability of rhythm. There were also a number of cries that were simply weak replicas of the conventional cry pattern, suggesting either that the infants were not disposed to cry, that the offense was relatively weak, or that the infants were "too weak" to cry, as in the case of premature infants.

The Causes of Crying

Most of the observations concerning proximal causes of crying were recorded serendipitously as responses to "naturally" occurring events in the home when these were of sufficient frequency over repeated observations in the same infant and across babies to warrant the inference of a direct causal relationship. Some of the presumed causes of crying were, however, sufficiently innocuous so that I could introduce experimental manipulations that were variations on presumed causes, that could be reproduced without doing any conceivable harm or having any adverse effect on the baby itself. These causes were examined systematically on one day each week reserved for the purpose.

Crying in Sleep. Half the infants of the sample occasionally gave single cries during state II sleep that seemed unrelated to any environmental events or identifiable organismic conditions. The cries occurred almost exclusively in state II and were never observed during state I. Sometimes, they were accompanied by cry grimaces, but the face almost always returned to a peaceful state immediately after the vocalization. Because the cries were rare, even in the first several weeks, I could not predict their occurrence, and could therefore not tape record the samples for spectrographic analysis and comparison with waking cries. By ear, they were, however, distinguishable from episodic squeals in state I or state II sleep, and they were never associated with cry or pre-cry grimaces. The only clue about possible causes came from experiments designed to elicit smiling in state II by various auditory stimuli. As indicated earlier, the number of responses to the voice, bell, rattle, Audubon bird whistle, etc. during state II were quite variable, ranging in type from smiling to mouthing, tonguing, and occasional grimaces that were reminiscent of a "pre-cry face" of the waking infant, but they never produced cry sounds. The overall frequency of cries during sleep decreased rapidly between the first and second month; by the third month, only two of the infants still made occasional cry sounds during sleep.

Hunger. Presumably the most common cause of crying, as well as of waking up and a period of activity in healthy infants is hunger or food deprivation (Kleitman 1963), a conclusion which is consistent with a considerable amount of both direct and indirect clinical evidence. Figure 7 already indicated that infants were significantly more likely to cry or fuss fifteen minutes before than fifteen minutes after a meal. However, the overall frequency of cry bouts diminished over the first three months; and by the sixth month, it was a rare occurrence, even in the waking infant. Moreover, crying became progressively dissociated from the time of last feeding; and by the third month, infants were often alert and actively playing, even when they had been without a meal for three or four hours. The significant decrease in base rate of crying bouts may have contributed to the lack of apparent temporal relation between feeding and crying. On the other hand, a number of observations summarized earlier suggest that hunger as determined by time since last feeding became progressively less disruptive of the infant's behavioral state or general disposition to attend to environmental events over the first three months. Thus, it is at least likely that the disruptive impact of hunger on behavior in general and crying in particular diminished over time, perhaps as behavioral states of waking became more stable and self-correcting. The same trend continues during childhood, and adults rarely cry because they are hungry, although they may feel disgruntled or irritable.

One clinical experiment on the interaction between sucking and behavioral state was carried out on a small group of infants who were being fed by gastrostomy tube during their recovery from surgical repair for a tracheo-esophageal fistula (Wolff 1972a). The results indicated that gastric loading by the tube was usually sufficient to reduce or arrest crying. By contrast, sucking on a pacifier without a concurrent gastrostomy feeding, or a sham feeding by mouth as the stomach contents were constantly removed by gastrostomy tube, did not arrest crying once the pacifier was removed. Such observations strengthen the hypothesis that hunger is a sufficient cause of crying and stomach loading an efficient means for terminating the behavioral state of crying.

However, from such observations it cannot be concluded that all episodes of crying which are terminated by a feeding are necessarily caused by hunger. Many mothers in the longitudinal sample fed their infant whenever it cried, even when it had been well fed within the previous hour and the mothers did not believe that their infant was actually hungry. More often than not, such a supplementary feeding terminated crying (see also Bernal 1972). In other words, the fact that feeding terminated crying is not itself prima facie evidence that the cause of crying is always hunger. By and large, however, the evidence is consistent with traditional assumptions.

Temperature (cold). The assumption held by many parents that babies are more likely to cry when they are cold gained some support from observations, particularly of Japanese babies in their homes, which were carried out during the fall and early winter in homes without any central heating. The infants slept in rooms which were cold enough so that Dr. Sadako Immamura, who collaborated with me on these observations, and I were usually dressed in sweaters and overcoats, while the infants were usually covered by mountains of blankets, as well as an amply protected electric heater placed at their feet. Three of the infants kept in this way slept considerably longer throughout the observation periods, and the other two infants who were not covered so generously with blankets and usually felt cold to the touch had a generally disturbed sleeping pattern. No conclusion can be drawn from such a small sample. Further support for the claim came from observations on eight full-term neonates kept in an incubator to control for ambient temperature, sound, and light. Sleep durations were compared when the infants were maintained at a relatively high temperature (85 to 90°F) and when the incubator was relatively cool (78°F). The infants slept longer and cried less in the warm than the cool environment. There were no differences in the duration of individual state I episodes or in the sequence of transitions from state I to state II, and most of the additional sleep time in a warm environment was due to more sustained state II periods. These results are consistent with the conclusion that ambient temperature has an effect on crying and restlessness, and that changes of ambient temperature greater than those which mothers usually permit, may be associated with changes in the total amount of crying.

The influence of abrupt temperature changes on crying was tested directly whenever babies were undressed in preparation for a diaper change or a bath. During the first month, being undressed caused babies who had not been crying before to break into cries in 44 percent of all observations but not to respond on 56 percent of observations. However six of the infants accounted for most of the effect even during the first month, as if they were particularly sensitive to nakedness or cold. By the end of the second month none of the infants responded with crying consistently to being naked. On the contrary they seemed to enjoy the experience, waving their arms, making noncry vocalizations, and smiling.

Wet Diapers. Many mothers independently arrived at the conclusion that wet diapers might be a sufficient cause to wake up a baby and cause it to cry. To sort out the possible confounding interactions between the sensation of wetness in the diapers and the cooling effect on the skin I carried out some manipulations in the newborn nursery to test the mothers' assumption. A change of diapers in the crying infant is frequently associated with an arrest of crying but this includes not only an exchange of diapers but also an active social interchange between baby and mother as well as a feeding following immediately after the diaper change. Therefore the observation on the effects of diaper change provides no persuasive evidence that wetness causes infants to cry. As reported elsewhere (Wolff 1969), I examined the influence of wetness by changing the diapers, keeping the wet diaper in the incubator to keep it warm, and testing whether the removal of the wet diapers arrested crying and subsequently whether redressing them in the wet diapers caused the crying to resume. The results of these "experiments" were clear-cut. Wetness per se had no significant effect as a cause of crying.

On the other hand, the response of infants to bathing suggested that sensations of wetness may be a sufficient cause of crying. Seven of the twenty-one infants frequently responded with loud crying or screeching when first immersed in a bath whose water had been adjusted to skin temperature. In this subgroup of babies, the protest to being bathed was persistent over the first month. Thereafter, they began to respond like other infants had from the start. Apparently they experienced the bath as a source of pleasure, lying placidly, cooing to their mothers, or else kicking happily with their legs. By contrast, most infants protested vigorously when first removed from the bath, again suggesting that the sensation of coldness or a rapid change of ambient temperature rather than the sensation of wetness may have been the essential factor. However, the process of bathing involves a complex set of perceptual events of which wetness may be only a small component, whereas sudden changes in skin temperature and the unfamiliar sensation of partial weightlessness may have contributed as secondary factors when infants cry as they are prepared for the bath.

In traditional Japanese homes, we noted that when babies were first covered with a towel that had already been soaked in bathwater adjusted to skin temperature before they were actually immersed, so that there was no sudden change of skin temperature, they never cried, although bathing was part of the everyday routine in each of the babies observed. On the other hand, many of the babies in Japanese as well as American homes, although perfectly content and even playing happily as long as they were in the bath, yelled loudly as soon as they were taken out of the water, until they had been wrapped in a towel and rubbed down. Rapid changes of skin temperature, especially from a warm to a cold environment, may thus be a sufficient cause of crying. On the other hand, the sensation of wetness as such probably does not contribute as a significant cause of crying.

Contact Comfort. Harlow's classic experiments on the behavior of caged-isolated infant monkeys has called dramatic attention to tactile stimulation as an essential ingredient of maternal care and as a critical determinant of normal development (Harlow and Harlow 1969), whereas Montague (1978) has summarized similar evidence on the importance of touching and being touched for human development. None of the infants in this study were carried about by their mothers for extended periods during the day, and direct skin contact was very rare except among breast-fed infants; yet they were developing reasonably well. Thus, the fact that they were almost always dressed with a diaper, a shirt, and a pajama bottom may have provided a continuous source of tactile stimulation analogous to Harlow's surrogate terry-cloth mothers.

To test the possibility that clothing is an important compensatory source of tactile stimulation for human infants, I introduced an electrically heated incubator into the homes of several infants one day each week, and observed their behavioral states while they were naked and their body temperature was controlled by the incubator. By the second week these infants had apparently become so accustomed to clothing that they frequently cried as soon as they were undressed and placed into the incubator; they also stopped crying as soon as they were redressed whether or not they were kept in the incubator. Since repeated attempts to readapt the infants to sleeping without any clothes were of no avail, I did not introduce the incubator into other homes, but tentatively concluded that, by two weeks, infants may be so accustomed to continuous tactile stimulation that they have a hard time falling asleep without it.

The assumption that tactile stimulation stabilizes the infant's behavioral states had to be qualified in light of other observations indicating that the quality as well as the quantity of tactile stimulation may be important variables. Traditional folk cultures have long used swaddling (i.e., tightly wrapping the infant in a cloth) to allow mothers to carry their young infants while leaving their hands free for other activities, and it has been reported that swaddling has a distinct quieting effect on the infant's state (Lipton et al. 1966). Therefore, I tested the effect of variations in swaddling on newborn infants. "Skilled" swaddling, which effectively immobilizes the limbs, in fact terminated crying and facilitated the transition to quiet waking or sleep. However, "poor" swaddling, which restricted the infant's limb movements without immobilizing them, exacerbated crying and sometimes provoked rage attacks. The effect could be demonstrated experimentally by loosening and then rewrapping the swaddling clothes. As soon as the swaddling clothes were loosened but not actually removed, the infants became agitated. When infants were reswaddled so that their limbs and trunk were immobilized, they usually calmed down and fell asleep. Although tactile stimulation has a soothing effect on the crying infant, the effect is neither simple nor linear. Apparently it has to be monotonous or rhythmical, and immobilization of the limbs has to be complete, perhaps in order to reduce the variable proprioceptive feedback associated with a restriction but not immobilization of the limbs.

Unfamiliar Tastes. Five mothers began supplementary feeding of semisolid foods (cereals, fruit, pureed vegetables) within the first month. All five of the infants repeatedly expressed their strong dislike of the cereal vocally, usually crying, arching their backs, and refusing to eat initially as soon as they tasted the first spoonful of cereal, but settled down as soon as they were offered the bottle or breast. Three other babies who were started on cereal during the second month also initially showed a strong objection to the cereal and expressed that objection with crying, whereas other infants when first introduced to cereal did tolerate it initially but seemed much more restless during that part of the feeding than once they received the breast or bottle. In part, this adverse reaction to cereal may have been the anticipation of a feeding and the disappointment when the nipple was not forthcoming. A competing assumption that the protest exhibited by many of the infants was, in fact, a response to the taste or texture of cereal rather than failure to receive the nipple, was supported by the observation that as soon as the semisolid foods included not only cereal but also pureed fruit infants responded very differently. For example, when they first tasted applesauce, pears, plums, or apricots their entire body posture, facial expression, and response to the spoon differed dramatically from their responses to the cereal. As soon as they tasted the first spoonful of fruit, all general motor activity stopped, their face became placid, and their mouth opened wide, as it received the next spoonful. None of the infants in the sample showed any hesitation in accepting fruit or subsequently even pureed vegetables. On the contrary, they tended to show irritation when the food was not presented rapidly enough. By contrast, the same babies began to fuss or cry again as soon as the spoon offered cereal. This specificity of food preferences was dramatically illustrated by a strategy adopted by several of the mothers who were intent on getting their infants to eat cereal and alternately presented a spoonful of cereal and one of fruit. In this way, they were usually able to get two spoonfuls of cereal in before the protest became too sharp, and once the infants tasted the fruit their attitude changed and they eagerly awaited the next spoonful. In all instances where a direct comparison could be made, infants showed a distinct preference for the fruit and, at least during the first month, a distinct dislike expressed as crying and fussing in response to cereal. Beyond these two major staples of baby food, infants showed many individual differences; some, for example, accepted pureed liver or other meat with indifference, whereas others initially rejected it altogether.

Anticipatory Signals That Provoke or Arrest Crying. Hunger was the most common proximal cause of crying during the first six weeks after birth. However, a number of events related to but not essential for feeding also provoked and terminated crying and are of interest from a developmental perspective because they suggest that the infant's capacity to anticipate environmental events may be exhibited first in situations surrounding the meal and only later in relation to other events. Most of the mothers usually fed their infants in a semi-reclining position, supporting the baby's bottom in their lap and the trunk and head in the crook of their arm, but typically shifted the baby to an upright position between bouts of sucking to bubble it. Such interruptions of feeding frequently provoked a brief protest of crying, although never a full-blown bout; and furthermore, the crying response to the interruption of feeding was more evident in the first and second months than subsequently. The protest cries were not necessarily related to a shift of posture in the feeding context, since the shift to the upright position was always preceded by a removal of the nipple; and even without a shift in position, removing the feeding nipple when the baby was still hungry itself provoked a crying response, whereas shifting the baby to the upright position while keeping the nipple in the mouth did not. The inference that changes of posture provide the infant with an important cues about feeding-related events came from their responses to being put into the drinking position again. Even before the feeding but also during the early and middle part, the drinking position usually terminated crying long before the infant saw the bottle or breast. Its limbs became quiet, and there was a sharp increase in mouthing, tonguing, and rooting behavior. By the end of the second week postural cues such as being placed in the semireclining position were usually sufficient to induce a condition in the baby that was favorable to feeding by a reduction in general motility and active mouthing. The strength of the association did not increase significantly after the third week. On the other hand, anticipatory responses were more marked when infants were presumably hungry than at the end of a feed. Not adequately described by any summary table were the finer details of mouthing behavior. Most common in this respect were lip smacking and tonguing, but on occasion the infants actually opened their mouths wide as if to receive the nipple long before they saw it, or they rooted wildly, even when there was no tactile stimulation, as if they were searching for the nipple. Such anticipatory behavior of the mouth was not noted before the twenty-first day, and it was neither a constant finding in any one baby or consistent across all babies, but was nevertheless dramatic when it occurred.

To isolate the effect of posture from sight of the bottle, I also tested the influence of seeing the bottle on the baby's general behavior. Again, the relationship was not consistent across babies. Five of the infants showed a consistent decrease of general motor activity and began to mouth or tongue avidly on seeing the bottle but stopped mouthing and started struggling again when the bottle was removed. After two or three such sequences, the manipulation had to be discontinued because the infants gave way to crying or the mother objected.

The inventory of proximal causes of crying has so far dealt with simple physical or physiological events, sensations, and changes of perceptual context. The effect of physical pain remains relatively invariant throughout early childhood, although the intensity of response gradually diminishes. Other provocations, like novel food tastes, being naked or sudden changes of skin temperature, are transient phenomena. Even during the first three months, infants who initially showed strong and reliable crying responses to these conditions became accustomed to unexpected changes and no longer responded with discomfort or vocal protest. The reasons for such developmental dissociations between physical causes and crying cannot be directly inferred from these observations, but when combined with other developmental changes summarized in previous chapters, they suggest a number of alternative possibilities. One important reason for the reduction in readiness to cry in face of discomfort may be the infant's increased tolerance for bearing discomfort without giving way to crying as was, for example, the case with respect to behavior-state changes after food deprivation. Similarly, older as compared to younger infants have at their disposal a more diversified repertoire of goal-directed actions, and the increased range of options for dealing with novel situations probably includes cry-provoking situations as well. At the phenomenal level, the necessary and sufficient conditions for provoking various expressions of emotion including smiling, laughter, and crying differentiate considerably over the first six months, so that simple stimulus conditions are no longer sufficient in the three-to-six-month-old infants. Such changes in context on expressions of emotion argue for a "cognitive" perspective on emotional expression as an essential element in any developmental analysis. However, the term "cognitive" is not self-explanatory, and can be specified more concretely after I examine the more complex social conditions that provoke crying.

Physical conditions for eliciting crying, although generally transient, are by no means a constant finding across all babies. Some of the infants never objected to being naked, and did not protest when put into the bath. Likewise aversion to new semisolid foods such as cereal was not a universal response, and apparent food preferences showed considerable individual variation. After repeated exposure, most of the infants eventually made their accommodation to such stimuli and stopped crying. These considerable individual differences may be conceived as representing the behavioral manifestations of prefunctional sensitivities or perceptual preferences which remain a stable characteristic of the individual, requiring no elaborate psychodynamic or learning-theory explanation.

Evolutionary perspectives on the expression of emotions assign a substantially greater functional importance to crying as the most effective means at the infant's disposal for alerting the social partner of its need than as the mechanical response to pain. Therefore, one might also expect significant changes in the social environment as sufficient proximal causes for the provocation of crying. Again, unobtrusive observations provided the basis of phenomena, some of which were subsequently tested by experimental manipulation. However, the nature of stimuli as well as of the response often made it difficult to set up precisely controlled conditions that would examine all potentially confounding variables.

Social "Intrusion." Quite unexpected was the anecdotal observation that the sight of a *familiar* person or the sound of a familiar human voice sometimes provoked fussing and crying in infants who had previously been quiet and apparently placid. The paradoxical emotional response was neither consistent nor predictable; and it was for the most part limited to the first month of observation. Among infants who showed this paradoxical response with regularity, it could be provoked experimentally on some days but not on others, so that the reasons for negative responses to, for example, the sight of the human being or voice did not emerge clearly from the observations. Nevertheless, it was a phenomenon of sufficient frequency that I recorded it in detail whenever it occurred.

Five infants showed such behavior reproducibly within the first two weeks after birth; eight others demonstrated it with some consistency during the first six weeks. Among the other infants, I never observed the phenomenon.

"Separation" as a Cause of Crying

The notion that infants cry when their mothers or other important persons abandon them has been investigated in great detail under "attachment theory" (Ainsworth 1973); but the home observations summarized here indicate that crying in response to "being abandoned" occurs at a considerably earlier point in development than one would infer from the notion of separation anxiety.

Being Put to Bed. All infants sometimes cried as soon as they were put to bed in a room different from that in which they had been playing when they were perfectly content beforehand. Only seven of the infants, however, did so on more than 30 percent of occasions, and the descriptions to follow pertain specifically to the subgroup of seven. Crying in response to being put to bed occurred whether the infant had been alert and content beforehand, drowsy and asleep on the kitchen table, or fussy. A tabulation of all episodes of being put to bed over the first three months indicated that the infants cried on 68 percent of occasions, with a mean age of onset 29 days (range: 8–70 days). There was no evidence that protest cries to being put to bed diminished over time; on the contrary, the protests became more vociferous. The latency between transfer and the onset of protest cries increased from the first to the third month, and the tendency persisted until at least six months, when the observations were terminated. During the first month, infants usually did not begin to cry until they had actually been put into their cribs, after they had lost physical contact with the mother, or after they had actually seen her leave. By two and a half months, however, these infants apparently anticipated what was about to happen, and they began to cry either as soon as they entered the bedroom or as soon as the mothers put them down but were still in full visual contact. As in the case of feeding signals, infants apparently learned to read the signals correctly, that they would be transferred from the social context to a relatively isolated room. Detailed descriptions of informal experimental manipulations illustrate the same point.

At 105 days, D. F. is perfectly content in the living room in his "easy baby." For the past twenty-four minutes, he has been inspecting the movements of his hands, bringing them to his mouth or across his visual field and cooing, although he cannot see either his mother or his brother who are playing in an adjoining room. For reasons not entirely clear, the mother decides that he must be tired, and decides to put him to bed. When she picks him up, he grins. As soon as they enter the bedroom, he fusses, arching his back while extending his legs, which is the response he also demonstrates when a feeding is interrupted prematurely. When she puts him down on his bed and is no longer facing him, he cries vigorously for three minutes. Mother places his favorite stuffed animal into the crib so that he can see it; he shifts to whimpering and moaning, and then quiets down, again playing with the toy.

At 45 days, K. A. has been happily playing on the kitchen table for the past thirty minutes. Although I see no evidence that she is tired, the mother decides it's time for a nap. As soon as K. A. is put to bed and is no longer in physical contact with her mother, she begins to cry, and continues until the mother relents and brings her back to the kitchen. As soon as she is picked up, she stops crying and remains alert on the kitchen table. Ten minutes later, the mother again tries to put her to bed, but the sequence is repeated. On the third occasion, the mother decides to offer her a feeding even though K. A. was well fed in the previous hour and there is no evidence that she is hungry. This time, after the feeding she becomes drowsy, is again put to bed, and falls asleep.

"Being Left." A somewhat different version of the same theme which could not be readily isolated from the effects of being put to bed was a more general phenomenon across most of the babies. This was the emotional response to seeing the mother leave, whether the baby was in the kitchen, in the bedroom, or elsewhere. The crying response to being left had to be distinguished from a condition of being alone, because many of the infants who cried predictably when they saw their mothers leave were nevertheless peaceful and content for long periods while they were alone, as long as they did not observe the actual departure of an important person. Again, the response was not invariant within or across babies. Mothers obviously entered and left the baby's perceptual field frequently as they did their housework, without causing the baby any distress. The inference that infants were, in fact, responding to the mother's disappearance was therefore limited to occasions when they actually stopped doing whatever had occupied them beforehand while they were alert and active, pursued the mother's trajectory with their eyes and head, arched their back in order to prolong visual contact, and then cried within five seconds after visual contact was broken. All infants observed for at least three months frequently but not always,

cried when they saw their mothers leave the visual field. The phenomenon did not become evident until the fourth week (mean age of onset: 34 days; range: 29–49 days), but in infants followed over six months the phenomenon was still evident and could be reproduced experimentally. By six months, the phenomenon became considerably more variable. Now infants frequently behaved as if they had noted the mother's departure but they remained peaceful and alert, returning to their prior activity as soon as she left and giving no evidence of any disturbance.

Using the criterion that infants stopped their activity to make a clear visual pursuit of the departing mother, I observed that infants cried briefly after the separation on 63 percent of occasions in the second and third months, and on only 24 percent of occasions from the third to the sixth month. The assumption of developmental changes was also tested by ad hoc experiments on individual children.

At 62 days, T. W. is alert and active playing in her "easy baby." She sees her mother leave the kitchen, twists around in her chair to follow the mother's path, and yells when she can no longer see the mother. She continues to fuss until the mother returns, and then immediately becomes quiet, alert, and resumes her play. However, she starts crying again as soon as she observes the mother leave, and grins again as soon as the mother returns. The mother's voice alone on the other side of the kitchen will not pacify her.

At 65 days, D. F. is alone, lying on his back in the crib and perfectly content, playing happily with a mobile, attempting to strike it with his fist or bringing it to his mouth. He can see me sitting next to him whenever he turns towards me; but for the most part, he is preoccupied with his mobile. When I leave his visual field so that he can no longer see me, making sure that he sees me leave, he immediately begins to cry. When I return, he stops crying and returns to playing with his mobile, checking only intermittently to see if I'm there. This sequence can be repeated five times. Each time, my departure, when made evident to him, provokes crying or whimpering, while my return induces quiet alertness, a smile, and a return to the previous activity. When I sneak out so that he cannot see me leave, he remains unperturbed and plays with his mobile.

At 113 days, D. F. is in the living room, alert and active, although he has not been fed for the last three hours. As soon as he sees his mother leave, he begins to cry. I deliberately enter his visual field; as soon as he sees me, he stops crying. His mother talks to him from another part of the room without showing herself. He turns his head to the source of the sound and, as soon as he sees her, grins and resumes his game.

Interventions to Stop Crying

The most efficient means to stop a baby from crying is obviously to remove the offending cause, whenever it is known (Hinde 1983). Examining the interventions used by mothers of all cultures in order to quiet their infants should therefore provide direct clues about the causes of crying. Any number of consummatory stimuli, such as holding, rocking, talking, cuddling, offering the breast or a pacifier will, however, comfort and calm the baby regardless of the proximal cause. What stops the baby from crying is therefore not necessarily a reliable index of its causes. In the observations to be reported, I focused on the kinds of events or self-initiated activities that would stop the baby from crying, without drawing any inferences about the antecedent causes. I also distinguished between interventions followed by a *transient* arrest of crying lasting only as long as the stimulus persisted (i.e., distractions), and interventions that inhibited crying for a substantial period beyond the time when the stimulus had stopped (i.e., the induction of a new behavioral state lasting for three minutes or more).

Sounds. Sound and touch were the most appropriate stimulus modalities for testing the effect of simple environmental events on crying. No attempt was made to standardize the intensity of various sounds (Eisenberg 1976); instead I used levels of sound approximating those to which the infant was accustomed in its everyday environment. The various experimental sounds were presented five times at five-second intervals, while infants were crying in rhythmic (basic) pattern; and responses were scored as effective when any one of the trials stopped crying for at least five seconds. After trying out a wide range of different sound patterns, I compared the effects of an ordinary baby rattle, an Audubon bird whistle, a high-pitched brass bell, and a high-pitched voice. Some sounds were consistently more effective than others during the first two weeks (see figure 13), but regardless of their differential effects in distracting the infant temporarily, infants almost always resumed crying as soon as the sound stopped, and the behavioral state did not change.

With increasing frequency after the second month, the high-pitched human voice, particularly the mother's voice, became most effective for the arrest of crying; by then mechanical noisemakers had lost all their effects unless presented very loudly. The voice

171

retained its privileged status as a means for the arrest of crying throughout the remainder of the observation period, and by the third month the high-pitched voice arrested crying at least temporarily in 80 percent of trials.

Visual Stimuli. Although it is generally assumed that the infant shuts its eyes tightly while crying, the early stages of crying were sometimes suppressed when a large target was moved across the visual field. The first response was a nonspecific "alerting" response or brief distraction, which inhibited crying and the associated diffuse motility. However, when infants could be made to pursue the target long enough, they shifted to an alert inactive state that persisted after the visual stimulus was removed. Again, the initial alerting response was apparently a necessary, but not sufficient, condition for the state transition, whereas prolonged distraction resulted in a discontinuous shift to a state of alertness. By contrast, when the visual stimulus was removed as soon as the infant stopped crying, crying usually started again.

Picking the Baby Up. Of the various means used by mothers to quiet their crying infants, picking them up is probably the most common in cultures where mothers do not carry infants all day long. On days of unobtrusive observation, in 90 percent of all observations, infants stopped crying within twenty seconds after their mothers picked them up, and the effect usually lasted for as long as the baby was held and comforted. As might be expected, the effect was less consistent on days when the infants were in physical discomfort because of intestinal cramps or an upper respiratory infection. The reasons why picking a crying baby up should have such a powerful quieting effect are probably complex. The act involves many stimulus modalities, including postural readjustments, vestibular stimulation (Korner and Grobstein 1966), contact comfort (Harlow and Harlow 1969), rhythmical rocking, and an increase of visual stimulation, various combinations of which may have accounted for the effect. By naturalistic observations it was not easy to isolate the individual stimulus modalities.

Because I was reluctant to interfere with the mothers' usual routine by asking them to put their crying babies down according to some fixed schedule, I used occasions of crying on days of experimental intervention to pick up the infants myself. Sometimes I put them back to bed within a minute, at other times after five minutes, and noted whether the intervention induced a change of behavioral state or served only as a transient distraction. The mere act of picking babies up caused them to stop crying in 88 percent of trials; but during the first two months, they almost always started to cry again when put back to bed after one minute. By the third month, a one-minute period of holding was enough to produce a change of state in 54 percent of trials.

When I held babies for at least five minutes without talking before putting them back to bed, the effect on state was substantially greater. One-month-old infants frequently fell asleep as soon as they were put to bed, while older infants stayed awake and alert as long as I remained in their visual field. The initial alerting response to being picked up was again a necessary, but not sufficient, condition for inducing a stable state transition; when a baby could be maintained in an alert state long enough by manipulation, this manipulation facilitated the induction of a new behavioral state.

Pacifier Sucking. The mechanical presence of a pacifier or nipple in the mouth is obviously incompatible with crying. The fact that inserting a pacifier into the mouth arrests cry vocalizations is of no interest. On the other hand, the conditions under which this transient and mechanical arrest of crying contributes to the termination of crying as a behavioral state is a question of theoretical interest for examining the factors that determine state transitions. For example, environmental events that produce a transient arrest of cry vocalizations must be distinguished from organismic or environmental interventions that induce a behavioral state change. The need to make such distinctions could also be demonstrated by letting bottle-fed babies suck on a pacifier for either one or five minutes before removing the nipple. During the first six weeks after birth, pacifier-sucking stopped crying as long as the nipple remained in the mouth. When the pacifier was removed after one minute, the infants returned to their previous state or became more agitated. When pacifier sucking was allowed to continue for at least five minutes, young infants usually stayed asleep, whereas three-month-old infants frequently stayed awake and alert (40 percent of trials) after the pacifier was removed. The termination of crying as a behavioral state therefore depended critically on a sufficient period of relative inactivity for the induction of the new state. The initial distraction suppressed disruptive motor activity, and when this suppression lasted long enough, a new behavioral state of stable sleep or wakefulness was organized.

Noncry Vocalizations

Whether or not neonatal crying contributes to the non-cry vocalizations of three-month-old infants (babbling) and the speech-sound production of older infants, remains a controversial issue in contemporary theories of language acquisition (see, for example, Jakobson 1940; Stark et al. 1978). Until recently, the prevailing view held that prelanguage babbling is essentially a marker of external phonetics without any developmental role in the acquisition of speech sounds. According to this view, babbling, which is already one step removed from neonatal crying, comprises the whole range of possible sound patterns available to the young infant that will later be encountered as variables in natural human languages (Lenneberg 1967). However, the sound patterns of lalling and babbling are essentially random occurrences. Only after twelve or fourteen months do they become orderly, systematic, and governed by general rules of speech-sound production that are required for language acquisition. This perspective implies that speech production does not *develop* from prespeech vocalizations, and that the latter are simply practiced until infants are ready to make use of component motor elements.

An alternative perspective has emerged from recent investigations on vocalization in early infancy which concedes that the noncry sounds produced by infants differ qualitatively from speech sounds of older infants and children with respect to temporal pattern, resonance, and spectral characteristics (Stark et al. 1978), so that the babbling sounds themselves cannot be construed as building blocks for the construction of expressive language. Nevertheless, there is assumed to be a logical relation between structure of babbling sounds in the first year and word production during the second year (Oller 1981). This perspective holds that the development of speech sounds is the successive recombination of phonetic skills, utilizing vowel-like cry and discomfort sounds produced during expiration which are variable in pitch and loudness, and brief consonant-like vegetative sounds produced either during inspiration or expiration. The transformation of these building blocks through practice in a language environment are the substrate from which speech sounds eventually emerge. Speech development is therefore conceived as the progressive recombination of primitive elements, their modification by such recombinations, and the superimposition of new elements like prosodic features (Crystal 1980) that are discovered in the context of an adult language environment. The latter perspective would imply that a detailed description of early transitions between crying

174

and noncry vocalizations may be relevant for the developmental analysis of speech-sound production, but the extent of such relevance depends on the level at which functional links are inferred. Infants are, in effect, speechless at birth. Whether infants below one year are "trying" to produce speech-like sounds, and whether they are preprogrammed with "subjective communicative intent," are questions that can, at present, only be addressed by speculation.

The physiological mechanisms involved in the control of subglottal air pressure during cry production probably overlap extensively with physiological mechanisms required for speech-sound production, and the human organism probably does not invent an entirely new machinery for speaking which differs qualitatively from that utilized for crying. For example, Lieberman (1984) has described striking similarities in the contours of the normal breath group used during phonation for crying and for speaking. He calls attention particularly to similarities in the rising and falling contours of the fundamental frequency from the beginning to the end of an utterance that are essential features of all natural languages during the production of declarative sentences but are also characteristic of the "rhythmic" or basic cry. From such similarities, Lieberman has inferred that the sound contours reflect the ability of the expiratory mechanism to maintain subglottal pressure at a high and relatively constant pressure until the lungs collapse, followed by an inspiratory reflex, a rapid fall in subglottal pressure, and a corresponding decrease of fundamental frequency in the voicing signal as the expiration comes to an end. At least on physiological grounds, one would therefore expect similarities in the sound contours of cry and noncry vocalizations.

The observations summarized here focus on the developmental transitions from crying to noncry vocalizations during the first several months after birth, on behavioral state as the organismic context that facilitates the emergence of novel sound patterns, and on noncry vocalizations as an important means of emotional expression and nonverbal social communication. I did not attempt to code the sounds of noncry vocalizations by conventional phonetic notation systems because the latter seemed ill-suited for the purpose. Similarly, an analysis of the acoustic signals by means of sound spectrography failed to distinguish reliably among the various sound patterns produced by young infants.

Instead, I characterized these sound patterns subjectively as I heard them, in order to determine whether they followed any orderly developmental progression. I also carried out some exploratory studies to determine whether, and how extensively, it is possible to influence the sound patterns, rhythms, and pitch contours of noncry vocalizations during conversations with the infant (Lieberman et al. 1982). Distinctions were made between guttural sounds such as /g g g g's/ produced at the back of the throat, vowel-like sounds such as /a a a a h/ and /o o o o h/, combinations of guttural sounds and vowels that might resemble cooing, and early attempts at labials resembling babbling. Although sound spectrographs were used as an independent criterion of these distinctions, trained phoneticians were unable to match the taped sound patterns reliably with spectrographs. When presented with actual sound tapes, they could group these samples reliably into at least global categories of the kind described above; and they invariably identified the acoustic signals as baby sounds. The illustrations of sound spectrographs will not be particularly illuminating about the distinctive features of various noncry vocalizations, but they provide an independent perspective on my attempts at verbal descriptions of acoustic signals.

General Description

The development of noncry vocalizations observed in the home followed essentially the same sequences that have been described in detail by others (Bühler and Hetzer 1928; Stark et al. 1978; Crystal 1980), although the onset of particular vocal forms was perhaps somewhat earlier than in previous descriptions because of the extended period of observations.

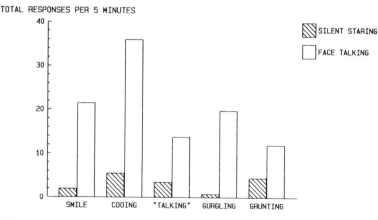

Figure 23: Noncry Vocalizations to Silent and Talking Face

176

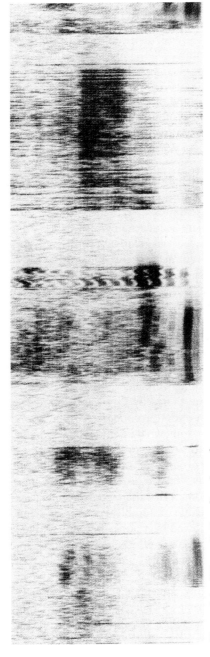

Figure 24: "Happy" Gurgling Sound

Stimulus configurations that predictably elicited smiling, such as the human voice or the combination of voice and nodding head, commonly elicited soft guttural sounds at the back of the throat (/g g h h's/ or /g a a h h's/ and, after the second month, vocal patterns that sounded like gurgling. Cumulative tabulations at one-month intervals (figure 23) indicated that during the second month the voice alone was likely to elicit a combination of vocalization, a search for the source of the sound, and then a smile when the infant discovered the face. By the third month, infants usually responded to the voice alone with a vocal response alone, whereas smiling was the preferred response to the silent nodding head (table 7; see also figure 25).

Discovery of New Sounds. The age at which particular infants discovered novel sound patterns was quite variable, and not all subtypes described here were represented in the vocal repertory of each infant. Yet, the development sequence in which novel sound types were discovered and practiced was relatively constant across babies. To give a somewhat coherent account of results from unobtrusive observations concerning spontaneous vocalizations or the infant's responses to the mother in everyday exchanges, I prepared a composite picture rather than systematically tabulating how many infants exhibited which particular sound pattern at what age, or what was range of individual variations. Guttural sounds (/g g h's/; /g g a a h h's/; gurgles; etc.) were common during the last week of the first month and the first two weeks of the second month (see figure 24). They occurred when infants were alert and active, either playing by themselves or being entertained by their mothers. Cooing sounds with a soft /k/ consonant and a prolonged /o o h h/ sound became part of the vocal repertory somewhat later (41–50 days), again when infants were playing by themselves or engaged in vocal interchanges with their mothers. At around the same time, a category emerged which mothers labeled as "fake cries," intermediate between fussing and noncry vocalizations, cries that were produced at times when the infants gave no visible or audible evidence of being in distress. Fake cries were not followed by a bout of crying, and mothers interpreted these sounds as the baby's efforts to attract attention when there was nothing wrong. I could also not relate them to any specific causal condition.

Loud squealing and single yells first emerged at around 40–50 days, and then usually occurred while the infants were physically active and engaged with a social partner, but rarely when they were alone, unless they were actively kicking or playing with a favorite

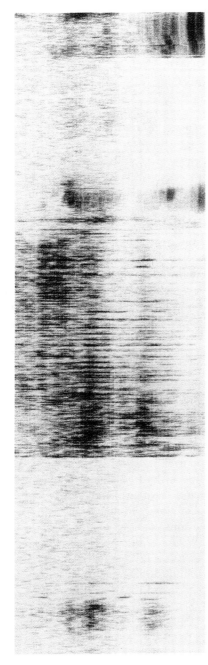

Figure 25: "Bronx Cheer"

179

toy. By 72–90 days, many of the infants had converted the original guttural sound (/g g h h/) into something resembling /g a a h h/ which they could repeat two or three times in a row, with or without social stimulation. By 140–70 days, several of the infants produced utterances resembling /b a a h h, b a a h h/ with distinctive labial sounds. Infants who made such sounds regularly repeated them in subsequent days and weeks.

Several of the babies also discovered how to clack their tongues while waiting for the next spoonful of semisolid foods they relished; thereafter they practiced tongue clacking while alone in their cribs. Other infants discovered the "Bronx cheer" (figure 25) sometime between 120 and 140 days, and practiced it while alone in their cribs or while playing with their mothers. However, once they were proficient in clacking their tongues or producing the Bronx cheers, they lost interest in making such sounds. In general, those sound patterns which infants had discovered by chance but which had no obvious relation to conventional sounds of their language environment gradually dropped out of the vocal repertory, whereas infants assiduously practiced those sounds which were even indirectly related to conventional speech patterns in their language environment. Most of these new sounds were discovered and practiced first when infants were alone, whereas discoveries in the context of actual conversations were an exception.

At 74 days, for example, D. F. is playing in his crib with a favorite toy animal, holding a long private conversation with it. Until now, he has not cooed. Suddenly, he makes a cooing sound, then repeats it three times, gurgles, yells intermittently, and returns to cooing, all the while reaching for the animal. The sounds are intermittent, but the conversation stretches out over seven minutes before he starts to fuss and eventually fall asleep. Similar private conversations are repeated at 83 and 120 days; cooing sounds become increasingly discrete and are intermingled with other familiar sounds. By four months, labial and babbling sounds have been added to the repertory of private conversations.

Similarly, T. W. holds long private conversations in her crib at 70, 93, and 112 days while she intermittently kicks her legs and swings her arms without directing them to any particular object. At 93 days she makes a sound that resembles /g a a a a h/, repeats it several times, and then intermingles it with other sounds she has already practiced. By 112 days, the /g a a a a h/ becomes a distinct vocal utterance (see figure 26). Similar patterns of prolonged conversations were observed in all the infants at three to four months when

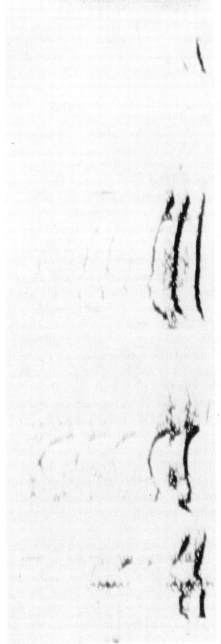

Figure 26: Noncry Vocalizations of a Four-month-old during Conversation (Narrow-band Filter; Real Time)

they were alone in their cribs and not distracted by the social partner. The range of vocal utterances increased with age, usually starting with /g g g g h/ sounds and progressing to /g a a a a h/, gurgles, squeals, and open vowels by the end of the third month. Thereafter, infants developed their vocal repertories along individual lines, but laughter was never heard when the infants were playing alone.

The temporal organization of discrete noncry vocalizations developed according to a more predictable pattern. Most of the sounds described so far ranged in duration from 0.4 to 0.8 seconds, as measured by spectrographs. Gurgles, labials, and squeals were typically of longer duration, but their length was quite variable (0.7–1.5 seconds). During early stages of discovering new sounds, novelties were usually produced as isolated events, but as the infant gained familiarity, the novelties were organized in strings of two to four repetitions. Such repetitions, in contrast to the initial discovery, were usually produced in the presence of a social partner, and particularly during a vocal interchange.

An acoustic feature of noncry vocalizations that distinguishes them sharply from the rhythmical cry pattern, was the contour of the fundamental frequency. Repetitive cries typically had U-shaped contours on the spectrograph, with an initial rise and a terminal fall in the fundamental frequency (see also Lieberman 1984). Many of the noncry vocalizations, once they were well established by practice, did not show this terminal fall but showed either a plateau or an actual rise near the end (see, for example, figure 27), this change in contour suggesting that the infants had gained control over the flow of expiratory air. However, differences between cry and noncry vocalization were not categorical. Many presumably "happy" vocalizations also showed the initial rise and terminal fall in contours, whereas many fussy sounds and some prolonged cries did not follow the inverted U-shaped contour. By themselves the contours of fundamental frequencies, as displayed by spectrograph, were not sufficient to distinguish noncry from cry vocalizations; and seeing the infant while listening to its sounds was still necessary for making such distinctions.

Near the end of the fifth month, some of the infants produced sounds that resembled moaning or early fussing, although they were apparently content, engaged in active play, and were ready to respond by smiling when confronted by the face. By the same token, many of the vocal preludes to actual crying were acoustically ambiguous (figure 28). Even when heard in context, these sound patterns could not be clearly classified as either distress vocalizations or "hap-

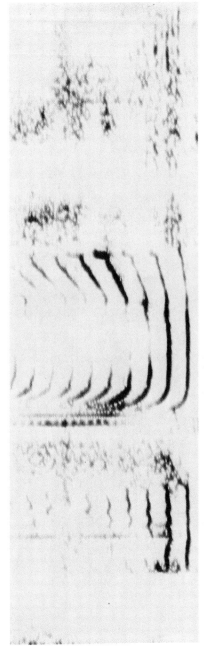

Figure 27: Noncry Vocalizations of a Five-month-old during Conversation

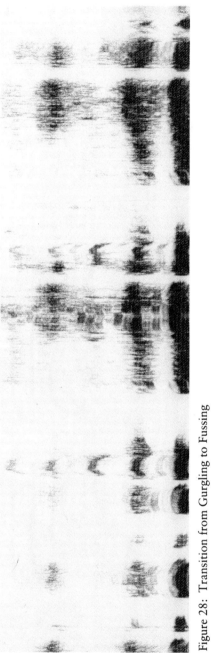

Figure 28: Transition from Gurgling to Fussing

py" noncry patterns. It may then be of theoretical interest to ask whether such intermediate vocalization patterns are simply random variations of nonspecific fussy noises, or whether they have a more direct functional significance for the invention of new sounds. By direct observation alone it is obviously impossible to address this question with more than preliminary impressions.

Behavioral State and Noncry Vocalizations. The relation between waking states and vocalization patterns indicated that the infant's general disposition, and particularly fluctuations between alert wakefulness and early fussing, may contribute to the discovery of new sound patterns. However, even experimental manipulations to test this point provided only indirect support for the hypothesis. During spontaneous transitions from alertness to fussing and crying, the infants frequently produced a variety of unclassifiable sounds which, by spectrographic analysis, sometimes had the fundamental frequency contours of a discrete noncry vocalization, at other times of precry sounds. The new sounds were first described in the running record at times when infants were no longer alert and active although not yet crying. These occasions were commonly followed by fussing or full-blown crying, but the "accidental discovery" of new sounds was sometimes followed by a repetition of that sound and a temporary return to alert activity. While none of the anecdotal observations were sufficient to make a persuasive case, ad hoc experiments gave some support to the claim that the transition between alert activity and fussing might be the organismic context that facilitates the discovery of novel sound patterns.

Experimental Vocal Interchanges

A part of the experimental protocol carried out one day each week addressed questions concerning the development of noncry vocalizations. For example, is it possible to increase the overall amount of vocal interchange with the infant by carrying out conversations or presenting the infant with carefully timed vocal stimuli? Is the type of sound produced during vocal interchanges different from the spontaneous vocalizations the infant holds in private? Can one, by imitating the baby's vocal repertory, influence the speech contour and temporal pattern of its utterances? Is it possible to induce the baby to produce presumably novel sounds? Can one convert fussy sounds to noncry vocalizations by distracting the baby with an active vocal interchange?

To answer several of these questions, I used five-minute tape-recorded samples of my own voice and of the mother's baby talk, such that each vocal stimulus was separated by an appropriate period of silence during which the infant would be able to respond. The infants' responses to tape-recorded samples were compared with responses during five-minute control periods of silence before and after the vocal interchange, as well as with the baby's responses to tape-recorded samples of crying. Because the timing of sound stimuli relative to the infant's own vocal responses was a critical factor in such "turn-taking" experiments, I later repeated the observations using my own voice rather than taped speech samples so that I could synchronize my utterances with the infant's vocalizations.

Until the end of the second month, there was no clear evidence that tape-recorded speech samples without an accompanying face increased the frequency of vocalizations or the kind of sound produced. Starting between 65 and 90 days, the results were more clear-cut. Taped speech samples significantly increased the overall amount as well as the variety of utterances, and with the tape there was a distinct shift from ambiguous sounds (moans and grunts) to discrete patterns (coos, gaahs, gurgles, chortles, and squeals). Tape-recorded samples of the mother's voice were more effective than those of my high-pitched voice. Tape-recorded samples of infant cries either had no effect or increased the frequency of ambiguous sounds and fussing (see figure 29).

A comparison of infant vocalizations to the silent nodding head and tape-recorded speech samples had similar results. By three months, but not before, the taped sounds produced more vocal responses, the silent nodding head more smiles. Although the latter also increased the level of vocalization relative to control periods without any social stimulation, the frequency and variety of discrete utterances were less distinct.

In other comparisons, I presented my face and voice simultaneously, timing my answers exactly to each of the baby's utterances, but trying to alter its speech pattern by selecting sounds from the repertory (or rather my imitation of that repertory), which it had not made in the immediately preceding "conversation." By carefully timing my sounds to those of the infant, I was able to elicit many more vocal responses than when playing the fixed sequences of tape-recorded speech. Even at an early age, a successful vocal dialogue therefore seems to depend on the temporal sequencing of component elements contributing to the structured interchange. The early vocal conversations are therefore an emergent property of coordinated ac-

TOTAL RESPONSES PER 5 MINUTES

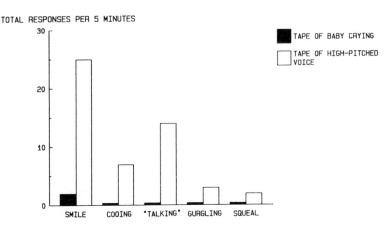

Figure 29: Smiling and Noncry Vocalizations in Response to Male Voice and Taped Infant Cries; Twelve Infants

tions contributed between two independent centers of causality, and are therefore a feature of early behavioral adaptation which is possible only with respect to the infant's relation to persons.

By numerical tabulations it was very difficult to document that infants tried to imitate the specific sounds from their own repertory that I presented to them, rather than simply increasing their overall level of vocalizations. Instead, I had to rely on the description of individual infants.

At 63 days, for example, T. W. and I are holding a conversation while she is alert, active, and smiling frequently. I coo four times, and she responds with two soft /g o o h's/ in a sequence. I then gurgle for about thirty seconds, and she responds with two clear gurgles. Then, I talk to her, calling her name, and she responds with two soft /g o o h's/. Again, I gurgle, but this time, she is silent and simply stares at me, eventually making a familiar /g a a h/ sound at the back of her throat. Again, at 79 days, T. W. is talking with her mother. The mother makes five /g u u h h/ sounds which T. W. has not uttered in the preceding three minutes, and she responds with three separate /y u u h/ sounds. Then, the mother says "hyaah" three times in a row (a sound which T. W. has never made), and T. responds with an open vowel resembling an /e e a a h h/ sound, which she has also never made. Then, the mother says "hurry up," and T. W. is silent, but smiles. Thereafter, mother asks her "What voice is that?," and T. W.

merely squeals. Finally, mother returns to the /y u u h h/ sound, which started the conversation, and T. W. responds with a /y a a h–g o o h/ sound several times.

At 56 days, J. F. is happy in his crib where he has been playing by himself for the past ten minutes. I sit at the side, so that he cannot see me, and record the number of his vocal utterances. During a five-minute control period, he makes three spontaneous cooing sounds. Then, I seat myself so he cannot see me, and talk to him for five minutes, alternating between /g a a h h/ and cooing sounds, as well as gurgles. He responds twenty-seven times during the five minutes, but continues to make only cooing sounds. I again leave his visual field and sit by his side. He moans briefly, and then returns to his play. During the five-minute control period, he makes nine discrete sounds that vary in type from cooing to gurgling.

Then, I resume talking to him so he can see me for a five-minute period during which he produces twenty-seven discrete utterances, but the sound /g a a h h/ does not appear in the repertory, although in preceding weeks he has frequently made such sounds.

Repeated efforts to enlarge the infants' vocal repertory by introducing sounds they had never produced before were uniformly unsuccessful. Infants vocalized significantly more when I talked to them than during silent periods, but the attempt to "teach" them new sounds invariably failed, although I may not have been sufficiently persistent in my training procedures. Once having discovered new sounds on their own while fussy, infants practiced these on subsequent days while alert; thereafter they used their new discoveries in conversations with a social partner, and could then also be induced to alter their pattern of familiar vocalizations according to the sound patterns presented to them by the social partner.

Even these experimentally induced changes in vocalization patterns cannot be interpreted as evidence for any simple, direct imitations. By spectrography, the sound patterns I produced when trying to imitate the baby's vocalizations differed qualitatively from the infant's own vocal productions (Wolff 1969). One can only conclude that the infants' successful imitations of vocal patterns presented to them by a partner involve extensive perceptual-motor transformations from model to sample.

I also tested whether infants are sensitive to the temporal characteristics of sounds produced by the social partner, by systematically varying the number of utterances of a familiar sound. Descriptions summarized earlier suggested that infants might be sensitive to the length of a string, responding several times to a repeated stimulus but only once to a single vocal event. However, when I systematically changed the number of distinct vocalizations intended to evoke a response from the baby, there was no one-to-one correspondence between the number of utterances I made and the number of responses the baby gave. A temporal pattern did emerge to the extent that any single utterance on my part was more often followed by single than multiple responses, whereas a string of utterances, regardless of their length, frequently produced two or three responses. In each case the distinction between single and multiple responses to my utterances was statistically significant.

Summary

The behavioral observations and informal experiments on the development of emotional expressions has not resolved any of the enduring controversies about the "nature" of emotions and their ontological status, or about the interaction of biology and experience in the formation of new emotions.

The relevant empirical observations of this section focused exclusively on expressive motor patterns, and even these were found to refer to a broad range of behavioral phenomena that may involve different causes, forms, and functions, so that they cannot be lumped into one homogeneous category. Some of the motor patterns were near-linear responses to organic discomforts (e.g., crying to pain or hunger); these did not depend on the social context for their emergence although they had a powerful effect on the social partner. Others were spontaneous motor patterns (e.g., smiling and other facial grimaces during state II sleep) which I attributed to subtle changes in the internal dynamics of a behavioral state. These had no obvious communicative function, although they pleased mothers and may provide developmental psychologists with material for speculation.

A third set of emotional expressions depended critically on the interaction between at least two individuals. They were neither spontaneous motor discharges nor "responses" to discrete organic or environmental events. Rather, they were the products of a hierarchically ordered interaction between two independent centers of psychological causality that could not be defined adequately in terms of the motor contribution made by either partner alone. These patterns of social communication, including eye-contact, laughter in response to tickling, vocal interchanges, and perhaps some forms of precocious imitation, are manifested in a recognizable form only when considered as component elements of a larger coherent structure that includes at least two individuals (Fentress 1982). Their formal investigation requires models of behavioral analysis that go beyond frequency counts, transition probabilities, or first-order Markov chains. They cannot be reduced to the linear sum of component motor actions contributed by each of the partners, but are truly the emergent properties of interactant units. Because no appropriate models were at my disposal for the formal analysis of co-ordered patterns of social behavior, I had to rely on describing these "dialogues" or expressions of emotion in terms of the temporal coordination of motor patterns.

Another group of emotional expressions that do not appear until the third or fourth month, are also "spontaneous" in the sense that they are not linear responses to particular environmental or organic events but appear to be self-initiated. At the same time, they differ qualitatively from the spontaneous sleep grimaces in younger infants. They are observed only when the infant is alert, and their relative unpredictability in response to an adequate social stimulus implies an element of choice. The same social encounter may elicit either qualitatively different expressions of emotion or no response at all, depending on the infant's behavioral state and on other activities which compete for his interests. Such emotional expressions should be of particular interest for a cognitive theory of emotions, since they may provide a conceptual bridge between the earlier obligatory and reflex-like responses which are more nearly consistent with a rigorous ethological interpretation of universal emotions, and later volitional social communications that depend on the differentiation of intellectual structures.

I proposed that the element of volition in such expressions of emotion may be determined in part by fluctuations of waking behavioral states that facilitate one rather than another expressive motor behavior in response to the same environmental (social) event; and in part by the availability of equally appropriate, but alternative, sensorimotor actions in response to the same environmental event. A detailed analysis of the interaction between waking behavioral states and expressions of emotion may thus provide one avenue for investigating the "meanings" associated with particular expressions of emotion in particular contexts; in other words, state may be the context which confers functional significance on both the motor expression and the environmental event that initiates it.

The interaction between state and emotional expressions was dramatically illustrated by laughter where the appropriate "priming" stimulus had a distinct effect on behavioral state which, in turn, influenced the kinds of emotional expression in response to subsequent stimulations. More generally, observations on the interdependence of state and emotional expression again emphasize the nonlinearity of input-output relations as a function of behavioral state, as well as the theoretical limitations of any direct learning or preformationist paradigm for the developmental analysis of emotions.

4

The Infant's Relations to
Things and Persons

Developmental change in the infant's relation to the social partner is one of the most actively pursued research topics in contemporary studies in early child development, providing the empirical basis for most current theories about human socialization, interpersonal communication, and psychopathology. Assumptions about the long-term effect of deficiencies in early social experience have also become the subject matter for enduring debates about the linear or epigenetic causal relation between antecedent events and social, cognitive, and linguistic competence in later development.

Some formulations assume that the infant is equipped by evolution with species-typical mechanisms for transmitting socially appropriate signals to the partner, while the parent is equipped with parallel mechanisms to perceive and respond appropriately to such signals. They further assume that there is a critical period in early infancy that irreversibly determines how early experience influences later development. Fortunately, no controlled isolation studies have been attempted to test this assumption in humans. On the other hand, clinical observations on feral, abused, and neglected children are usually so confounded by uncontrolled factors of brain damage, mental retardation, psychosis, malnutrition, and distorted historical information, that these "experiments of nature" provide only weak support for the claim that particular kinds of social experience during a critical period are vital for normal mental and intellectual development of humans.

A very different perspective on the role of early social experience for later development comes from social-learning theory, which assumes that most of what the infant will become in its social world results from drive reduction, the linear accretion of contingent reinforcements, imitation, and other socializing processes. On the basis of the available evidence it is safe to conclude, I believe, that neither

192

of these general hypotheses is sufficient as a theoretical basis for investigating the infant's differential relation to things and persons.

An extensive body of simple but reliable reports by parents, as well as results from controlled behavioral experiments, converge on the conclusion that infants act on and respond to persons in a qualitatively different way than they act on physical objects, at a very early age. While this observation may seem self-evident, it remains a legitimate topic of inquiry to examine how the young infant's relations to persons differ from those to physical objects; what are the necessary and sufficient conditions that allow young infants to make such discriminations; and how these are elaborated during development.

Piaget advanced the hypothesis that the infant's relations to the social partner do not differ inherently from its relations to physical objects. Persons acquire a privileged status in the infant's world of values only because they are a uniquely rich source of "aliment" for its various sensorimotor schemes (Piaget 1952, 1954). The theory further assumed that the differentiation between action and object depends critically on the number of distinct action patterns at the infant's disposal for "triangulating" on objects (Piaget 1954). Persons, in contrast to things, provide multiple opportunities for alternative actions on the same object, and therefore acquire a privileged status over physical objects, not because they constitute an inherently different class of objects for the infant, but because they are the nodal points around which actions are first differentiated from objects. Evidence from other sources indicates that the naive infant's responses to the social partner differ inherently from those to physical objects, and do not depend exclusively on cognitive experience.

To address these competing views in more detail, I designed a number of observations and experiments to test the infant's differential interactions with things and persons.

Things

Piaget's (1954) account of the development of object permanence subsumes six distinct phases over the first eighteen months, which have been summarized repeatedly by various commentators (Wolff 1960; Flavel 1963), and tested in a number of replication studies on a larger number of subjects. They generally confirm the original observations when the same methods of observation are applied (Corman and Escalona 1969; Uzgiris and Hunt 1975). However, the interpretation of findings differs considerably among commentators who start with different theoretical orientations (see, for example, Harris 1983 for a review). The central focus of the present investigation was not to attempt a systematic replication of the infant's intellectual development during the first half-year, but to address a set of very different questions. Nevertheless, an adequate description of the infant's relations to persons required parallel observations on their relations to things, persons, after all, also being physical objects along important dimensions. In keeping with Piaget's clinical method, I examined the infant's search for objects as they moved across the visual field in the vertical and horizontal directions, looked for evidence that the infant might be anticipating the future position of objects by looking in the direction of its trajectory, and tested whether the infant made an effort to reconstruct the full object from seeing a portion of it when the rest was partially occluded. A quantitative dimension was introduced to examine for how long in any one session infants continued to pursue the moving target, intended as a partial response to the criticism that infants may lack the motor ability to search for objects rather than lack the concept of object permanence (Piaget 1956; Wolff 1972b). As a part of other investigations on the relation between behavioral state and goal-directed behavior, I also compared the persistence of pursuit movements during different behavioral states.

In earlier sections I used observations on visual pursuit as variables for defining waking behavioral states, for investigating dual-task performance, and to examine the onset of "voluntary action." All of these behavior patterns probably contribute indirectly to the development of object permanence. To investigate the development of object permanence more directly, I also examined visual pursuit when infants tracked or reached for moving and disappearing objects, using Piaget's original observations as behavioral criteria for defining the early development of object permanence.

Visual Pursuit of a Moving Target. Table 6 summarized data on the duration of sustained pursuit of a moving visual target when it was displaced slowly in the horizontal or vertical direction but never moved entirely out of the infant's visual field. During the first two weeks, conjugate eye movements were more proficient than coordinated head-eye movements. The mean duration and maximum length of uninterrupted pursuit, as well as the proficiency in head-eye coordinations, progressed steadily over the first three months, and by the second month the coordination of head and eye movements had effectively replaced conjugate eye movements as the preferred mode of visual pursuit during alert states. Similarly, head-eye pursuits in the vertical direction, which initially were poorly coordinated, improved substantially during the second month.

Auditory Pursuit. When sounds were presented to the left or right side of the head without letting the infant see the origins of the sound, all of the infants occasionally turned their head to the appropriate side when they were alert and inactive. Auditory pursuit to the brass bell, the Audubon bird whistle, and the voice could be elicited in all infants within the first twelve hours after birth, depending on their behavioral state, but the number of occasions when head-turning responses to sounds could be reproduced in a string was limited. The maximum number was three rotations (180°) by four weeks, five in the second month, and six oscillations from side to side without interruption in the third month. Persistent auditory pursuit was not tested systematically after the third month because of the many distractions in the environment that might have confounded the results.

In general, the results of visual and auditory pursuit suggest that the motor apparatus for pursuit movements and for prolonging the "permanence" of an object by perceptual search is fully intact within the first two weeks after birth; and that coordinated head and eye rotations extend object permanence considerably by the end of the first month. The results further indicate that some quantitative dimension, whether attributed to an increased capacity for attending or to stabilization of coordinated motor patterns, increases substantially over the first three months.

Piaget defined the second stage of object permanence in terms of the infant's tendency to search at the place where the object was last seen before it vanished. When I used this criterion to examine the permanence of inanimate things, the results were difficult to interpret. The length of time for which the infants stared at the place where the object disappeared could not be distinguished from random staring or spontaneous search. Search for disappearing familiar persons, by contrast, could readily be identified even during the second month, and will be further described in sections on the infant's relations to persons.

The third stage of object permanence (between four and eight months) was defined as the infant's ability to anticipate the trajectory of moving objects and to search for occluded portions of a partly hidden object. Again, direct observations were not precise enough to distinguish between visual anticipations of moving physical things and random eye movements, but the game of peek-a-boo, involving persons rather than things, suggested that one-to-two month-old infants were, in fact, able to anticipate future positions of a disappearing person.

At twenty-eight days, I play a game of peek-a-boo with D. C. Four times, I change my position, either at the foot and the head of the crib or on the left and right sides of the crib, disappearing rapidly from sight so that he cannot follow my trajectory, but I call to him at the place where I reappear. On the fifth occasion, when I reappear on the side opposite to the one where I disappeared, he shifts the direction of his gaze to the place where he had seen me reappear in the past, as if he were now anticipating that the alternations would continue. A week later, the same anticipation occurs after five prior alternations of position with a vocal cue.

At forty-one days, D. C. is lying prone, so that he can see either of two stuffed animal toys lodged between the bars of his crib but must rotate his head in order to look directly at each in turn. Four times in succession, he slowly turns his head back and forth between the two animals, as if deliberately trying to see both. At sixty and again at seventy-three days, he looks at each of the animals in turn, in four to six deliberate sweeps, although I have moved the animals further apart so that his head has to turn more laterally, and he completely loses sight of one animal when looking at the other. The alternation of gaze is slow, and apparently deliberate. At least the movement patterns suggest that the directed gaze is not the result of random head rotations and occasional chance discovery of the two animals. Instead, it is a slow, smooth rotation of the head in the appropriate directions.

When D. F. is seventy-seven days old, I play the game of peek-a-boo with him which, until now, has been totally unsuccessful. I alternate the place of my disappearance five times, between his right and left sides in a predictable pattern, and call him each time from my new position when I reappear. On the sixth occasion, I reappear in the same position but say nothing, and then reappear on the opposite side, again saying nothing. Both times, he looks at the place where I will reappear before I get there. When I continue the game, he loses interest or forgets the sequence. As in the case of D. C., D. F. only anticipates after I have already played the game five times beforehand with vocal cues.

Such observations suggest that infants can anticipate the place where moving objects are likely to reappear. The anticipations are usually of persons; and they depend on the infant's having played the game before, using unambiguous clues such as the voice, in order to indicate the position of the reappearing object. There was no evidence to indicate that infants at this age were able to anticipate the trajectory of physical objects when given similar cues.

Reaching for Objects. Another behavioral criterion that defines Piaget's third stage of object permanence involves the coordination of sensorimotor schemes so that the infant grasps what is seen and looks at what is held in the hand. Although reaching behavior was not investigated in any detail in this study, the observation of spontaneous manual activities and reaching responses to experimental manipulations provided indirect clues about the development of hand-use preference and its role in the development of object permanence. The mean age at which infants began to reach for objects in a controlled way was seventy-two days, with individual variations ranging from thirty-four to eighty-seven days.

From his second week, D. F. had been provided with a stuffed animal lodged between the bars of his crib, and the animal had been his constant companion since the second week, so that, by two months, he seemed to have formed a special attachment to it. The toy in question was a fluffy lion with a large mane and a bright red ribbon around its neck. At fifty-six days, D. F. stares at the lion, smiles, and then reaches out one arm and hand until he makes contact with it. Contact with the texture of the lion's mane leads to momentary stroking of the animal, but then he withdraws his arm. Four times subsequently on the same day, he reaches for and touches the lion, but from his behavior it is not clear whether he reaches for the mane or for the red ribbon. At eighty days, the direction of reaching seems clearer. His hand gets hold of the red ribbon, and he pulls at it so that the lion falls into his crib. On subsequent days, the same "chance" contact with the ribbon occurs repeatedly. The net result is that the lion is frequently pulled into the crib, after I have replaced it to its original position. Thereafter, I move the lion to a different spot between the bars, so that D. F. must redirect his vision as well as his grasp. Again, the head goes towards the lion, and the hand reaches out and touches the mane, but he has to make several efforts before he can grasp the red ribbon again. This time, the lion is too firmly lodged between the bars, and he starts playing with his hands instead, making mouthing movements. During subsequent weeks, the same game is frequently repeated; and by 120 days, D. F. often gurgles at the lion while he reaches for it, plays with its fur, and pulls at the red ribbon. By direct observation, the finer details of hand motor coordination involved in the maneuver could not be documented. However, during the early weeks of reaching, there was no evidence that the hand prepared itself for grasping (opening) before it actually reached the ribbon (Bruner 1968). Instead, the effort to pull on the ribbon came after he had made contact with the lion and after he began to manipulate the texture and shape of the stuffed animal.

Six of the bottle-fed infants began to help their mothers to hold the bottle by placing one or both hands on the bottle itself or on the mother's hand holding the bottle between six and twelve weeks. One mother actually allowed her infant to "hold" the bottle by eleven weeks, giving only partial support to lessen the weight of the bottle. Similarly, when I recorded vocalization patterns by placing a shiny black microphone close (five inches) to the baby's mouth when it was vocalizing, the microphone frequently elicited directed reaching behavior, starting at around sixty and continuing until at least ninety days.

T. W. and M. C. both exhibited grasping behavior to objects that did not lend themselves to grasping. At 150 days, for example, T. W. sees a brightly colored balloon tied to her bed on a short string so that she can easily reach it. Her hand opens wide, as if to grasp the large object, but hand contact causes the balloon to bounce out of her reach. She looks surprised, and then begins rhythmical mouthing movements, smacking her lips and making other apparently unrelated motor responses. In subsequent weeks, I provide her with other balloons in similar circumstances. For two weeks, she continues to make grasping movements with her wide-open hand, and mouths vigorously when she can't get hold of the balloon. Thereafter, she loses interest in the game.

M. D., to whom I have introduced a similar balloon experimentally, starting when he is 120 days old, makes similar unsuccessful grasping movements as soon as he sees the balloon. Over the next four weeks, he develops a procedure "to make interesting spectacles last" (Piaget 1952). His initial efforts to grasp the balloon are gradually transformed into what appears to be a game. Instead of continuing the grasping effort, he hits the balloon with his hand and arm in a swiping motion. At first, the movements of the balloon absorb all of his attention, but over several weeks he makes wide-mouthed grins and begins to vocalize intermittently when he has been successful in making the balloon bounce. In contrast to T. W., he never displays mouthing movements when he fails to grasp the balloon.

Although the study of hand preference was not a primary goal, I carried out a series of experiments in which I recorded which hand or hands were involved in spontaneous and elicited movements. These observations also provided incidental information about early hand-preference for particular tasks. For one experiment on the co-ordination of looking and grasping, I placed an object (either a rattle or my finger) into one or the other hand when the infant was alert and relatively inactive, and both hands were resting on the mattress. The purpose was to determine whether the infant systematically turned its head to the side where the object was placed or brought the hand holding the object preferentially into its visual field (i.e., in order to look at what the hand was holding). The same procedures were used to examine Piaget's notion of "circular reaction" as a mechanism for the self-activation and gradual refinement of motor patterns by self-stimulation.

All of the infants demonstrated some degree of manual specialization sometime toward the end of the first month, a specialization that became more pronounced from the second to the sixth month of observation. However, what appeared to be a distinct preference for a particular action over a two-to-three-week period would frequently be reversed during the next month in the same infant. Hand preferences were also to a large extent task-specific. One hand might be used preferentially for sucking, scratching the head, or pulling the ears, while the other was used preferentially for visual inspection and for transporting grasped objects into the visual field. Finally, the preference exhibited for a particular task was not consistent across babies, some using the left hand preferentially for inspection as it moved across the visual field, whereas others showed a similar preference for using the right hand.

From twenty-six to seventy days, for example, K. F. typically uses his left hand for investigating his mouth, finger-sucking, face-wiping, etc., or to play with his ears, scratch his head, etc., while the right hand preferentially plays in the visual field, so that he spends more time inspecting his right than his left hand. At the same time, his head is more often turned towards the right than towards the left side. By sixty days and again at sixty-three and seventy-four days, the right hand is more adept at holding a rattle, bringing it into the visual field, and shaking it, as if to make noises while it is in the visual field. By contrast, when I place the rattle in his left hand, he either holds it in a fixed grasp at the side without shaking or moving it into the visual field, or else drops it, only rarely bringing it into the visual field. Yet, by eighty-five days, the pattern of hand preferences has reversed. The right hand now goes preferentially to the mouth, ears, or face, where it makes gentle scratching movements, while the left hand is used more often for reaching to objects and for bringing such objects into the visual field for inspection.

By contrast, S. H. shows a preference for the left hand as the instrument for visual pursuit and grasping, the right hand being more commonly used for self-touching (hand-sucking, ear-scratching, and the like), even though the preferred head position during the first several weeks is to the right. Moreover, specialized usage of the two hands for different functions is less well established in S. H., and he exhibits intermittent reversals.

At thirty-five days, he shows greater facility of the left than right hand for putting the hand to the mouth and sucking his fingers. By fifty-seven days, and again at sixty-four and seventy-one days, he holds the rattle for longer periods with the left than right hand; and when it is in his left, he brings it more consistently into the visual field to inspect its movements than when I put the rattle in his right hand. On the same days he brings both hands into the visual field whether I put the rattle in the right or left hand. From sixty to ninety days, whenever the head is turned to the left, it is usually the left hand which enters the visual field for inspection and delicate finger manipulation, whereas the right hand plays with the ears or hair outside the visual field. When the head is turned to the right, the right hand is not preferentially used for reaching behavior.

The development of hand-use preference was expressed more clearly in older infants who sat upright or in a partially reclining position so that both arms and hands were free for reaching and grasping. By four months, D. F. had spent several weeks in a "trampoline" suspended from a rubber spring, which left his arms free and also allowed him to bounce up and down by flexing and extending his legs against the ground. When I present him with a bright red ball on his left side, he reaches for it with the left hand; when I present the same object on his right side, he reaches with the right hand. The game can be repeated in the same way for as long as he is willing to play. Each time the appropriate hand reaches out, but when I first present the rattle in midline he is confused and puts his hand to his mouth. On subsequent days, he reaches more often with the right than left hand when the object is presented in midline.

Similarly, K. C. has been accustomed to sitting in an "easy baby" chair since the third month. By the fourth month, she frequently plays with both hands in the midline, one hand grasping the other, while the individual fingers of each hand play against each other, or one hand holds the other when it is contracted into a fist. At

124 days, when I present her with a familiar bright-colored toy animal on her left side when her hands are in midline, she releases the
right hand and reaches out with the left. When I present the same toy
on the right side, she again releases the midline contact, and reaches
with her right hand, and the pattern is consistent. When I place the
animal in the midline, she typically reaches out with both hands
when they were grasping each other beforehand, but such bimanual
grasping is not a coordinated movement pattern. Instead, one hand
seems to interfere with the other, and usually one hand (the right)
gets to the animal first and then makes contact. From such observations, it is difficult to draw firm conclusions about the development
of hand-usage preference during the first six months of life, since the
period of observation may have been too short to demonstrate a stable hand preference. Several tentative conclusions can, however, be
drawn from these scattered observations. All children in the sample
demonstrated directed unimanual reaching sometime between forty
and sixty days, their manual reaching behavior increased in confidence and skill over the first three months. Hand-use preference appears to be task-specific rather than subject-specific during this time,
and the distribution of right- or left-hand use-preference did not conform to the distribution of handedness in the population at large.
With respect to the question of object permanence, the reaching behavior began to make a substantial contribution between the second
and fourth months; but from my observations, it could not be concluded that infants had programmed foreknowledge about how the
hand should be shaped in order to seize the desired object. Instead,
practice in handling the object once they have made contact appears to be an essential component of the development in grasping
behavior.

The Recovery of Partially Occluded Objects. The last component in
the development of object permanence about which I was able to
make some partial observations was the stage in which the infants
upon seeing a portion of a familiar object when the rest is hidden
behind a cover make an apparently deliberate effort to reconstitute
the full object, for example, by removing the cover or changing their
position to see the hidden portions of the object. In none of the uncontrolled observations over the first six months or the experimental
manipulations was there any evidence that infants deliberately removed a cover so they could see those portions of the object which
had previously been hidden. This observation would be consistent
with Piaget's description, as well as with systematic replication stud-

ies of his findings. Complex behavior in which there is removal of the cover and subsequent directed grasping of the desired object in a distinct action-pattern of temporally, spatially, and causally appropriate means-ends sequences is not clearly manifested in infants until around eight or twelve months (Piaget 1954). Yet, there are isolated observations referring to the infant's visual reach for the remainder of an object, when seeing only part of it, that may be early analogues of later means-end behavior.

One behavior pattern that has nothing to do directly with searching for the occluded portion of an object, but probably contributes to the construction of a permanent object, was exhibited by almost all of the children during the third to fifth weeks. At nineteen days, P. R., for example, is lying on the kitchen table where she is accustomed to spend much of the waking hours during the day. On her right side, I construct a tower made up of colored jars of powdered milk, coffee, and jam. When she turns her head to the right side, she sees the base of the tower, but slowly directs her gaze further upward, as if searching for its upper boundaries. When her gaze reaches the top of the tower, she stares at it in a fixed gaze. Using the same components, I build various towers of different heights, and each time her gaze is directed to the top at which she stares for several seconds in a fixed pattern. The shape or color of the object residing at the top seems to be irrelevant, since her gaze eventually always comes to rest at the upper boundaries, even when such looking requires her to exert herself, stretching her body, or arching her head and neck.

At twenty-seven and again at thirty-eight days, her gaze gradually shifts to the top of seven towers of different heights and constructions, but always stays at the top. By contrast, at seventy-eight and eighty-four days, the same towers elicit a qualitatively different visual scanning pattern. She is no longer fixated at the top, but slowly moves her head and eyes up and down several times (three, five, six times), as if to scan the full length of the tower, and there is no longer any evidence that she is compelled to look only at the top.

Similarly, F. E. has been provided with a clothesline strung from one side of the crib to the other and from which the mother suspends colored objects which are within his reach, and can be made to move when they are touched. I remove the colored objects and replace them with four wooden clothespins equally spaced between the two sides of the crib. At 112 and 121 days, he slowly scans the extent of the line, moving both head and eyes back and forth, apparently along the trajectory of the string. In subsequent weeks, the same tracking behavior is extended to a variety of spatially distributed long objects when the boundaries of the objects extend beyond his visual field, and such boundary behavior can be observed repeatedly as a spontaneous event; but it is difficult to induce behavior on days of experimental manipulation in order to detect, for example, whether scanning patterns systematically stop at points where I have attached colored objects or clothespins. On one day, for example, he sees the black telephone cord as his mother telephones near his crib, and he seems to follow it away from the telephone to the periphery of his visual field. But when I try to reproduce the behavioral sequence under controlled conditions, he is readily distracted by other activities, and I cannot induce such slow, deliberate scanning. In all infants exhibiting the scanning patterns as if they were tracing the full length of an extended object, it seems as if the search behavior occurs only in a delicately balanced subset of waking behavioral states which for want of a better name might be called a "contemplative" or reflective disposition in which the infant is motorically at rest, not engaged in repetitive movement patterns, nor looking for social contact, and neither fussing nor sleeping. The objective behavioral correlates of such a disposition are difficult to define, but seem to be relatively late acquisitions, not emerging until the fifth or sixth month. Even towards the end of the sixth month, such a "contemplative disposition" was transient and elusive, so that it hardly qualifies as a distinct category of behavioral state. Yet, it is of interest for a developmental analysis of behavioral states as a possible analogue for periods of alert wakefulness that are no longer critically dependent on ongoing motor activity when "thinking" begins to replace activity as the necessary organismic process for maintaining wakefulness.

For a developmental description of the infant's relations to things and acquisition of an object permanence, observations concerning the tendency to trace the outlines of a spatially distributed object to its periphery and then to remain fixed at its boundaries may be no different than the "stimulus boundness" described in earlier chapters. However, between five and six months, this scanning pattern has been replaced by a tendency to inspect the full length of the object in a deliberate pattern back and forth along its outlines, which is perhaps similar to the previously described "emancipation" from stimulus boundness. The underlying physiological processes of visuomotor control that determine such a shift are clearly beyond the scope of my behavioral descriptions. Such distinctions do, however, highlight the important interactions between behavioral state and adaptive behavior during phases in development when the infant is in a transition from a well established to a more differentiated form of coordinated action.

Whenever possible, the same experimental manipulations were carried out also when the infants were fussy or drowsy. As might be predicted on the basis of earlier descriptions, the presentation of objects which elicited deliberate searching behavior was accompanied by a transient arrest of fussing or mild crying but was usually ignored when the infant was vigorously crying. Novel motor patterns in process of formation which were transient phenomena even under optimal organismic dispositions usually did not divert the infant from a fussy condition. Well-practiced motor patterns relating to object permanence, such as head and eye pursuit of a moving target, were consistently more effective in transforming fussiness to alert activity or inactive states. Such observations, however, demonstrated little more than the relative distractibility of infants along a near-linear continuum, depending on their disposition. In contrast to the rooting responses described in the neonate by Prechtl (1958), and in contrast to expressions of emotion in response to particular stimulus configurations, variations of waking behavioral states were not associated with qualitative changes of motor coordination in response to a stimulus array. In other words, behavioral-state variations altered the probability and proficiency with which infants acted on inanimate objects but not the form or quality of motor responses, as in the case of expressions of emotion.

Persons

Visual Pursuit of Human and Inanimate Objects

Since unpredictable movement is a feature that distinguishes persons from most inanimate objects, I systematically compared the infant's preference for persons and things when they were moving and when they were stationary. On each day of experimental observation, I compared and contrasted, for example, the infant's gaze preference for a human face and blanket, jacket, or other physical object of comparable size with detailed contours that were more complex than a piece of plain cardboard. The two sets of objects were always compared when both were stationary but in different regions of the infant's visual field; when one object was slowly displaced across the visual field in the horizontal axis, while the other remained stationary; and when both objects were moving slowly in opposite directions. To make such comparisons, I either recruited familiar persons in the home such as older siblings and parents or, on occasion, introduced strangers to make such comparisons. After the third month, I also compared looking preferences to my face and to the mother's face when both were nodding, silent and moving.

During the first month after birth, the fact of movement, or the displacement across the visual field, was primary in determining where the infant looked when confronted by two objects, only one of which was in motion. When things were displaced slowly across the field starting at a position where the infant could easily see both the objects, the face usually drew its gaze away from the stationary face. By the same token, moving faces almost invariably drew the baby's attention away from stationary things. When both objects were displaced in opposite directions across the field, a clear trend emerged by the fourth week. The infants usually pursued the moving face. When the thing moved while the face remained stationary, infants usually first pursued the moving thing. By the end of the fifth week, they rapidly redirected their gaze to the place where they had seen the face, as if they now "knew" its position and were compelled to return to it. Renewed contact with the face on such occasions frequently elicited a smile, and occasionally a vocalization. A similar return to the place where the object had last been seen (Piaget 1952) was never observed when the thing was stationary while the face had moved across the visual field. Thus, by the end of the first month, there was already a preference for looking at faces over things, which gradually replaced the initial preference for anything that moved over anything that was stationary. By six weeks, the preference for moving things over stationary things had shown a dramatic decline. Looking at the face, particularly when it included eye-eye contact, now captured and held the infant's attention more often than any moving thing displaced across the field. This preference for stationary faces, particularly when there was eye contact, increased in frequency until the end of the fourth month, after which infants were likely to redirect their gaze to other events in the environment or to return to their ongoing activity while intermittently checking whether the face was still there. Until the third month, when they did pursue the inanimate object displaced across the field in preference over the stationary object, they usually abandoned the search for the object after it had crossed the midline, and immediately returned to the stationary face (see figure 30).

One essential variable that may have conferred privileged status on the human face was the phenomenon of eye-eye contact,

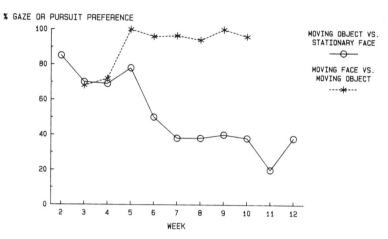

Figure 30: Looking Preferences for Faces and Objects

which is an important but elusive nonverbal communication between older social partners that may also be an essential feature by which infants learn to distinguish human faces from nonhuman objects.

Search for the Missing Object

The operational criterion by which Piaget traces the concept of object permanence in the young infant pertains to the infant's attempts to recover a disappearing object by directed visual search, or visuomotor search, and the changes in the infant's strategy for pursuing such search over the course of the first year of life. Using analogous criteria, I compared the search strategies of infants in response to disappearing persons and disappearing things at bi-weekly intervals.

During the first two weeks, infants gave no evidence of having noticed that objects had disappeared. Between two and four weeks, they often stared at the place where the object had disappeared as soon as it left the visual field, but then usually returned to their previous activity. From these observations, it was not possible to tell whether the staring was simply the consequence of "stimulus-boundness" shifting from one object to another in the same environment, or whether it constituted an active search. Throughout the first month, there were no differences in the infant's response to the disappearing person and thing. By nine weeks and increasingly thereafter, infants searched actively, rotated their heads smoothly in two or three full horizontal arcs, or attempted to raise their trunks in order to enlarge their visual field when the disappearing object was a person. At the same time, the duration of their search for persons was more persistent (mean time: 10.4 seconds; range: 6–32 seconds) than their search for the missing inanimate object. Increasingly after the tenth week, there was a dramatic difference in searching behavior for persons and things.

Preceding descriptions of the adequate cause for crying have indicated that visual awareness of being left commonly provoked crying, and that such a response was stable until at least the end of the fourth month. By contrast, the disappearance of physical objects hardly ever produced crying. On the very rare occasions when there was an apparent association, it was difficult to tell whether the association was causal or the onset of crying was coincidental. If we leave aside cry vocalizations as the response to being "abandoned," the duration of active search for the disappearing person without crying was also considerably longer than the search for things, from the second until the fifth month (Wilcoxon signed-ranks Test, p < .01 in each month).

Preceding chapters indicated that the infant's observation of its mother leaving was the sufficient cause to provoke crying in a significant number of instances; that the response was specifically related to the process of being left and was not the response to the condition of being alone. Protests to being left reached a peak at around three months, after which infants became more tolerant of being left, even though they clearly were aware that their mother was leaving, as judged by their visual pursuit. Although infants never cried when they saw things disappear, even when they had previously been inspecting or holding them, there was a special class of things to which some infants had formed a privileged relationship. When these disappeared, their responses were intermediate between those to the disappearance of things and to the disappearance of persons. These things were favorite stuffed animals that were commonly present in their cribs, such as a stuffed toy lion or a dog with distinctive colors and forms that made it relatively easy to distinguish from other things in the baby's immediate visual environment. When older infants and children form such attachments to blankets and toy animals, the object in question is commonly referred to as a "transitional object," and the assumption is made that such favorite toys are imbued by older infants and children with symbolic significance or treated as a substitute for the parent. However, the infants were probably not yet capable of mental imagery and symbolic representations at a time when they already showed a distinct preference for particular toy animals. Ony five of the infants in the longitudinal sample demonstrated any such preference during the first six months, but each of them was already devoted to one particular animal and would not be placated by substitutes.

D. F. was generally accustomed to a toy lying in his crib since the age of three weeks. The toy in question was a fluffy stuffed animal with a large head and a mane, as well as a red ribbon around its neck; the toy was usually inserted between the slats of his crib and had all the appearance of a lion. By seven weeks, when D. F. was alert and inactive or active in his crib, he began to gurgle and coo regularly at the lion as long as it was present, and he smiled at it when he first reencountered it, having turned his head away just before. By twelve weeks, he had the habit of talking to his lion consistently when in his crib; he reached out for it and pulled at it repeatedly with apparently directed grasping movements which were sometimes successful in pulling the lion into the crib because he had gotten hold of the red ribbon. Whenever I replaced the lion to its customary position, he pulled at it again; sometimes we played the game for ten minutes intermittently while he gurgled and smiled with each new encounter.

At seventeen weeks, he cries when put to bed without seeing his lion, but when the lion is put into its usual place, he stops crying immediately and goes to sleep. At other times when presentation of the lion has stopped his cry, I remove the lion, and he starts to cry again, stopping as soon as it is put in its place. Again at twenty weeks, he is fussing in his crib. I place the lion so he can clearly see it, and he gurgles happily, reaching for it until he pulls it down. The same observation at twenty-three weeks. Taking the lion away causes him to start crying again, while bringing it back stops the crying. This sequence can be repeated three times, but then he gives way to inconsolable crying, and the mother has to come. At twenty-four weeks, the same sequence is repeated. If he is fussy, the lion makes him stop crying; he begins to smile and coo, sometimes reaching for it, while taking the lion away makes him cry. When I remove the lion while he is happily looking somewhere else or playing with his arms and then turns back to the place where the lion was, there is no negative response. When I introduce a very different stuffed animal which he has not seen before, it does nothing to console him or to make up for the crying in response to removal of his favorite lion. Similarly, a large woolen blanket in the place usually occupied by the lion does not console him when he has cried, having seen the lion disappear. However, reintroducing the lion is clearly effective, and he becomes happy.

A. F. Since he was three and a half weeks old this boy has been accustomed to a black stuffed dog, which is a replica of the Disney character, Pluto, and has prominent mouth, teeth, and floppy ears. The dog usually occupies the same place, inserted between the slats of his crib within reaching distance. At five weeks, he turns to the dog, grins and gurgles, blowing bubbles with his mouth. Such vocal behavior stops when the dog is removed, but removing the animal does not provoke crying. By seven weeks, he is alert in his crib, inspects the dog in a slow scan and with apparent deliberation, coos at it and reaches for it, but does not succeed in displacing it. I remove the toy, and he begins to snort and fuss. As soon as I replace the dog, he becomes quiet and alert. When I remove it a second time, he begins to fuss, although not yet really crying, but becomes quiet and gurgles again as soon as the dog is replaced. At nine weeks, removal of the dog causes full-blown crying. When the mother puts him to bed and he starts to cry without having seen the dog, placing the dog so he can see it stops him from crying. Three times in succession, I can provoke a cry by removing the dog and bringing him back to an alert active state by replacing it. I remove the dog while he is not looking at it, so he does not notice its disappearance, and he is occupied with some other activity, and when he turns his head to the place where the dog usually sits, he does not respond adversely.

At ten weeks, he is happily playing with his hands on the kitchen table where he can see his mother coming and going. I bring in the dog; he smiles at it but goes on with his hand play, and is not perturbed when I remove the dog, as long as he can see or hear his mother in the room. As soon as he sees his mother leave the room, he turns to the dog, and then continues with his play. If he sees me removing the dog while his mother is away, he begins to cry, and replacement of the dog gives him comfort. He gurgles at it and reaches for it. When I remove the dog while the mother is out of the room, he starts to cry. A few minutes later, when I remove the dog while the mother is present, it has no adverse effect on him.

Two other children of the sample were accustomed to having the same animals in their cribs. Starting at the fourth or fifth week, they began to show similar preferred relationships to the stuffed animals towards the end of the second month. When they saw the toy disappear, they began to fuss or cry if they were not in the presence of their mother, whereas the mother's presence buffered the effect. Both infants vocalized actively and smiled intermittently when encountering their favorite toy while alone in their cribs, and they were significantly more responsive to the familiar toy than to novel stuffed animals introduced intermittently for experimental comparisons. The age when they first showed such special attachment and when the disappearance of the object predictably provoked crying differed by two to three weeks across the four infants, but the social greeting behavior (smiling and cooing) usually started between seven and eight weeks, whereas the crying response to the disappearance of the object did not start until twelve or fourteen weeks. A fifth infant showed a distinct preference for an inanimate object that would not typically be classified as a toy or transitional object, but seemed to have special meaning for at least this one infant.

M. R. spent a great deal of her waking day in the kitchen, where most of the family activity during the daytime occurred, lying on her back on the kitchen table supported by blankets which allowed her considerable freedom of movement. Above her head on the kitchen wall, suspended from a nail, was a thick black wire figure in the shape of a dancer. By chance, the mother discovered when M. R. was four or five weeks old that the pendular movement of the black figure provoked great interest in M. R., quieting her predictably when she was fussy and amusing her when she was content. As long as the wire figure was moving back and forth, it had the ability to pacify the crying infant and produce smiling and vocalization. As soon as the oscillating movements slowed down or stopped, the object was no longer effective. If the infant was fussy, it began to cry as the arc of the pendulum movements decreased in amplitude beyond a critical value, but stopped crying whenever the movements of the black figure were again accelerated.

One possible explanation for these findings might be that the oscillating black figure simply served as a distraction that temporarily arrested the infant's crying because it was an "interesting spectacle," and in this sense, functioned as a counterirritant perhaps analogous to the white noise which during the newborn period was consistently effective in reducing the crying of infants. Some other "interesting spectacles," or spectacles which I thought would be at least as dramatic and interesting for the baby, could not distract her from crying once the black figure had stopped oscillating. Yet, as soon as the black figure was set in motion again, she stopped crying, gurgled, and eventually smiled. Thus, the movements of the black figure had taken on a special meaning that might in some primitive sense be compared to other "transitional objects." The very idiosyncrasy of this particular favored spectacle suggests that inanimate objects do not need to have particular perceptual characteristics (such as furry texture or the configuration of an animal) to take on a special role in the child's world of objects, although the other descriptions suggest that stuffed animals do apparently lend themselves more readily to this role.

Others in the group gave no evidence that they had formed a special relation with a favorite toy; and a comparison of variations in the social environment between the two groups gave no clues why some infants did, while others did not, form such a special attachment. The number of siblings in the families of the two groups did not differ. Mothers spent about the same time playing with their infants; and in at least one case, one of the infants observed for the first three months had formed an attachment to a stuffed animal while the brother who was observed later did not. The only clue, and not a very persuasive one, was that some of the mothers made a concerted effort to encourage such attachment by always keeping a single animal in the crib in such a way that the infants could see it and reach for it whenever they wanted.

The specificity of privileged relations to a toy animal was demonstrated partially when I imported totally unfamiliar stuffed animals that had been selected deliberately to differ in color, shape, and size from the preferred toy. When removal of the latter provoked fussing or crying, the substitution with a strange animal did not pacify the infants, whereas the return of the familiar animal did. Introducing the strange toy could result in a transient arrest of fussing and momentary exploration, but then the infants usually returned to their prior discontented state until a familiar person appeared in the visual field or the familiar animal was returned to them or their discontent gradually subsided and they returned to their prior activity. In parallel, I tried to pacify infants from the other subgroup who had demonstrated no preference for a particular toy by showing them one of the animals in my collection when they were alone in their crib and fussing. The appearance of the unfamiliar toy again could provoke transient interest and an arrest of crying, but had no stable change of state.

The experiments also emphasize differences between being alone and being left as necessary condition for the provocation of crying during the early months. Infants who had a favorite toy were perfectly content to play alone in their crib as long as the toy itself was not present in the visual field and as long as they did not observe either the toy or a person leaving them. They became discontent when they were "reminded" of their animal which was then removed from the field at a rate of movement which allowed them to pursue its departure. By contrast, when the toy was removed so quickly that they could not pursue its track, they were relatively neutral to the departure.

A few pilot explorations further suggested that the behavioral state of the infant may be an essential factor contributing to the responses exhibited by the infant when a preferred toy is removed from the crib. In the fourth and fifth months, when infants were fussy or in a transition between alert activity and fussing, disappearance of the favorite animal was much more likely to provoke crying than when the infants were alert and engaged with spontaneous explorations at the time when I showed them that their animal was being removed. Again, some analogue of state transitions between alert activity and crying seemed to be an essential variable which contributed to the ways in which infants responded to an event which at other times caused them to cry, as if variations of behavioral state codetermine the meaning or value the infants attribute to their everyday experience.

Eye-to-Eye Contact

In preceding chapters, I had referred to the phenomenon of eye-eye contact, which played an essential role in the provocation of smiling and vocalization to the silent face in older infants. In part it also accounted for the prolonged latency before the onset of smiling in response to the static face because the infants scanned the various distinct features (hairline, mouth) before locking in on the face and then smiling. After the seventh week, infants were inclined to search the landmarks of the face when first confronted by the silent familiar face, and to smile only after they encountered the eyes. The mean age at which eye contact before smiling was first recorded was sixty-nine days (range: 46–79 days). Infants who were relatively slow to maintain consistent periods of alertness, or late in acquiring a stable smile to the voice or face, were also relatively late in responding to eye contact in the manner described.

Eye-to-eye contact and its correlate of gaze aversion are among the most important nonverbal cues by which adults in relatively close proximity gauge the status of their communication (Kendon 1967; Argyle and Cook 1976). The term "eye contact" has often been confused with or equated with face-to-face encounters (Robson 1967), but phenomenologically as well as objectively there is a qualitative difference between them. At present, there are no decisive objective criteria for measuring when two pairs of eyes are actually in contact, although the subjective experience is always powerful and unmistakable. What is experienced subjectively as eye contact, in fact, involves a complex, dynamic interaction between two autonomous centers of causality, each partner looking intermittently at the eyes of the other, then away to other parts of the face, then back to the eyes. The actual time spent in eye contact may be relatively short. Deliberately staring into the eyes of the other actually creates an unnatural situation that makes the partner uncomfortable and usually forces the latter to avert the gaze. This dynamic shifting of the eyes back and forth to and from the eyes of the other constitutes an essential component of all social encounters between two individuals in close proximity. Anyone can easily test the importance of eye contact as part of the "natural encounter" by experimentally looking at another person within the conventional interpersonal space but deliberately avoiding eye contact and staring instead at the partner's forehead, chin, or neck while carrying on a conversation. Yet, independent judges have great difficulty scoring eye contact accurately, even when they sit near the partners they are observing; and at a distance of ten feet or more, such assessments become virtually impossible. Judges can also not give an accurate description of subtle variations in gaze direction during eye contact, including a wide range of expressed emotions and nonverbal signals that depend on carefully orchestrated sequences of eye contacts and gaze aversions, which have been described in detail by Argyle and Cook (1976; see also Hutt and Ounsted 1966). While eye contact appears to be a basic vehicle for the expression of human emotions, its various meanings cannot be catalogued without taking the broader social context of the encounter into consideration. Even then, two individuals engaged in eye contact probably communicate a wide range of subtle social messages that will escape any third person.

Given the overriding importance of eye-eye contact in the non-verbal communication of children and adults, I explored the possibility that it might also contribute in important ways to the social development of young infants; and that it might serve as one mechanism by which infants distinguish between persons and things. With the help of several associates I first attempted to use two video cameras, one placed immediately above my head, the other above the infant's head. The infant's gaze pattern and motor behavior were recorded when I looked directly at its eyes, looked deliberately at its ears or hair line but not its eyes, and when I focused on a virtual image behind the infant's head so that it could see my eyes but I did not make eye contact. From a replay of the tapes on one split video-screen, it was impossible to tell either where I was looking or how the infant's behavior changed as a function of my gaze. The addition of infrared reflectance oculography might have given more satisfactory results, but the elaborate instrumentation needed for such a procedure would probably have distorted the phenomenon beyond recognition.

Instead I relied on my subjective impressions about where the infant was looking and systematically varied the direction of my gaze, while an independent observer, who did not know where I was looking, scored changes in motor activity as I varied the direction of my gaze. The levels of motor activity were scored on an ordinal scale as I watched the infant in a mirror so that it could not see my face or eyes; as I faced the infant but deliberately looked away from its eyes; and as I looked into its eyes with an unwavering gaze. Eight infants were examined for two-minute episodes under each of the three conditions at two, five, eight, and twelve weeks while they were alert and active, and the different gaze patterns were presented in a counterbalanced design. At two and five weeks, the direction of gaze had no measurable effect on motor activity. However, at eight and twelve weeks, the level of motor activity was reduced significantly when I looked directly into the baby's eyes instead of looking in the mirror ($p < .01$). The level of motor activity also differed when I looked into the baby's eyes and when I deliberately gazed at its hairline, the ears or the nose, but avoided eye contact ($p < .05$). The effects were of short duration, and the differences were statistically significant only when scored for the first minute of each presentation.

"Strangeness Anxiety"

Toward the end of the second month, subtle distortions of the familiar face began to elicit emotional responses of discomfort ranging in type from surprise and an arrest of limb activity, to frowning, fussing, and occasional full-blown crying (see figure 17). Such social responses probably differed in kind from the phenomenon of "stranger anxiety" (Spitz 1950; Bowlby 1969) that is reported to occur later in development (eight months?), and that by definition refers to the infant's responses to actual strangers. "Strangeness anxiety," on the other hand, was defined as the infant's response to minor alterations in the facial appearance of familiar persons. Although the particular context of its occurrence was specific to each infant-mother couple, at least half the mothers in the longitudinal sample had independently observed some variation of the general phenomenon; and when I asked other young mothers, they confirmed the impression that the phenomenon is widespread.

In order to test the phenomenon, I first prepared a catalogue of concrete examples that I had observed directly or that were reported to me by mothers. From the most commonly reported examples I prepared a protocol that was subsequently tested both in other children of the longitudinal sample and in a separate group of infants examined by cross-sectional design.

Four mothers of the longitudinal sample noticed "strangeness anxiety" in their four-to-five-month-old infants when they wore a shower cap that hid their hairline. The infants stared without smiling and remained relatively immobile, but returned to their previous level of activity when the shower cap was removed and stared again when the shower cap was replaced. A five-month-old girl cried when she first saw a man with a full beard (her father was clean-shaven), while a six-month-old boy fussed repeatedly when held by a man with a prominent moustache, but let himself be held by clean-shaven strangers without any signs of distress. One nearsighted mother who usually wore thick horn-rimmed glasses when feeding her child, reported that her four-month-old boy turned his head away deliberately and refused to eat when she fed him without her glasses, but settled down comfortably to the meal as soon as she put her glasses back. Another mother reported that her infant looked very surprised when she wore glasses for the first time. A six-month-old boy stopped sucking on the bottle, stared at his mother's face with a puzzled expression when she started to weep silently during the meal, and did not resume sucking until she had wiped away her tears. This anecdote is of particular interest because it suggests that changes in facial appearance required to elicit strangeness anxiety can be very subtle indeed.

In an earlier chapter, I described the strong aversive responses to a clear plastic mask worn by a familiar person; cardboard models of the face or latex masks of a clown and a Frankenstein monster produced no distress, although they reduced the overall frequency of smiling. Because the clear plastic mask provoked aversive responses in almost all of the infants examined, it was compared with other facial distortions. Table 8 compares emotional expressions to the natural silent nodding face, the face wearing a latex Frankenstein mask, and the silent nodding face wearing the clear plastic mask, when infants were alert-inactive or alert-active at the start of the examination. In none of the trials did the plastic mask provoke crying in alert babies, but in 20 percent of confrontations infants fussed when looking at the mask worn by either the mother or by me. Across all trials, infants smiled significantly less to the plastic mask than to the natural face; they never talked, and until the end of the fourth month they usually stared with immobile limbs and a puzzled frown until the mask was removed. Expressions of distress were exaggerated considerably if the infant was already fussy before the masked face was presented, and on such occasions it provoked crying in about a third of the cases. Neither the familiar silent nodding face nor the latex masks ever produced crying, even if the infant was already fussy.

As an independent test of the phenomenon, Mrs. Barbara Rowbotham and I recruited a sample of twenty-four healthy "naive" infants ranging in age from five to ten months who were not part of the longitudinal study. Infants below seven months at the time of first testing were retested at nine months; the others were tested only once. Subjects were examined in the familiar surroundings of their homes to eliminate the confounding effects of a strange environment. Each stimulus configuration was presented to the infant when worn both by the mother and by a female observer who was a stranger to the infant. The natural silent smiling face was always presented first. The distortions used for this experiment included flesh-colored eye patches covering either one or both eyes, mirror sunglasses that reflected an image of the infant, a paste-on black moustache (provided the father was clean-shaven), a pink latex head-covering that hid the hairline, the clear plastic mask described earlier, and various combinations of these stimulus configurations; and the order of presentations was counterbalanced. Babies were tested only when they were awake and alert at the start of the examination, and testing was discontinued when the infants became agitated. Each social stimulus, including the natural face, was presented for three five-second trials, but the clear plastic mask was always presented last so that the experiment could be completed even when infants were frightened by the mask. Emotional responses were classified as broad smiling and grinning, hesitant smiling, noncry vocalizations, blank staring with an arrest of limb activity, fussing, crying, and gaze-aversion.

Table 9 indicates that infants smiled and vocalized more to their mother's than to the stranger's natural face, and that the stranger's face provoked more frowning and occasional fussing. Distortions of the face had a more dramatic effect when worn by the mother than by the stranger, but the effect was probably due to differences in base rates of smiling to the natural face. By far the most dramatic effect on all infants was produced by the clear plastic mask; in all trials these effects were more pronounced than those to any combination of other distortions.

When combined with findings from the longitudinal study,

Table 9: Strangeness Anxiety; Cross-Sectional Sample ($N = 21$)

Natural Face Compared to Altered Face, Both in Mother and Stranger	Smile X^2	Noncry Vocalizing X^2	Frown X^2	Cry/Fuss X^2
No Distortion				
Mother vs. Stranger	14.0***(a)	6.5*(a)	8.4**(b)	—
Bathing Cap				
Mother	2.8	—	4.4*(d)	—
Stranger	—	—		—
Ordinary Sunglasses				
Mother	5.5*(c)	—	—	—
Stranger	1.8	0.9		—
Eye Patches				
Mother	8.4**(c)	1.9	5.5*(d)	—
Stranger	—	—		—
Mirror Glasses				
Mother	18.7***(c)	1.9	—	—
Stranger	—			—
Clear Mask				
Mother	16.3***(c)	2.3	14.9***(d)	—
Stranger	6.4*(c)	0.9	9.7**(d)	—

* p .05
** p .01
*** p .001

(a) responses to mother greater
(b) responses to stranger greater
(c) responses to natural faces greater
(d) responses to distorted faces greater

these results identify some of the essential variables contributing to the phenomenon of strangeness anxiety. The mere fact of physical difference was not sufficient to account for the findings, since more extreme physical distortions of the familiar face (such as the monster masks) did not have the same aversive effect. On the contrary, subtle distortions had a more dramatic effect than either strangers or gross alterations of the familiar person. For example, the plastic mask provoked more distress than the opaque latex monster masks; tears in the mother's eyes were more disturbing to at least one infant than pink eye-patches which covered both eyes.

The infants acted as if they could register the fact of a difference but could not identify exactly what the difference might be, whereas they had no difficulty identifying more blatant differences which did not disturb them. "Cognitive factors" obviously played an important role in causing the phenomenon, since a schema of the familiar face had to be constructed and then compared with the perceived face. At the same time, the phenomenon could not be reduced to cognitive processes, since it was observed only in relation to persons. A series of parallel distortion experiments involving familiar inanimate objects, including favorite stuffed animals, never elicited anything resembling strangeness anxiety, but either had no effect at all or or elicited exploratory efforts that did not differ from explorations of the same object in the familiar form.

Imitation

A precocious analogue of imitation, which is observed primarily although not exclusively in response to persons, was originally described in a number of infant biographies (summarized in Werner and Kaplan 1968), and has, in recent years, been systematically reinvestigated (Meltzoff and Moore 1977). Infants below one month will sometimes reproduce a movement pattern, gesture, or sound made by the social partner in a way that suggests they are capable of reproducing the analogue of complex perceptual configurations by their motor activity. Such imitations are observed long before infants differentiate between themselves and other persons, or between action and object. Moreover, such imitations appear to be form-specific rather than random movements initiated by heightened arousal.

One dramatic instance of precocious imitation described by Zazzo (1957), involves the infant's attempt to "imitate" tongue protrusions when the social partner makes a similar gesture, at an age when the infant has probably never observed itself in the mirror and when the mother has probably never reinforced spontaneous tongue protrusions. Such imitations raise important theoretical questions about the mechanisms by which infants can recognize similarities between what they see and what they do. Tongue protrusions, which have probably been studied in greatest detail (see, for example, Meltzoff and Moore 1977; Fontaine 1984; and Koepke et al. 1983 for a failure to replicate), may also be the most dramatic illustration of precocious imitations. However, the imitation of other facial grimaces including smiling, limb gestures, and the imitation of vocalizations confront us with very similar unresolved questions.

Piaget (1951) called such behavior "pseudo-imitations" to distinguish them from later emerging "true imitations," on the assumption that pseudo-imitations lack intentionality and should therefore be included among the "primary circular reactions." The latter term implies that selected stimulus configurations, whether self-induced or presented by the external environment, are assimilated to existing sensorimotor schemas and serve to maintain the cycle of activity exactly like other forms of self-activation, without, however, giving any indication that the infant intends to imitate. While this explanation is not sufficient to account for neuropsychological mechanisms by which the infant can match its actions with complex perceptual models, alternative hypotheses which have been advanced to explain the phenomenon are also inadequate.

Given the wide range of forms and muscle units which may, in various combinations, be involved in these imitations, it is unlikely that they are controlled by prefunctional (species-typical) coordinations between perceived visual or auditory patterns ("innate releaser mechanisms") and preprogrammed motor patterns ("fixed-action pattern"). One would, then, have to assume that human infants are equipped by evolution with discrete mechanisms for tongue protrusion, lip pursing, smiling, hand waving, and the like. For similar reasons, it is implausible that the form-specific imitations are simply diffuse motor discharges in response to heightened arousal. On the other hand, the age at which the phenomenon can first be demonstrated makes it unlikely that infants have been reinforced by their parents to imitate the motor patterns according to laws of learning.

Infectious Crying

From a developmental perspective, the earliest references to pseudo-imitation reported in the literature pertain to infectious crying. Peiper (1963) summarized a number of anecdotal reports by others indicating that when one infant in the neonatal nursery begins to cry, there is a tendency for other babies to begin crying as well. Since the babies in most of these studies were probably fed on a rigorous schedule, it is unclear how much the presumed phenomenon of infectious crying may have been confounded by the cyclical recurrence of hunger and hunger satiation. Simple counts on the number of infants crying at various points between two feedings in both American and Japanese newborn nurseries indicated clearly that the number of infants crying at any one time was substantially greater a half-hour before a meal than during the three-quarters of an hour after all the babies were returned to the nursery, having been fed by their mothers. Within the first hour after a meal when one infant in the nursery cried, there was no apparent "infection" (and the probability that single infants were crying was as great as that two or more were crying at the same time).

By contrast, Piaget (1952) has reported that the infant who has repeatedly heard its own voice while crying will also cry when it hears the crying of other infants. He assumes that the infant fails to distinguish between self and others or between motor activity (crying) and perception (hearing a cry). Thus hearing the sound and actively producing it are merely different aspects of one sensorimotor schema, the pattern of cry vocalizations by others being assimilated by the infant to its schema of crying, in a "circular reaction." This explanation serves Piaget as a prototype for a variety of pseudo-imitations during the early months after birth.

Because of the important theoretical problems for developmental psychology raised by the phenomenon of pseudo-imitation, I carried out cross-sectional studies to test the phenomenon of infectious crying under more controlled conditions. Samples of crying for each infant separately, as well as the symphony of cries in the newborn nursery within a half-hour before a meal, were tape-recorded and played back in a sound-isolated room to individual one-week-old infants while they were not crying at various intervals between two meals. Twenty healthy three-day-old well-fed infants who were not part of the longitudinal study consistently failed to respond by crying to the sound stimulus when they were asleep (irregular sleep), drowsy, or awake but not fussing. This lack of effect was unrelated to the time since last feeding. When the stimulus was presented to "waking active" or fussing babies, it occasionally induced full-blown crying within thirty seconds after the tape was turned on, but the occasions were sufficiently rare so that they could not be distinguished from spontaneous crying or the effect of a nonspecific disturbance which might have accelerated the onset of crying during the transition from waking to crying. Parallel observations on ten five-day-old Japanese infants in a newborn nursery, all of whom were breast-fed, gave essentially the same results. The combined findings suggest that infectious crying during the first week after birth is not a real phenomenon, and that other variables presumably associated with hunger are probably the necessary and sufficient conditions to induce group crying in the newborn nursery.

Cry specimens made by individual infants were saved and used at regular intervals during the longitudinal study to determine whether infectious crying might emerge at a later time. During the first month after birth, the results were essentially the same as those noted in the neonatal nursery, even when behavioral state and time since last feeding were controlled. By the sixth week, hearing a tape-recorded cry sample could occasionally trigger vigorous crying in otherwise noncrying infants, although the effect was clearly still state-dependent, and could be demonstrated only when infants were already restless, "waking active," or fussy. Under such conditions, cry samples provoked vigorous crying in 20 percent of trials and in eight of twelve infants tested repeatedly, regardless of the time since last feeding. The effect was significantly greater than chance when compared to a period of fussiness during which no tape-recorded sample was played, but the effect could not be clearly differentiated from a nonspecific response to disturbances and sound patterns which might have provoked an infant already in a transitional disposition.

Therefore, I also compared the effect of turning the cry samples on and off, and compared the influence of cry samples produced by the same infant with samples of noncry vocalization such as cooing and gurgling. The observations suggested that between the second and third months, infectious crying might be a real phenomenon as well as an illustration of pseudo-imitation. Experiments were carried out with eight infants to test the assumption, but the details of the procedure had to be varied according to the infant. The results were therefore quite variable and could not be translated into numerical values; instead illustrative descriptions are presented.

At sixty-three days, for example, A. R. is silently exploring her hands and feet. A tape-recorded sample of her own crying distracts her temporarily from ongoing activities while she turns to the source of the sound, but then she returns to playing with her hands. Three minutes later, a tape recording of my imitation of noncry vocalizations again distracts her from playing as she looks at me, and she begins to vocalize, but then she returns to exploring her hands, making only occasional noncry vocalizations. An hour later, she is moaning and beginning to be fussy. The same tape recording of her own cry now provokes crying in less than thirty seconds. However, as soon as the recording is stopped, she also stops crying but continues to fret. The tape recording of my noncry vocalization changes her mood; she begins to squeal and gurgle, but no longer produces any cry vocalizations. When the tape recording of her cry is played again, she begins to cry again, and this time can no longer be consoled by silence or a tape of noncry vocalization but appears to require her mother.

At 102 days, J. F., who hasn't been fed for at least two hours is lying on the kitchen table, actively moving his hands before his eyes and grunting intermittently as if responding to his own motor effort. He has not cried or fussed for the preceding hour. When I play a tape recording of his own vigorous hunger cries which were made one week earlier, he stops all limb movement, stares towards the sound source with a cry face, and begins to whimper. I stop the cry tape and play instead a sample of his laughter and cooing. He, in turn, stops whimpering; his face relaxes; and he resumes his hand play while making intermittent cooing noises. A minute later, I again play the cry tape. This time, he begins to cry vigorously within thirty seconds, but when I stop the tape he also stops after a few sobs, and begins to gurgle and smile as soon as I play a sample of his own noncry vocalizations.

Even among infants who showed infectious crying consistently, the effect was not invariant. Sometimes, the first exposure to the tape evoked crying that could not be consoled by turning off the machine or playing noncry vocalizations. Sometimes, the infants ignored the stimulus altogether, or turned briefly to the sound source before resuming their prior activity. Such indifference was more common when infants were drowsy or alert-inactive than when they were already intermittently active (alert activity with vocalization) before the start of the experiment. A comparison of frequency with which infectious crying induced crying in these seven infants as a function of behavioral state indicated that failure to produce any infectious crying was substantially higher during conditions of drowsiness and the alert-inactive state than when the infants were alert-active ($p < .01$). Playing tape-recorded samples of crying while infants were in state II sleep produced only mouthing movements and occasionally cry grimaces when other kinds of sounds had no longer had any effect; but taped samples of crying never provoked cry vocalizations in state II sleep. In sum, infectious crying appears to be a real phenomenon, but it emerges during development rather than being present at birth, and it is strongly state-dependent rather than being an automatic response to the appropriate sound stimulus.

Imitation of Noncry Vocalizations

Earlier description of noncry vocalizations indicated that infants respond to taped samples of their own gurgling and cooing with noncry vocalizations (see figures 23, 29). The observations were tested systematically by preparing one-minute tape samples of my imitations of baby talk, and alternating these with one-minute samples of silence and harpsichord music. The tapes were played to the infants while they were alert inactive or active, and their vocal responses were recorded on a second recorder for later comparison and analysis; two complete sequences of the tape were played to the infant on each day of testing. Ten infants were tested once a month, starting at four weeks and continuing until the end of the third month. The overall frequency of noncry vocalizations was significantly greater in response to my taped baby talk than to recorded silence or musical passages (p < .01, by Friedman two-way analysis of variance); the frequency of vocalizations to the music did not differ significantly from that during silent periods. Thus, human speech was evidently more effective in generating noncry vocalizations than complex non-human sound patterns, even when the speech samples were distorted and when they were not synchronized to the infant's spontaneous vocal productions.

Infants also vocalized more during the second than the first control period (p < .05), as if the first exposure to taped speech carried over or "primed" the infant to continue vocalizing into the second control period (see figure 31). The specificity of vocal answers to auditory models was tested in infants who were particularly responsive to the tape recordings. Taped samples of their noncry vocalizations were first classified as sounds coming from the back of the throat (gurgles, "ga-ga"), from the front of the mouth ("bah," "da-da"), and grunts or squeals. Although trained phonologists could not match the infant's vocalizations with my imitations on the basis of sound spectrographs, they could match sets of sounds when listening directly to the tapes. Despite the obvious physical differences in the acoustic signals, the sounds produced by the infant and my efforts to imitate these were evidently sufficiently similar to warrant the assumption that they were "imitations" (see also Wolff 1969).

Thereafter, I engaged eight alert infants in direct conversations, rather than relying on fixed tape-recordings, and determined whether

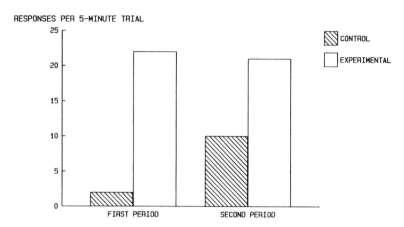

Figure 31: "Priming" Effect of Vocal Imitation

vocalization patterns could be modified by presenting them with imitations that differed in kind from those they were making at the time. When pooled across the eight infants, the results were entirely inconclusive. Yet, an inspection of individual records suggested that infants may have been attempting to imitate the vocalization patterns under the conditions described.

At sixty days, for example, K. A. is lying in her crib playing with her fingers. I approach her so she cannot see me and make a series of sounds at the back of my throat (gurgles). She turns and looks at me, then makes a sequence of three sounds at the back of her throat. Then I make three hyah-hyah sounds, which are already a part of her repertory. She squeals with a wide-open mouth but does not attempt to copy my sound. I return to the cooing sound, and she makes two coos followed by a squeal. I speak to her, using actual words and a high-pitched voice. She squeals two times but then loses interest, and returns to inspecting her hands.

At ninety-one days, T. W. is actively grunting in her crib. I present my face and make a low murmur. She responds with two coos and a long moan, but then stops paying attention to me. I coo three times in succession and she makes three guh-guh sounds in succession at the back of her throat. Then she becomes fussy and I interrupt the experiment.

At seventy-one days, J. P. has discovered a new vocal pattern which sounds like "da-da." On that day and for several days thereafter, I try to imitate his da-da sound but he responds with gurgles and smiles, and makes no obvious attempt to imitate my da-da sounds. Several days later, he is lying in his crib and seems to be practicing the da-da sound. I approach him, making cooing sounds which are already a part of his repertory. He immediately turns to me, and makes a series of cooing sounds and then begins to smile.

In earlier sections I speculated that fussiness during the transition from waking alertness to crying might be the context in which infants discover new vocalization patterns that will eventually be transformed into stable noncry vocalizations by repetition and practice and are then used in other behavioral states. To explore this assumption further, I examined whether the imitation of familiar or novel sound patterns is also state-dependent. By simple comparisons, infants were significantly more likely to respond with noncry vocalizations to a model during the early phases of fussing than when while alert and inactive, and these vocal imitations frequently delayed the onset of crying. There was no evidence that infants were more likely to copy familiar or novel sound patterns when they were fussy than during alert periods.

Pseudo-Imitation of Gestures and Facial Expressions

While observing newborn infants in the nursery (Wolff 1966), I had the strong subjective impression that they yawned much more often within a short period (ten seconds) after I yawned than at other times, and that they made brief but distinct head oscillations not observed at other times, when I shook my head deliberately in the baby's visual field. Attempts to confirm this anecdotal observation by a systematic protocol applied to all newborns were inconclusive. The phenomenon was so elusive and state-dependent that it was difficult to distinguish between chance observations and real effects. In a few infants the phenomenon was, however, sufficiently striking so that the description of individual cases lent weight to the subjective impression.

At ten days, N. W. is alert and inspecting his environment. I present my face and he smiles several times. During a three-minute control period, I count the number of tongue movements. He protrudes his tongue three times during the control period and the tongue is flat rather than contracted in a pointed shape. Five times in succession, I then slowly protrude and retract my tongue in a rhythmical sequence, look at him quietly, and again record the tongue movements and other behavior patterns. While I am protruding my tongue, he stares at my face with immobile limbs. As soon as I stop he slowly protrudes his tongue seven times in an apparently deliberate fashion, all the while looking closely at my mouth. His lips are pursed and the tongue is shaped in a pointed form in the center of the mouth. Two minutes later, I again count two tongue movements during the control period and repeat the experiment. As soon as I stop, he makes four slow tongue movements while staring at my face. The tongue is again pointed and protrudes from the center of the mouth while the lips are half open and held still. Similar imitations are observed at twelve and fourteen days, but thereafter the response fades.

Similar observations on other infants were all consistent with the hypothesis that very young infants are capable of copying facial patterns which they have probably never seen on themselves in the mirror. Twelve infants from the longitudinal study were therefore tested systematically while alert and active during the first hour after the meal. The experiment was always limited to five minutes to reduce the possibility of training effects, and parents were explicitly asked not to play similar imitation games in my absence. After infants were placed in a semi-reclining position, I presented my relaxed immobile face for a one-minute control period and scored the number and types of tonguing or mouthing movements, smiles and vocalizations, by a protocol described in detail below. At the end of the control period I protruded and retracted my tongue five times in succession, and again scored the infant's facial movements for one minute, using the same categories as before. After a two-minute delay, the procedure was repeated.

In the first month, only two infants responded with increased tonguing to the model. In the second and third months, seven of the other ten infants also showed a systematic increase of tonguing in response to the model (p < .01 for the whole group, by Wilcoxon signed-ranks test). The imitation effect could be demonstrated more clearly when the tongue protrusions were subclassified to distinguish apparently random mouthing activity, in which the tongue was flat rather than shaped, from midline tongue protrusions, in which the lips were pursed and the tongue was shaped to a point. The latter type was observed only in response to the model, whereas the flat and random tongue movements were observed as often after as before a presentation of the model. The frequency of tonguing movements was also significantly greater during the second than the first control period. Since the initial exposure to a model may have primed the infant's tonguing activity, the first experimental trial in any imitation experiment may provide the most reliable and least contaminated results.

The peak period in development for tongue imitations differed considerably across babies. One infant showed the phenomenon clearly between seven and ten days, while others exhibited it most clearly between twenty-three and fifty-two days. In all twelve infants the effect had disappeared by seventy days.

Head-Rolling to Make a Spectacle Last. In a preceding section describing "transitional objects," I described the behavior of one infant, K. F., who rolled his head to the left and right of the body axis after watching the oscillations of a wire figure suspended above his head. The head-rolling usually began when the pendular movements of the wire figure came to a halt. The infant's body was at a sixty-degree angle to the wall in the supine positions, so that the axis of his head movements differed distinctly from the axis of oscillations made by the wire figure. In other words, his head rotations did not actually prolong the spectacle in a circular reaction, although the motor response suggested something akin to the other precocious imitations.

At sixty-seven days, K. F. is alert and active on the kitchen table. When I start the black figure oscillating, he stops moving and looks with great interest at the figure. As the latter slows down but before it has come to rest, he begins to roll his head from side to side with vigor, and I count at least twelve lateral head oscillations before he resumes his former level of activity. When I restart the oscillations of the figure, all his limb activity stops and he watches with great interest. As the figure slows down, he again rolls his head back and forth vigorously. This sequence can be repeated ten times over half an hour with little variation. As long as the figure is swinging in a full arc, he stares intently. As it slows down he rolls his head laterally or, rarely, up and down, as if nodding, although these efforts are clumsy and unconvincing. This phenomenon can be reproduced at weekly intervals until the end of the third month, when observations on this child are stopped.

Assuming that lateral head-rolling is another instance of pseudo-imitation, I introduced similar black wire figures into two other homes, and requested parents to hang the figure on the wall above the baby's head in a room where the infant spent most of the day. I also asked them to make the figure move back and forth intermittently, when the infant was both happy and fussy, but withheld any information about my reasons for doing the experiment until afterwards. Once the infants had been familiar with the wire figure for at least two weeks, I made systematic observations.

At fifty-two days, D. R. is lying on the kitchen table in an arrangement similar to the one described for K. F., kicking his legs, blowing bubbles with his saliva, and gurgling intermittently. I give the wire figure a push and all his activity stops while he stares with fascination at the moving figure. His eyes can be seen to follow the trajectory of the black figure back and forth in smooth pursuit. When the figure stops, he stares for five seconds and rolls his head vigorously back and forth four times. When nothing further happens, he loses interest and returns to his former activities. A week later, I repeat the experiment while he is fussy. He immediately quiets down, and tracks the oscillating figure; when it stops moving, he smiles, and rolls his head six times slowly and rhythmically, but then starts to fuss. At sixty-seven days, the experiment is repeated while he is alert, and he makes seven slow rhythmic head-rolling movements. This time head-rolling is accompanied by smiling and intermittent noncry vocalizations.

A third infant never responded to the figure with similar head-rolling movements, although the figure provoked great interest and a transient arrest of all random activities.

Cross-sectional Observations of "Pseudo-imitation" for Tongue Protrusion

Tongue protrusion would, if it could be persuasively demonstrated as a real phenomenon, constitute the most dramatic instance because it raises the puzzling question of the process by which the infant links what it does with what it sees, when it has no opportunity to observe its own action. Mrs. Dorothy Marcus and I therefore carried out an exploratory study of an imitation of tongue movements which may simply be another attempt to replicate findings reported by others.

The study sample comprised fifteen healthy infants born after uneventful pregnancies who were neurologically normal at birth. They were all studied when they were between four and seven weeks old, and they were brought to the laboratory by their mothers at a time during the day when, according to prior experience, they would be most likely to be awake and alert. When necessary, testing was postponed until the infant was in an optimal behavioral state. Five of the infants were eliminated from the study because they were fussy or drowsy throughout the examination, and the final sample included six girls and four boys.

Methods. Infants were accompanied to the laboratory by their mothers and placed in an infant seat set in a reclining position (45° angle). The experimenter or the mother, who sometimes served as the experimenter, stood directly before the infant and operated a control button which activated a light behind and above the infant's seat to indicate whether or not the infant was making a direct eye-to-eye contact with the observer. Two video cameras were placed so that one focused directly on the infant's face and upper torso, while the other focused on the experimenter. Images from the two cameras were projected together on a split screen and a timed signal at the bottom of the screen indicated the duration of each trial in minutes and seconds.

Procedure. Before the start of the experiment, the experimenter stood quietly in front of the baby, speaking softly and reassuring but not touching the infant, while making eye-to-eye contact. This "control period" lasted for two minutes. Thereafter the experimenter protruded her tongue five times in a slow continuous motion so that the tongue protrusion lasted for a total of ten seconds; the responses were scored for the next sixty seconds.

Coding. The videotapes were scored for mouthing activity either with both halves of the screen showing or with the image of the experimenter's mouth movements occluded. Independent judges were used to determine whether seeing what the model did biased the scoring of the infant's activity. Mouthing responses were scored in five categories as:

1. Mouth open with tongue visible inside the open mouth.
2. Lips loosely pursed and mouth slightly open with tonguing visible, moving towards the lips or touching the inside rim of the lips but not protruding beyond the mouth-opening.
3. Pursing of the lips without visible tonguing.
4. Definite protrusion of the tongue outside the lips with mouth open.
5. Lips pursed and partially open with definite tonguing movements protruding beyond the boundaries of the lips.

The number of mouthing types observed throughout the one minute were scored for the control period (divided by 2 to control for differences in duration of observation time) and compared under the control and experimental conditions.

Results. Three independent observers, two of whom saw only the infant's image, while the other observer saw the full screen showing

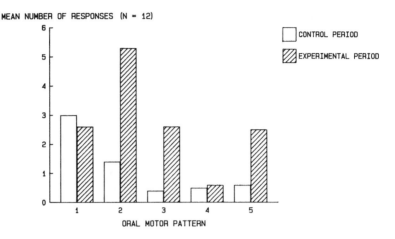

Figure 32: Imitation of Tongue Protrusions; Cross-sectional Sample

both partners, scored the video tapes for tongue imitations and other motor patterns. Interobserver reliability was satisfactory (0.90+ for categories 2, 3, 4, and 5; 0.75 for category 1). As figure 32 indicates, the model generated a significant increase of lip pursing with the moving tongue visible (category 2) or with the tongue not visible (category 3; $p < .02$; $p < .03$, respectively), as well as tonguing movements outside the lips ($p < .02$). There was no significant effect on nonspecific mouthing movements (category 1) or on flat-tongue movements outside the mouth (category 4). The most pronounced effect was on "pointed" tongue movements outside the lips while the mouth was pursed (category 5; $p < .008$).

Such observations call attention to a dimension in early human behavior that cannot be adequately explained by extant theories of psychological development. The concept of innate releaser mechanisms fails to account for the flexibility of variations in precocious imitation relative to experimental changes in the form of the model, which have been reported by others (Meltzoff and Moore 1977). Explanations in terms of conditioning and contingent reinforcement are critically challenged by the unlikely event that four-to-seven-week-old infants have practiced sticking out their tongues in front of the mirror, or that they have been "reinforced" by a social partner. In fact, mothers whose infants clearly exhibited the phenomenon reported that they had never played such a game with their infants. They were amused by the question since the possibility of tongue imitations at this age had never occurred to them. The alternative hypothesis that the alleged imitations are simply diffuse movements in response to heightened arousal are similarly called into question by reports concerning the form-specificity of the precocious imitations.

Summary

Comprehensive theories of human social development generally assume that the naive infant's relations to persons differ categorically from the infant's relations to physical objects. Ethology and sociobiology have focused exclusively on the infant's earliest social and emotional ties to the social partner. They assume that biological mechanisms for the control of social behavior differ qualitatively from those for instrumental behavior, but they have never actually investigated the infant's relationship to physical objects. Comprehensive theories of intellectual development have focused primarily on the infant's veridical relation to objects in the real world, whether the term "object" refers to persons or things. Some cognitive developmental theories further assume that social-emotional development depends exclusively on the development of cognitive structures, whereas other theories have not addressed the question explicitly.

From free field observations and informal experiments summarized in the preceding sections, I concluded that neither a strictly cognitive nor a rigorously "sociobiological" theory of emotional development are adequate points of departure for empirical studies on the infant's differential relation to persons and things. Both formulations start with primitive categories that beg the question, instead of recognizing the need for its empirical investigation. For the same reason, I assumed that it would be unproductive to subdivide the phenomena of early behavioral adaptation into one major category pertaining to social-affective behavior and another pertaining to cognitive development, as if these were autonomous domains from the start which remained invariant throughout development. On the basis of observations, I concluded instead that either the two "developmental lines" emerge from a common matrix of organism-environment interactions or behavioral forms which are later categorized as cognitive or affective adaptations cannot be so classified during the early months after birth.

The latter alternative is supported by observations on the critical interdependence between waking behavioral states and the particular emotional expressions manifested during social transactions. A priori distinctions between the infant's relations to persons and things were blurred as soon as the essential transfer function of waking behavioral states was taken into account. The conventional distinction between social-affective transactions with persons and cognitive actions on things is probably not self-evident even in children and adults. What appear to be logical, objective rules of cognitive adaptation turn out in practice to be idealized abstractions that hold only during brief periods under optimal circumstances. In everyday adaptations, waking states and their fluctuations frequently alter the substance of apparently logical and invariant actions on objects, persons, and ideas qualitatively, although the discontinuities in function are less dramatic than in the young infant. By the same token, what appear to be idiosyncratic patterns of social-affective behavior may, under the concept of waking behavioral states, be susceptible to systematic investigation, for which one does not have to depend exclusively on introspection, clinical intuitions, or specialized training in the interpretation of private meanings.

5

Conclusions

Three major themes emerged from the earlier discussions that inter-
sect with many topics of empirical research in child development
which are currently under active investigation. When considered as
parts of a larger framework, the themes also raise broader theoretical
issues that are relevant for all the developmental and historical sciences, although they are rarely discussed within developmental psychology proper. This concluding section therefore affords an opportunity to pull together loose threads from preceding chapters;
to integrate the findings under a comprehensive psychobiological
frame of reference; and to outline some programs of behavioral research on early human behavior that would be congruent with generic principles of psychobiological development.

The themes in question were:

1. *Behavioral states,* as mutually exclusive ensembles of motor
patterns and physiological variables that contribute critically to the
nonlinearity of input-output relations between organism and environment, as well as to the asymmetric distribution of spontaneous
motor actions.

2. *Expressions of emotion,* as motor patterns that alert the social partner to the infant's physical and social needs, and presumably
promote their common nonverbal transactions.

3. *The infant's relations to inanimate things and persons,* as a
point of departure for investigating the differentiation of, and differences between, social-emotional and cognitive domains of mental
functioning during infancy.

Each theme in its way raised questions about the processes of
developmental induction and ontogenetic transformations that remain essentially unresolved in all the developmental sciences. For

example, by what mechanism are novel behavioral forms and functions induced from antecedent conditions which do not contain such properties (Gottlieb 1976)? Within what limits can the whole be considered as greater than the sum of its parts (Weiss 1955, 1967)? In what sense can later developmental forms be said to possess properties that are not present in their constituent antecedents? How is it even possible to think rationally about development as a constructive process without inadvertently reintroducing autonomous central executives or nativist principles that prescribe a priori all the essential adult qualities in a hierarchic top-down control mode; or without assuming that all adult qualities are produced by the shaping effects of an arbitrary but omniscient environment?

Naturalistic observations of young infants in their homes, even when supported by informal experiments, are obviously not sufficient to draw firm conclusions about any of these larger theoretical issues, but they do provide a baseline of empirical observations from which we can propose research programs on early human development that would not follow from more conventional perspectives.

The Induction of New Behavioral Forms

Current studies of infants use the state concept as a descriptive taxonomy for ordering what otherwise appear to be random collections of movement patterns, capricious fluctuations of physiological variables, and unpredictable responses to environmental stimuli. Despite residual technical controversies about the definition and classification of behavioral states, many laboratories have independently arrived at the same four or five mutually exclusive organismic conditions as the minimum, and probably the optimum, number of behavioral states for describing and ordering spontaneous and event-related motor activities of young infants. In this sense, the state variable has proven invaluable as a tool for the clinical assessment of normal and high-risk infants. It has also provided an empirical basis for redirecting normative infant research from a preoccupation with reflexes, learning paradigms, and environmental manipulations to a perspective that recognizes the internal dynamics of the organism as essential factors in adaptation and development.

The concept of behavioral state has sometimes also been used to connote the surface manifestations of underlying organizational principles of human brain-behavior interactions, and as a theoretical basis for investigating the nonlinearity of input-output relationships (Prechtl 1974; Wolff 1984). In this latter sense I defined behavioral states as functional properties of the organism that emerge from a sufficient density of interactive components (physiological measures and sensorimotor patterns), to induce dynamically stable self-organizing conditions. Of all the logically possible combinations among state variables of the infant, only a small number of dynamically stable and mutually exclusive combinations are predictably observed in healthy infants; these were defined as behavioral states. From this definition it should also follow that state changes will not be smooth transitions or linear processes, but discontinuous jumps accompanied by qualitative changes of input-output relationships. Such an inference is, in fact, congruent with most investigations on state transitions and input-output relations in human infants (Theorell et al. 1973; Prechtl 1974; see also above). Each behavioral state was therefore assumed to represent a unique ensemble of component variables scaled at particular parameter prescriptions, whose "transfer function" or input output relations change discontinuously, rather than continuously, with state transitions.

This conception of behavioral states borrows extensively from formal statements about the irreversible thermodynamics of open biological systems (von Bertalanffy 1968; Katchalsky et al. 1974; Kugler et al. 1982; Szentagothai 1984; Prigogine and Stengers 1984), although concrete application of this conception to biological phenomena has, for the most part, been limited to simple systems where many of the critical variables can be rigorously controlled. In the case of direct observations and experiments on intact human infants, by contrast, such conditions can rarely if ever be met. Therefore, formal concepts such as *self-equilibrating systems* were used throughout as metaphors rather than as explanatory models. However, even in this restricted sense, the metaphor proved useful as a reference point for addressing some of the enduring theoretical problems on developmental induction and structural transformations that are common to all the historical sciences. Moreover, it allowed me to organize unobtrusive observations and experiments under a coherent psychobiological frame of reference that differs in principle from traditional and more widely accepted perspectives, which have not dealt effectively with the inherent problems of development as a transforming process.

For example, the proposed metaphor provided a means for examining the development of early behavior, without relying in circular fashion on a priori "ghosts in the machine," genomes, central neural programs, and maturational timetables, in order to "explain" by rational argument exactly those developmental phenomena that must be investigated empirically if we are ever to resolve the enduring problem of developmental induction. The concept of self-organization has long been applied to developmental issues by theoretical biology (Eigen 1971), embryology (Waddington 1969), experimental neurology (Purvis and Lichtman 1985; Szentagothai 1984), as well as by theories of motor coordination in normal adults (Kugler et al. 1982). In each case, the concept was introduced to account for those ontogenetic transformations in which an almost infinite number of independent degrees of freedom must be controlled, but where no a priori prescriptive program could possibly anticipate all the finer details of form and function (Changeux 1980).

Fifty years ago, von Bertalanffy (1933, 1968) had already identified the need for a theoretical biology based neither on a machine metaphor nor on the assumption that behavior is constructed from the summation of elementary units and properties, reflex arcs, reflex centers, brain loci, etc., reacting linearly and exclusively to extrinsic impulses. With the formulation of mathematical tools of sufficient power to model nonlinear physical and biological systems (Prigogine 1980; Thom 1972), it also became possible to explore many of the unresolved conceptual problems raised, for example, by investigations into the mechanisms of developmental genetics (Lewis 1978), enzyme interactions in biochemical solutions (Eigen 1971), the functional integration of physiological functions (Yates and Iberall 1973), and the construction of neuronal networks during early ontogenesis (Easter et al. 1985; Edelman 1984). The same models should, in principle, be applicable to the investigation of behavioral development in human infants (Piaget 1975). However, the methods of data collection on normal human infants are still too imprecise to determine whether such models of development can in fact be applied in more than a metaphorical sense.

The Spontaneity of Behavior

Behavioral states, state transitions, and the emergence of new behavioral waking states were described in considerable detail on the premise suggested that a quantitative analysis of states and state transitions may be one concrete entry point for testing whether the model is, in fact, relevant in more than a metaphorical sense; whether it can be used, for example, for planning concrete experiments. The concept of self-organizing systems is intimately related to the concept of *spontaneous* motor activity. Neurophysiology and developmental neurology have long regarded spontaneous behavior to be a phenomenon eminently suitable for the experimental analysis of underlying biological mechanisms, without invoking gratuitous notions of vitalism (Weiss 1967; Jeannerod 1985). In fact, von Bertalanffy considered spontaneous behavior to be a defining criterion of all living organisms: "Spontaneous activity is the consequence of the fact that the organism is an open system being able to maintain a state distant from equilibrium and to extend existing potentialities either in spontaneous activity or in responding to releasing stimuli. Biological, neurophysiological, behavioral and psychological evidence equally show that spontaneous activity is primary; that stimulus-response is a repetitive mechanism superimposed on it. The organism is therefore not a robot or automaton, and originally holistic behavior becomes progressively but never completely mechanized" (1968).

Although the term "spontaneous" does not have the same connotation for the natural and cognitive sciences, the different meanings may share common theoretical assumptions (Popper and Eccles 1977). In previous chapters, for example, the term "spontaneous" sometimes referred to the observation that all normal and many pathological newborns and young infants exhibit discrete motor patterns which cannot be related to known exteroceptive stimuli, and many of which are organized in near-periodic sequences at base frequencies specific to each type of motor activity. Their periodicity was taken as a clue to their "spontaneous" causation. At the very least, it argues against the competing behaviorist assumption that all motor behaviors are reflex responses to exteroceptive stimulation, in other words, that they are responses to precisely timed environmental stimuli emitted at the appropriate intervals without any stimulus-response "cross-talk."

The conclusion that temporally ordered motor patterns sometimes occur as spontaneous phenomena does not exclude the possibility that the same motor patterns can also be elicited by exteroceptive stimulation. By varying the stimulus intensity to elicit the motor patterns in full-term infants in various behavioral states, I was able to show, for example, that motor patterns occuring most frequently as spontaneous phenomena in one behavioral state can also be elicited in that state as responses to the relatively lowest stimulus intensity, whereas greater stimulus intensities of the same kind are required to elicit the same motor pattern in other behavioral states where such motor patterns rarely or never occur spontaneously (Wolff 1959, 1966). The stimulus, instead of "causing" the response, apparently facilitated the production of motor patterns that can also occur as a spontaneous phenomenon. In the absence of known exteroceptive stimuli, the same motor patterns were probably induced by shifts in the internal dynamics of the interactive motor patterns, resulting in periodic instabilities, "catastrophes," or "bifurcations" (Prigogine and Stengers, 1984). In sum, the "spontaneous" causation of motor patterns does not differ in principle from its afferent causation. In both cases, behavioral state contributes an essential transfer function that renders input-output relations nonlinear. In both cases, transient perturbations, created either by the environment or from within the organism, are causally related to the provocation of the same "spontaneous" motor action or "response" to exteroceptive stimulation.

By excluding exteroceptive stimulation as the necessary and sufficient cause for all motor behavior, we have, however, not provided an adequate explanation for the causation of spontaneous or "epileptiform" motor activity (Weiss 1955). One hypothesis advanced for the causation of rhythmic or near-periodic motor patterns, holds that they are activated by central clocks discharging periodically to trigger episodic or near-rhythmic movements. Such clocks operate as relatively autonomous executive agents, but they can be updated periodically by peripheral events to come under partial environmental control (Strumwasser 1974).

Many enzyme systems function as rate-limiting variables on metabolic processes and may in this way influence the timing of complex behavioral functions, but their effect is likely to be an indirect vectorial product of many individual clocks operating concurrently and becoming mutually synchronized. Similarly, in the brains of various animal species neural cell aggregates have been identified whose only function seems to be to emit pulses at regular intervals (Sollberger 1965; Strumwasser 1974). They too may contribute to the timing of motor events. Again, however, they cannot be said to *cause* the periodic motor patterns in complex organisms, because the relevant nerve-cell assemblies are widely distributed across the central nervous system and function as pace-makers only by virtue of their dynamic interactions (Michon, 1967). More generally, the periodicity of spontaneous motor actions is probably an emergent property of collections of discrete oscillations each of which operates at a fixed frequency, and several of which acting in concert induce qualitatively new temporal patterns that are not represented in any single oscillator (Pavlidis 1973).

In earlier sections, I also used the term "spontaneous" to connote episodic coordinated motor patterns in waking infants, which would probably be called "voluntary actions" if they occurred in children or adults, although we are reluctant to attribute volition to three-month-old infants. These motor patterns were spontaneous only in the sense that they could not be systematically related to exteroceptive stimulation, but the influence of environmental events could never be excluded entirely because the actions were observed only when infants were awake, alert, and "open" to uncontrolled environmental events. Nevertheless, I applied the term "spontaneous" to these motor actions in order to suggest that there may be theoretically important conceptual links between the spontaneous activity that characterizes all living organisms (which was manifested in infants during sleep as discrete and near-periodic movement patterns), and the episodic goal-directed and apparently volitional actions of waking infants. Both appear to be internally caused, rather than driven as machine-like reactions to exteroceptive stimuli.

The distinction made here concerning various spontaneous and stimulus-elicited motor patterns in young infants can be illustrated, for example, by considering the ontogeny of smiling. The "cause" of spontaneous smiling in sleeping newborn infants is obviously different than the quasi-obligatory facial response of six-week-old waking infants to faces and voices. In fact, the latter might fulfill the criteria of a near-linear reflex response, if it were not for the essential modifying effect of behavioral state. By contrast, the smiling response of the four-month-old infant to the same social encounter is highly selective even within the same behavioral states. Sometimes four-month-old infants will smile to the socially adequate stimulus; at other times the same stimulus elicits no emotional expression, although the infant has evidently noted the event since it temporarily arrests ongoing activity or else responds with another appropriate social greeting such as vocalization. The four-month-old infant seems to be making "choices" of whether or not to smile, and in which way to acknowledge the encounter. While such choices are clearly not what is meant by volition or intentional action in the adult, they imply totally different rules of input-output relations than do the obligatory smiling response of the waking four-week-old infant. The apparent unpredictability of such motor actions in alert four-month-old infants may be causally related to variations in behavioral waking states. In other words, one might speculate that subtle fluctuations in waking behavioral states contribute in significant ways to phenomena we call volitional actions in older children and adults, which may be "volitional" in a similar sense in three-month-old infants.

As indicated earlier, the taxonomy of behavioral states appropriate for neonates was particularly inadequate for characterizing wakefulness in the one-to-six-month-old infant. Such inadequacies probably become more apparent after the first year of life, when subtle fluctuations in waking disposition may not be evident to direct observation but can nevertheless play a critical role in modulating input-output relations. A systematic developmental analysis of behavioral states, and of their presumed transfer functions in regulating organism-environment interactions might therefore provide an observational basis for investigating the development of "voluntary" actions, attention, and the like.

The concept of behavioral states as self-organizing conditions also implies a perspective on human brain-behavior relations that is usually accepted in principle by theories of psychological development but honored in the breach when it comes to planning observations and interpreting their results. This perspective holds that the central nervous system is always active in all of its parts, and that such (spontaneous) activity is always dynamically organized (for example, in terms of neuronal modules; Goldman and Nauta 1977). If this perspective portrays central nervous system activity accurately, the reflex concept can no longer be accepted as the self-evident basic building block for all complex behavior. Any discrete movement, action, or goal-directed behavior pattern that seems to conform to the laws of the reflex must in fact be the vectorial property of an environmental event superimposed on many neural and skeletomuscular elements interacting in one of a limited number of combinations that induce a behavioral state. Both discrete exteroceptive stimuli and internal "perturbations" can produce a dynamic shift in the far-from-equilibrium conditions referred to here as behavioral states, but neither of them *causes* the observed motor action (Kelso and Tuller 1983). Even in the waking adult, fluctuations in waking behavioral states may then contribute in important ways to voluntary actions in everyday situations, partly accounting for the "unexplained variance" of behavior under experimental conditions, although such state fluctuations will be less obvious to direct observation than in the young infant.

The Problem of Developmental Induction

Earlier I suggested that the induction of novel behavioral forms may be the single most important unresolved problem for all the developmental and cognitive sciences. Yet surprisingly little effort has been devoted to examining the problem empirically. Instead the problem is usually either dismissed as of no interest or else addressed by rationalist argumentation (Piattelli-Palmarini 1980). There is an almost unlimited body of experimental data demonstrating how environmental events can maintain or accelerate behavioral changes; and how the development of behavior can delay, degrade, or disturb the course of behavioral development. By contrast, there is little if any systematic evidence indicating how environmental mechanisms cause healthy organisms to proceed from a condition of primitive undifferentiation or chaos to a condition of greater order that exhibits properties and functions not observed in the antecedent condition (Gottlieb 1976).

Given the lack of carefully studied examples of developmental induction, and the absence of nearly adequate theoretical explanations for the phenomenon, one might of course conclude that induction is a pseudo-problem; that all later properties of the organism are anticipated as potentialities in the genome, and that these potentialities have only to mature to achieve their adult steady state (Monod 1972). The historical conflict between nativism or biological reductionism and organicism suggests that the controversy will not be resolved by currently available evidence. In fact, the tension between competing perspectives on induction has probably been more productive of new knowledge than any "final" solution. Each formulation leads to particular lines of investigation, and both are essential for resolving the many enduring theoretical issues in developmental biology, molecular genetics, and the development of behavior. Neither, however, has any ultimate claim on truth.

Extant theories of behavioral and psychological development have addressed or circumvented the problem of induction in so many different ways that any exhaustive review of the many competing solutions would go well beyond the intentions of this book. Yet there may be some profit in reviewing three generic solutions or "root metaphors" (Pepper 1946) within psychological theory as a point of departure for examining, for example, how novel behavioral states emerge, or are induced. At the same time, a brief review of extant solutions will demonstrate the need for a qualitatively different perspective on development which will address some of the unresolved theoretical problems in human developmental psychology alluded to earlier.

Preformationism or the nativist perspective on the origins of differentiated behavioral forms in the mature adult has reclaimed considerable lost territory in recent years. This renaissance was no doubt motivated by a renewed interest in Darwin's evolutionary worldview, the emergence of ethology as a distinct discipline, and of sociobiology as a popular although controversial "solution" to the induction of new behavioral forms (Wilson 1975). Renewed interest in nativism was probably also motivated by the dramatic advances in molecular genetics and the attendant expectation that the morphology, physiology, and behavior of complex organisms will ultimately be reduced to their elementary components, particularly to the remarkable characteristics of the nucleic acid molecules (Sheldrake 1981).

Traditional nativist perspectives on human behavioral development posited that the organism's species-typical capacities are represented as potentialities in the germ plasm, embryo, or fetus long before function or experience exercise any significant influence. The same a priori capacities, once embodied in the germ plasm, are now represented, instead, in the form of central neural programs, modules, or maturational timetables (Fodor 1983; Haroutunian 1983), and more recently in the genome and DNA sequences (Monod 1972). In each case it is assumed that the actual manifestations of behavioral structures and functions as well as their underlying "computational rules" or "operational principles" are prescribed a priori and remain essentially unaltered by experience. Experience can accelerate or slow down maturational rate; it can fine-tune the elementary behavioral forms; and it can trigger the maturational unfolding along one, rather than another, path. Neither experience per se nor the interaction of experience and biology induces novel principles of operation or new forms of behavior. Nativism appears to have an enormous strategic "advantage" in that it provides a simple and all-inclusive explanation for linguistic, cognitive, socio-emotional, moral, and aesthetic competence in the adult, and seems to eliminate the core problem of developmental inductions altogether. However, the power of this explanation is also its inherent weakness. Its major conclusions can neither be tested nor falsified. Particularly as a frame of reference for investigating phenomena that are generally attributed to developmental processes, it is therefore totally unsuitable since it treats the problem of induction as if it had been solved, which is clearly not the case.

A directly opposite solution to the origin of mature behavioral forms has traditionally been the environmentalist perspective and the explicit theories (including nontheories) of reflexology, operant conditioning, and instrumental learning theory based on this perspective. Relatively pure versions of the environmentalist perspective (of which only a few remain) assume that, except for a "biogram" of basic reflexes, the infant is infinitely plastic at birth; and that it can be shaped into almost any end product, as long as environmental contingencies are appropriately programmed. Watson, for example, proposed: "Give me a dozen healthy infants, well formed, and my own specified world to bring them up in, and I will guarantee to take any one at random and train him to become any type of specialist I want" (1928). Two decades later, Skinner proposed a similar program when he concluded that "From the point of view of scientific methods, the description of behavior is adequately embraced by the principles of the reflex" (1938, 1953). Using the reflex as the basic unit of all behavior, he then proceeded to show how complex behavioral forms can be elaborated by building progressively longer (and presumably more "complex") stimulus-response chains according to the laws of operant conditioning and contingent reinforcement. So much has been written about the logical contradictions and theoretical vacuity of these formulations as a basis for understanding the origins of human cognition, language, philosophy, morality, skilled motor action, and the like (Chomsky, 1959; Lehrman, 1971), that a review here would serve no purpose. Whatever may be the heuristic value of behaviorism as a method for controlling behavior in the laboratory or clinical situation—and it may be substantial— the general behaviorist program is of little help either in solving the problem of developmental induction or in clarifying the concept of behavioral states as self-organizing phenomena emerging under far-from-equilibrium conditions.

The developmental perspective that has been most often represented in contemporary theories of cognition, communication, language, and social-affective adaptation is probably the epigenetic-constructivist-interactionist point of view, even when it is not explicitly identified as such. It assumes that each organism is equipped at birth with a limited species-typical repertory of biological mechanisms which insure a species-typical line of development. In contrast to the nativist perspective, it does not assume that biologically given structures and functions ultimately determine the adult steady state, but rather that the organism acquires new information about the environment by acting on it, restructuring itself as it changes the environment. The qualitatively new forms and functions which appear during development are predictable constructions resulting from the interaction between antecedent structures, experience, and (specified or unspecified) invariant operating principles, and can therefore be analyzed systematically in terms of their antecedent conditions. The epigenetic perspective further assumes that each phase in development prepares the causal conditions for all subsequent stages; each stage actively integrates and transforms (or schematizes) prior acquisitions, and all earlier stages are progressive approximations of the adult steady state.

This perspective has probably been articulated in greatest detail under three comprehensive or "grand" theories of mental development that have served as the umbrella for most current clinical formulations and cognitive theories about normal and deviant development. These include Werner's comparative developmental approach (1947, 1957), Freud's classic psychoanalytic theory of the instinctual drives (Rapaport 1954), and Piaget's sensorimotor theory of operational logic (1975). Vygotsky's theory (1962) on the functional relation of thought, language, and society was unfortunately never elaborated in sufficient detail to justify any retrospective extrapolation here to the preverbal period of early infancy when language and cognition can not be clearly distinguished.

The three theories share an interactionist perspective on human behavioral phenomena that distinguishes them in principle from rigorous preformationist or behaviorist perspectives. They all posit that development is always totally determined by intrinsic biological structures or functions, and totally determined by experiences that transform the manifest structures according to their underlying operational principles. On the other hand, the three theories differ qualitatively in the domains of human adaptation which they emphasize, their basic assumptions about organism-environment interactions, their methods of data collection, and their canons for the interpretation of findings (see, for example, Wolff 1960). Nevertheless they provide the context for considering why an alternative or "fourth" solution may be required as a theoretical framework for investigating the induction of new behavioral forms in self-organizing systems.

Werner's formulation on development is probably not helpful for our particular purposes because it programmatically insists that the essential task of any developmental psychology is the *description* of developmental phenomena at various genetic levels, rather than their causal analysis, which is the proper task of other branches of psychology (Langer 1970); but the induction of new developmental forms (e.g., mechanisms of stage transition) is essentially a problem of causal mechanisms, and was therefore not addressed specifically. Yet, Werner's conception of developmental *stages* may be relevant in an indirect sense as a basis for discussing the induction of new behavioral *states*, even though behavioral states are never explicitly mentioned. The formulation conceives of developmental stages as hierarchically ordered, reversible dispositions of the organism that comprise a finite number of discrete and internally coherent ensembles of part-whole relationships. The more mature, as compared to the less mature, individual can shift back and forth among a relatively greater number of discrete levels of developmental differentiation: "Even if such states of consciousness as the dream are disregarded, the normal man does not always function on the same level of mental activity. The same normal individual, depending on inner or outer circumstances, may be characterized by entirely different levels of development—primitive modes of behavior in the normal adult not only appear under certain extraordinary circumstances but are constantly present as the basis of all mental being" (Werner 1957).

Formal analogies between *stages* of development and behavioral *states* may be relevant for this exploration in the sense that both refer to the organism's dynamic organization of behavior patterns as discontinuous ensembles of elements inducing functional properties and structural features that are not contained in any of the elements and could not be predicted from knowledge about their constituents. Both state and stage are also assumed to modulate qualitative changes in organism-environment interactions or input-output relations.

Piaget's sensorimotor theory sets itself the more specific task of explaining the ontogeny of operational logic as being constructed from relatively simple sensorimotor transactions with the physical environment. It specifies a finite set of a priori structures (reflex schemata) ready to function at birth but continuously transformed during development, and eventually left behind. It also posits invariant functions or causal mechanisms (assimilation and accommodation) that operate on and continually transform a priori behavioral structures throughout development, regulating the organism's interaction with an ever-expanding world of action potentialities. The invariant functions guarantee that at least under ideal circumstances mental development invariably achieves the mature steady state which is characterized by the theory as the acquisition of operational logic, that presumably represents the stablest and most nearly equilibrated interactions between the "epistemic" organism and its material and intellectual environment (Piaget 1975). An epigenetic-constructivist perspective is essential to Piaget's general hypothesis, insofar as novel mental structures are assumed to be elaborated during the course of sensorimotor actions on the world of concrete objects, rather than being specified a priori in the genome.

As in Werner's formulation, behavioral *states* have no specific conceptual status in Piaget's sensorimotor theory. On the other hand, the *stage* concept again implies hierarchic levels of organization among discontinuous ensembles of part-whole relationships. However, in contrast to Werner's perspective on development, the temporal relation among stages is elaborated into an explicit theory of invariant stage sequences which are irreversible except under pathological conditions of neurological differentiation. Piaget proposes equilibration as an explanatory mechanism for stage progressions (i.e., the induction of new forms and functions), but in any specific instance it is very difficult to infer how equilibration could induce novel properties which are not already given implicitly in the invariant functions themselves. In other words it is difficult to imagine how ensembles of schemas could possibly "know" which new feature of an object or relationship (i.e., the "aliment" that modifies the schema by a process of assimilation) must be assimilated at any moment, and how the schemata must change themsleves (by accommodation) to achieve a relatively greater equilibrium of organism-environment interactions that defines development.

Under the concept of the instinctual drives, psychoanalysis posited an intrinsic maturational factor that differs categorically from the inherent executives of development hypothesized by sensorimotor theory. The instincts were construed as mental representations of theoretically unspecified physiologic or metabolic mechanisms. These determine the human organism's essential relation to the environment and specify its selective relation to privileged objects or sources of drive reduction or gratification. Drives are thus construed as executive agencies acting on and organizing ideas (thoughts), actions, and affects, but extrinsic to the mental structures on which they operate. Therefore, although the concept of psychosexual stages, particularly Erikson's formulation of modality-specific developmental sequences, imply an epigenetic formulation of qualitative, discontinuous changes in psychological organization, the epigenetic-constructivist perspective is not an inherent characteristic of the "classical" theory. Instead, instinctual drives are conceived as immutable maturational factors or autonomous executives that operate on behavior, as it were, from the "outside," without being progressively transformed by experience.

On the other hand, clinical psychoanalysis has provided a unique body of observations that may provide important clues about the long-term developmental outcome of behavioral states as reversible dispositions or "part-whole relations" of mental processes (Rapaport 1951a,b). By the clinical methods of free association and the systematic investigation of dreams, psychoanalysis has collated a body of detailed observations on the variations in psychological content (meaning) that may be associated with altered states of consciousness, ego states, and affect states. These observations suggest that not only psychiatric patients but normal waking adults may alternate among two or more semistable and reversible ensembles of mental processes or reversible states that share organizational features with the behavioral states of infants.

More generally, the epigenetic-constructivist perspective on human behavioral and mental development has generated a rich body of findings that portray the human newborn infant in a very different light than that implied by rigorous behaviorism or nineteenth-century nativism (Stone et al. 1973; Osofsky 1979). Despite its explicit interactionist position, however, even this perspective has not entirely eliminated its nativist core or its ultimate appeal to a priori executive agencies that anticipate the direction and end-stages of mental development. To be internally consistent, the epigenetic component of this perspective must assume that some architectural ground plan has implicit foreknowledge of the general directions that the development of intelligence, language, skilled action, and social adaptation will follow in order to achieve the adult steady state; in other words this ground plan must be equipped with basic operating rules that can determine which experiences in the real world can, and cannot, direct development to the anticipated end-point. For example, Piaget's theory of operational intelligence principally rejects all nativist assumptions. Nevertheless, it reintroduces a priori concepts when it assumes that the invariant functions (which are presumed to be biological givens) assimilate only those functional properties of real objects that will equilibrate unstable schemas, and will accommodate such schemas in accordance with schematic representations of the objects (i.e., aliment) rather than the objects themselves, as might be the case of organic aliment or nutrients. How do the functions of assimilation and accommodation "know" prior to experience which aliments of objects (i.e., their functional properties) will further the overall scheme of intellectual transformations, unless these functions contain some vague outline of what a stable equilibrium of logical operations must look like?

In a similar sense, the intrinsic developmental factor in psychoanalysis (i.e., maturation), although never precisely defined, must contain foreknowledge of objects in the environment that will afford drive gratification, and of other objects in the environment that will afford partial or substitute gratification when the biologically given drive object is not accessible. Although psychoanalysis introduces the "accidental" factor of experience as the counterpart to the invariant forces of maturation, the influence of experience in determining what will become substitute objects for drive gratification is neither random nor accidental, as it might be in a behaviorist theory of drive reduction and reinforcement. The instinctual drives are assumed not to be promiscuous in their acceptance of any object as suitable for drive gratification. On the contrary, a considerable clinical literature in psychoanalysis describes in detail the sometimes bizarre mental transformations of drive objects that may be encountered in practice as sexual perversions, fetishes, dream symbolisms, and the like. These are not random representations which depend exclusively on accidents of experience. Their function as substitute pathways for gratification always depends on a variable of similarity, as well as on temporal contiguity with the need state, that directs behavior to certain classes of "objects" (persons, parts of persons, and symbolic representations of persons). In other words, the intrinsic maturational factor has built-in knowledge about the direction which development must take to achieve a psychologically healthy adult steady state.

When considering, and then rejecting, the various alternative solutions to the problem of developmental induction, I am assuming that any appeal to a priori autonomous central executive agencies, including those implicit to the epigenetic-constructivist perspective is ultimately unsatisfactory as a basis for "explaining" development. Further, I am assuming that it may be timely and appropriate to propose a very different perspective on developmental transformations and induction. As indicated earlier, the alternative perspective to be explored here has been applied with some success to problems in theoretical biology, physiology, morphology, genetic embryology, to the study of motor coordination, and more indirectly to problems in evolutionary theory that were not anticipated by Darwin (Gould 1977). Before examining the possible relevance of this perspective for the analysis of infant behavior, it may, however, be useful to consider some of the empirical data of experimental biology that motivated a radical shift in contemporary models of development, including the introduction of concepts such as irreversible thermodynamic processes in far-from-equilibrium conditions, spontaneity of behavior, and self-organization.

The epigenetic formulation on behavioral development assumes that *all* antecedent forms are incorporated into *all* later developmental acquisitions. Yet the empirical findings from recent advances in developmental embryology and developmental neurology indicate that developmental sequences which appear on the surface to be well-ordered ontogenetic progressions, often turn out on closer examination to consist of multiple arrests, deletions, regressions, the elimination of earlier behavioral forms, and the emergence of qualitatively new forms whose antecedents are by no means self-evident (Oppenheim 1981). In other words, as a universal description of all antecedent-consequent relationships during development, epigenetics is not tenable.

Experimental studies in embryology combining behavioral observations and neuroanatomical examination have demonstrated, for example, that a number of behavior patterns specifically adapted to fulfill essential functions during a limited period of early development are then deleted from the repertoire; and this deletion is closely correlated in time with the physical dissolution of corresponding neuroanatomical substrates by mechanisms of cell death and the like. Such anatomical-behavioral regressions are neither accidental nor functionally neutral. On the contrary, their failure to occur may interfere with the smooth progress of later development. For example, experimental manipulations to "prevent" such regressions (ontogenetic adaptations) can be shown to produce functionally competent neural pathways, which result in grossly maladaptive behavior (Schneider 1979). Although the majority of relevant experiments have been conducted on nonmammalian vertebrates, similar phenomena are known to occur in higher mammals, including humans (Oppenheim 1981).

Once it has been shown under controlled experimental conditions that at least some early behavioral forms with transient adaptive functions are not incorporated into later structures but eliminated as "ontogenetic adaptations" (Hamburger and Oppenheim, 1982), the epigenetic formulation is obliged to investigate which earlier structures and functions are, and which ones are not, incorporated into later developmental stages. In practice, this turns out to be a very difficult task, particularly in intact human infants where the crucial surgical experiments are out of the question. Consequently, one can never be sure which later acquired structures of human development are directly "caused" by antecedent conditions; which earlier forms are eliminated as ontogenetic adaptations; and which later acquisitions are the emergent properties from antecedent conditions to which they seem totally unrelated.

Both the epigenetic and the nativist solutions to developmental induction are challenged even more critically when we consider what kinds of mechanisms could possibly control the number of independent degrees of freedom that must be regulated during ontogenesis for any of the more complex organs of the body or mind to achieve its adult steady state. For example, by current cell-count estimates, the human central nervous system contains approximately 50×10^{10} neurons, and each neuron may be supplied with up to 10^4 dendrite connections. Without some organizational principle not specified a priori in the genes or a maturational timetable that can internally reduce the independent degrees of freedom in the system, development would, in effect, be "impossible." The human brain would have to regulate 10^{15} independent degrees of freedom in order to achieve the appropriate neuronal connections of the adult brain (Purves and Lichtman 1985). In addition, the a priori prescriptions would have to determine the timetables of cell migration, cell differentiation, cell adhesion, and cell death, as well as the continual rearrangements in neuronal networks that compensate for unexpected alterations in the brain's environment throughout early ontogenesis (Easter et al. 1985). By available estimates, there are, however, at most one million genes in the fertilized egg, and the number of "true" structural genes coding for proteins is estimated to be around 10,000–30,000 (Changeux and Mikoshiba 1978; Changeux 1980). In other words, there are not nearly enough structural genes to regulate the connectivity of the human brain, not to mention the structure of other organs and their interaction. How then can such a limited number of genes (3×10^4 at most) regulate the enormous complexity of the developing human nervous system (at the least 10^{15} degrees of freedom) without considerable assistance from processes that are not specified beforehand? The developmental sciences, particularly developmental neurobiology, have therefore turned to theoretical models that incorporate the concept of self-organization under nonlinear far-from-equilibrium conditions, as a possible clue to the degrees-of-freedom problem and to the induction of novel properties in biological systems.

An increasing body of experimental evidence from developmental neurobiology on the specificity of neuronal connections during early stages of brain development, for example, indicates that many of the essential central neuronal networks of the mammalian brain are not coded a priori either in the genome or in the neurons by genetically programmed mechanisms of cell recognition and chemoaffinity (Sperry 1963). Instead, one major organizing principle appears to be a continuous rearrangement of neuronal connections by cellular and molecular interactions which occur during, rather than before, ontogenesis (Weiss 1941, 1955; Szentagothai 1984; Edelman 1984). There is also strong evidence that the eventual configuration of central nervous system circuitry is determined to a large extent by chemical transactions during, rather than prior to, embryogenesis (Changeux and Mikoshiba 1978). Such transactions are highly *selective* but not necessarily *specifically* prescribed beforehand (Edelman 1984). While the dynamic patterning of neuronal connections must ultimately reside in regulatory genes that control cell differentiation, such control does not determine cell patterning. For example, cell adhesions due to the packing and physical proximity of individual elements may be more critical for the control of cell patterning than prefixed neural addressing by specific neuronal markers, each of which controls its own degrees of freedom. Similarly, competitive interactions in the formation of neural connections depends in part on the secretion of synaptogenic molecules that determine the survival of the innervating neuron, and therefore also the formation of axonal arborization patterns, thus imposing internal constraints on the number of independent degrees of freedom of cell interactions that are not prescribed a priori (Easter et al. 1985).

The most persuasive experimental demonstration of self-organizing neural networks comes from tissue cultures, in which the spontaneous activity of individual neurons can be recorded. By this technique it can be shown that neurons not only develop into physiologically competent units which respond to stimulation, but when aggregated as a group, they also construct functional linkages or neural networks which will generate *spontaneous* pulses periodically, when they are packed at a sufficient density to insure mutual interaction (Crain 1976). Even before there was a technology of tissue culture, related experiments on amphibian embryos were carried out, in which neural tissue fragments and limb buds were deplanted to foreign sites in the same embryo. Such experiments indicated that the deplanted limb bud can be innervated by motoneurons from the foreign neural tissue, and will eventually show coordinated, although totally nonfunctional, movements (Weiss 1955; Szentagothai 1985). Such movements are evidently not triggered by afferent stimulation, because the limbs are not innervated by afferent fibers. Nor could the deplants be activated by mechanical stimulation. Quantitative histological analyses of such experimental preparations indicate that neural deplants with as few as ten or twenty neurons are sufficient to generate spontaneous activity in the supernumerary (deplanted) limb (Szentagothai 1985). A sufficient density of elements capable of dynamic interaction (for example, as "limit-cycle oscillations") is therefore sufficient to prepare the conditions needed for the induction of novel functional properties with distinctive temporal characteristics. Some of the deplantation experiments, in fact, indicate that the patterns of motor coordination (interlimb coordination) can closely approximate "natural" patterns for motor activity (Brändl and Szekely 1973); but these coordinated movements can obviously neither be preprogrammed in the genome and DNA sequences, nor shaped by exteroceptive stimulation. Such experiments, and others like them, provide indirect but persuasive evidence for self-organizing tendencies of "dissipative" biological structures when the component elements (e.g., neurons) oscillate spontaneously in near-periodic sequences and become mutually synchronized.

This model, which is derived from experimental neurobiology, allows us to consider the phenomena of spontaneous and rhythmic motor behavior in sleeping young infants from a very different perspective that provides the basis for planning concrete experiments. For example, it should be possible to test the hypothesis that a critical density of coordinated motor patterns and physiological variables must be scaled within a limited range of parameters in order to coalesce as self-maintaining states; and to examine systematically how experimental alterations of parameter settings on essential variables (for example, changing respiratory rate with a body plethysmograph) will either enhance or diminish the self-equilibrating potential of a behavioral state when its stability is challenged by exteroceptive stimulation. Similarly, experimental manipulations of episodic and repetitive motor actions in the waking infant should help to define the organismic conditions under which infants can interact optimally with specific events in their environment (e.g., "attend"), and carry out two or more goal-directed activities at the same time. In one such experiment, for example, we found that *nonnutritive* sucking markedly enhanced the infant's visual pursuit or "attending" to a moving target (Wolff and White 1965; see also Bruner 1968). More generally, one might test the hypothesis that waking states become optimally stable when no single state-criterion is any longer essential to maintain the infant in an alert condition; when the number of potentially interactive sensorimotor patterns has reached a sufficient density so that the perturbation of any single "essential" state criterion or the provocation of a potentially disruptive motor pattern is no longer sufficient to disrupt the self-correcting tendencies of waking behavioral states.

This conception of states as self-organizing conditions also suggests a series of clinical comparison studies that might help to explain the instability of behavioral states, the unpredictability of state transitions, and the presumed deficiencies of "attention" in infants who are at higher than usual risk for developmental disabilities (Prechtl et al. 1973). Clinical studies indicate that the boundaries between behavioral states are less well defined in such infants, and state transitions more diffuse. At the same time the periodicity of state-related motor patterns such as respiration, nonnutritive sucking, and limb movements is significantly more variable, and two or more near-periodic motor patterns are less likely to become mutually synchronized (Wolff 1967, 1968a; Dreier et al. 1979). Assuming that repetitive motor patterns function as mutually synchronizing "limit cycle oscillators" (Kugler et al. 1982), one would predict that greater variability of any rhythmic or near-rhythmic motor patterns, as well as extreme fluctuations in nonperiodic state variables, will interfere with the stability of behavioral states, notably wakefulness. Consequently, high-risk infants should be more vulnerable to intrusions from the stimulus environment, and more susceptible to spontaneous or externally caused state disruptions, giving the clinical impression that they are "temperamentally" irritable, "slow to organize," or distractible. However, under the proposed perspective the causes for the clinical phenomena would be attributed to measurable variations in the co-ordering of motor patterns, rather than to ambiguous and often untestable etiological factors such as minor neurological dysfunction, brain damage, or attentional deficits.

The Expression and Development of Emotions

Observations on the expression of emotions in human infants confront us with similar unresolved questions about developmental induction, as did previous discussions on behavioral states, although in a different form. For example, are the basic or essential emotions programmed prior to experience, so that they require only intrinsic maturational processes and the triggering effects of exteroceptive stimulation to achieve their adult steady state? Is there, instead, a subset of "basic" or culture free emotions that are not present in the full-term infant and are constructed during ontogenesis? Should basic emotions be defined only in terms of patterns of motor coordination, while the associated or underlying feelings are constructed during social-cognitive development? In that case, by what mechanisms are innate motor programs and acquired cognitive structures integrated? On the other hand, if the term "basic emotion" encompasses feelings and motor expressions as a single entity, how does a

253

strictly evolutionary perspective account for the radical dissociation between feelings and expressions that may occur during development? By what process does the same motor patterns serve both as a direct expression of inner state, and as an instrumentality for deceiving the social partner by communicating emotions different from those experienced (Solomon 1983)?

Nativist theories of human emotions generally take Darwin's hypothesis as their point of departure, that emotions are essential adaptive mechanisms for survival of the species. They assume that humans, like other animal species, are endowed by evolution with a finite set of species-typical (basic) motor patterns, postures, and gestures from which the social partner extracts crucial information about the infant's internal condition and expectable actions in the foreseeable future. Since basic emotions are developmentally invariant, it follows in principle from this perspective that all the essential emotions of the adult can be identified in young infants.

The environmentalist perspective on emotional development need not be considered in any detail because the definition of emotional behavior under this perspective is so intimately tied to its global formulation concerning all behavioral forms, that emotions can hardly be distinguished from other learned stimulus-response patterns except by content. Yet emotional content has no meaning in the constraints of that theory.

The epigenetic-constructivist perspective on emotional development is most extensively elaborated in cognitive theories which assume that emotions are developmental constructions emerging in parallel with, and functionally dependent on, the construction of cognitive mechanisms. Emotions are always about something and directed at someone (Lazarus 1968), so that the development of emotions can only be examined as the product of a social-cognitive context that confers form and content on the emotions. What, exactly, emotions are or do in this formulation; or whether they can even be defined concretely as units of behavior, remains entirely unclear. One strong cognitive formulation of adult emotions, for example, summarizes the current status of cognitive theory as follows: "Emotions are generally conceptualized and studied as an organic mix of action, impulse and bodily experience, drives positive or dysphoric (subjective), cognitive, affective states and physiological disturbances" (Lazarus 1984). On the basis of this definition it would be virtually impossible to propose concrete experiments for making any selective study of those behavioral phenomena generally subsumed under the concept of emotions. Contemporary definitions and functional specifications of the emotions in early infancy are equally ambiguous (Sroufe 1982). In an exhaustive review of the literature on infantile emotions, Campos and his colleagues (1983), for example, stress the logical impossibility of defining emotions altogether, but then proceed to formulate a functional taxonomy of what emotions *do* rather than what they *are*. Specifically, emotions are assumed to "organize" perceptual, motor, cognitive, and social functions during development, but the means and mechanisms for achieving this monumental task remain theoretically unspecified. In effect, the emotions would have to replace the genome or the maturational time table as the central executive that contains all the basic computational rules necessary for differentiating cognition, perception, and motor action, not to mention their organization. Moreover, such an emotional executive would have to direct each of these domains of mental development to its anticipated adult end state. Thus emotions as organizers would become equivalent to the entire process of human behavioral development, again leaving it unclear what, exactly, the emotions "do."

Piaget has advanced at least three specific formulations about affectivity, but since they are in some senses mutually exclusive, it remains unclear which of the various formulations is most congruent with the central intent of his theory of intellectual development. In volumes on the sensorimotor period of intelligence (1952, 1954), for example, affects are most often discussed as units isomorphic with the sensorimotor and symbolic structures of intelligence. Affectivity represents the dynamic, valuative, or subjective dimension of every sensorimotor schema, that persists as long as the sensorimotor schema itself remains in a condition of relative disequilibrium and new affects or values are constantly generated as new coordinated sensorimotor patterns are constructed. Affects are therefore not construed as psychological structures with their own rules of developmental transformation.

Yet, in other passages, Piaget (1951) makes an explicit distinction between affective and intellectual schemata, defining affective schemata as adaptive structures that organize the infant's or child's "intimate permanent concerns of secret and often inexpressible desires" (in other words, ideas about the differences between the sexes, copulation, excretory functions, and the like): "Affective life, like intellectual life, is a continual adaptation; the assimilation [of affective encounters] give rise to affective schemes or relatively stable modes of feeling or reacting and continual accommodation of these schemes to the present situation" (1951). This account does not indicate what makes some experiences "intimate," what could be the origins for "permanent desires" within the constraints of his theory of motivation (see, for example, Wolff 1963b), how "private experiences" differ from public experiences, or by what mechanism the former are selectively organized under affective rather than intellectual schemata. Yet, these are precisely the enduring concerns both in psychology and philosophy for which psychoanalysis proposed detailed accounts in its clinical theory.

In still another discussion, Piaget proposes a very different formulation of affectivity and its development which may provide a theoretical basis for the empirical investigation of differences between intellectual and affective development in human infants (1956; see also below). In this third formulation, Piaget formally contrasts the individual's relation to physical objects or geometric relations in the real world that can be described by the mathematical language of logical operations, with the individual's affective relations to persons that always involve two independent psychological centers of causality. The latter always remain probabilistic (i.e., they are never equilibrated as logical structures), and their developmental analysis requires totally different mathematical models than those appropriate for describing the development of operative knowing (see also Wolff 1972b, 1985).

In this very cursory review I have tried to consider some of the ways in which selected theories of development have dealt with the enduring problem of emotions and their development, using three "root metaphors" to identify the main perspectives on the question. If the review is even approximately correct, it would appear that we have not made a great deal of progress in elucidating the ontogenesis of emotions and emotional expressions from a psychobiological perspective. Instead of attempting to formulate still another global theory of emotions, I will limit the discussion to what might be inferred from direct observations of infants in their species-typical environment, and focus on those features of early expressive motor behavior that are susceptible to empirical investigation in nonverbal infants who cannot tell us what they think, feel, or believe.

There is, for example, consensus that all human neonates are born with a limited repertory of discrete coordinated motor patterns which can be recognized by the social partner either as indicators of some underlying state or as social gestures (Leyhausen 1967). Whatever else expressions of emotion may be or do, they are also patterns of motor coordination. As such they can be objectively described in terms of physiologically and psychologically plausible units of motor function. Experimental investigations of complex patterns of motor coordination in humans and animals have made it clear that directly observable limb displacements are, from the perspective of motor coordination, only the tip of the iceberg. Visible movements are always codetermined by an extensive range of "underlying" variables of postural control, co-contraction of apparently unrelated muscles, motor synergies, and the like which all play an essential role as mechanisms of support and fine tuning (Belen'kii et al. 1967; Gel'fand et al. 1971) that is at least as important to smooth performance as the limb displacement itself. In principle, the same rules should hold for the motor coordination in infants, and by extrapolation for expressions of emotion. Yet the majority of studies of emotional expressions in infants have focused exclusively on the visible displacement of the facial muscles, assuming that since the human facial muscles have evolved specifically for the expression of emotions, the face should also contain all the essential information which allows the social partner to make the biologically relevant discriminations among various expressive patterns.

By contrast, Darwin's descriptions of emotional expressions in animals and man were by no means limited to a classification of facial expressions. Particularly in animals, they included detailed accounts of posture and movement in the limbs, trunk, and head as well of the face. Even in the human case, a kinesic analysis of facial muscles may therefore not be sufficient for the systematic functional investigation of emotional expressions as coordinated motor patterns. For example, crying, which is generally classified as an expression of emotion, involves not only a universally recognized facial grimace (cry face) and cry vocalization, but in a critical sense also respiratory movements, postural adjustments, and patterned limb movement (see also Stark and Nathanson 1973).

Even expressions such as smiling, which seem obviously anchored in the facial muscles, may nevertheless involve more widely distributed muscle ensembles that may provide a necessary context of coactivations. In the waking one-month-old infant, for example, smiling usually occurs only when the limbs are at rest, as if active limb movement and smiling were mutually incompatible. By contrast, the smiling of the three-or-four-month-old infant is frequently accompanied by rhythmical movements of two or more limbs, episodic action (e.g., reaching), and vocalization. When analyzed only in terms of the facial-muscle configurations, the smiling patterns at the two ages might appear to be identical, although even this assertion requires detailed investigation. However, when analyzed as "co-

257

ordinated structures" or "muscle collectives," the smile of the one- and four-month-old infants would probably be judged as being qualitatively different (Greene 1972; Kelso et al. 1981). The investigation of emotional expressions as coordinated motor patterns should also help to resolve the enduring debate whether smiling and laughter are qualitatively different expressions or merely variations of the same basic emotion manifested at different levels of intensity. As a pattern of motor coordination that involves respiratory, vocal, upper trunk and limb muscles, laughter obviously differs qualitatively from smiling.

More generally, the proposed perspective would predict that the various expressions of emotion, like various behavioral states, differ in the degree to which they are self-equilibrating or self-maintaining or else susceptible to environmental interventions. Anecdotal observations on infants, children, and adults alike indicate, for example, that hysterical crying or laughter are relatively self-maintaining and immune to disruption by exteroceptive perturbations, whereas emotional expressions that involve two independent centers of psychological causality, such as vocal interchanges between mother and infant, eye-to-eye contact, and precocious imitations are acutely sensitive to disruption by any changes in the sensory environment or in the timing of movements by the social partner (see also Fentress 1976). Finally, a formulation which treats emotional expressions as patterns of motor coordination may provide us with an important conceptual link between affective behavior and the behavioral states that leads directly to empirically testable hypotheses about the mechanisms which might be related causally to the critical state-dependence of emotional expressions.

Relations to Persons and Things

Assumptions made by theories of human behavioral development about the infant's relation to persons and things should, in principle, also define that theory's perspective on the structural-functional relations between intellectual and social affective development, i.e., whether the two domains of mental development are determined by different a priori structures, and follow autonomous pathways; or emerge from a common matrix. Instead, however, most theories of human behavioral development tend to emphasize one domain at the expense of the other. Consequently the young infant's relation to persons and things has rarely been compared and contrasted systematically under a coherent theoretical framework. Ethology for example, starts from the premise that evolution has provided humans with specific mechanisms for recognizing members of their own species, but it draws no parallel conclusions about the status of prefunctional structures for cognitive competence. Similarly, psychoanalytic formulations concerning the infant's relation to the external world are defined almost entirely in terms of the infant's relation to persons (drive objects), their part representations, or their acquired symbolic equivalents. On the other hand, the theory does not discuss in any detail the infant's or adult's specific relation to inanimate objects and geometric-physical relationships. Although psychoanalytic ego psychology proposed the preliminary model for such a formulation under the apparatuses of primary autonomy (Hartmann 1939), this was never elaborated or integrated as part of the "classical" psychoanalytic formulations. Moreover, no empirical observations on infants were collected from which one could infer what might be the particular psychoanalytic perspective on the infant's differential relation to persons and things.

By contrast, Piaget's sensorimotor theory compares the infant's relation to things and persons explicitly. It assumes that newborn infants possess no prefunctional mechanisms for distinguishing between persons and things but become aware of such differences as they elaborate the appropriate structures of sensorimotor intelligence (1952, 1954). Persons, like things, are initially experienced by the infant as objects of action. However, unlike things, persons come and go repeatedly through the infant's visual space, can be felt, sucked, grasped, heard, and tasted all at once. Moreover, they obey causal laws that differ in kind from those regulating physical things. In this way persons provide "aliment" for many action patterns at once, and are therefore differentiated from action earlier than physical objects, which may be the aliment for only one action pattern. The qualitative difference in causal characteristics between things and persons also confer on persons a special status of probabilistic relationships, whereas physical objects usually conform to stable physical laws that can be subsumed under the rules of operational logic. However Piaget's formulations were concerned primarily with the development of intellectual operations, and therefore did not draw extensively on observations from which one could analyze the infant's and child's privileged relations to persons that have been the primary focus of clinical psychological theories. Instead we must turn to focused observations of infants in their natural environment and experiments based on these, rather than relying on theoretical inferences, to examine what might be the qualitative or quantitative differences in the infant's relations to persons and things.

Four-to-five-week-old infants smile almost automatically to human faces, voices, or the combination of faces and voices, but they rarely smile to physical objects. This commonplace and perhaps trivial observation would suggest that humans, like the young of other mammalian species, are endowed by evolution with behavioral mechanisms for detecting the unique features of their species-typical social partner. Ahrens (1954), for example, reported that two-to-three-month-old infants smile systematically to flat pieces of white cardboard on which large black circles and lines representing the eyes and mouth parts were represented in the proper geometric orientation (see also Kagan et al. 1966). Infants became increasingly particular about the stimulus qualities to which they would smile, and in fact the oldest infants in the study smiled only to the "natural" three-dimensional face. This study has often been cited as strong evidence for innate releaser mechanisms and fixed action-patterns as the prefunctional basis for the infant's special social relationship to members of the same species. However, the species-specificity of such human innate releaser mechanisms, as well as its prefunctional invariance remain open to debate. The earliest smiles to the flat cardboard face models in the Ahrens experiment occurred at an age that was considerably beyond the age at which the home-reared infants first smile to the "natural" three-dimensional, mobile face, when they are still indifferent to the cardboard model or use it merely as an object for visual regard (see above; also Field 1979; Kaufman and Kaufman 1980). Thus the three-dimensional face may contain specific perceptual properties not present in the flat cardboard model, and it is unclear what are the critical variables of such an "innate releaser." For example, the heterogeneous summation of multiple stimuli may account for the observed differences between mobile faces and static models (Bower 1966) without invoking fixed evolutionary mechanisms that are specific to the geometric configuration of the human face. Moreover, the natural human face, unlike the cardboard model, is never static, and movement per se may be an essential clue for distinguishing between persons (animate objects) and things. Observations reported earlier indicate that, shortly after birth, the infant's gaze is selectively drawn to any object that moves, whether it is a human face or an inert object. By the age of one month infants begin to show a strong gaze preference for natural three-dimensional faces over inanimate objects, even when the latter are displaced while the former are kept steady, perhaps suggesting that social experience shapes differential behavior to persons and things by contingent reinforcement. On the other hand, even when the head is held still, the natural three-dimensional face is never immobile, so that subtle internal movements of the facial musculature and of the eyes may provide the critical information by which infants distinguish between persons and things. Such a conclusion, which is consistent with the results of our experimental comparison between natural faces and the same faces frozen by a clear mask as stimuli for eliciting smiling and vocalization (see also Papoušek and Papoušek 1982), also seems intuitively correct, since all of us use internal displacements of moving or static objects as one defining criterion for deciding whether something or someone is alive or not.

Along similar lines, the precocious imitation of gestures (or "pseudo-imitations"; Piaget 1952, 1954) such as tongue protrusion, might constitute persuasive evidence for the infant's prefunctional capacity to distinguish between persons and things (Meltzoff and Moore 1977). Studies on the imitation of tongue protrusion have been replicated by some investigators but not by others (Koepke et al. 1983). Moreover, according to some reports, the same imitation of gestures can be elicited by presenting infants with physical models which exhibit the same vectorial properties (Werner and Kaplan 1968). Therefore it has been suggested that there is nothing specifically social about the phenomenon of early imitation, in other words, that it is not imitation in any sense of social learning theory. While such experiments with physical models are interesting in their own right, they merely shift the level of analysis to a different plane, calling attention to the fact that there is nothing mysterious, or resistant to analysis, about stimulus properties which are uniquely human. The experiments do not eliminate the essential question of whether the naive infant is sensitive to specific qualities of the human partner, what those qualities are, and how they may contribute to the infant's differential relation to persons and things. On the basis of observations reported earlier concerning the infant's smiling responses to voices and other sounds, analogous questions can also be raised about the specificity of the infant's relation to the auditory human and nonhuman stimuli.

An extensive body of anecdotal and experimental observations supports the conclusion that naive infants respond selectively to persons over things, but the phenomenology has not been investigated in sufficient detail to clarify what are the structural and functional foundations for these earliest discriminations between persons and things, or between animate and inanimate objects, although answers to this question would be of central importance for any theory of cognitive or affective social development. The phenomena summarized above are probably too complex to admit any extreme sociobiological interpretation in terms of innate releasers and fixed action-patterns. At the same time, infants in all cultures and growing up under very different circumstances, as well as infants with significant neurological impairment, are able to make such discriminations with great consistency, so that the phenomena also do not fit under any purely cognitive interpretation.

A partial resolution of competing views may come from a more detailed consideration of the different kinds of emotional expressions that are observed in young infants and of their variable effect on the social partner. Motor patterns commonly classified as expressions of emotion, or nonverbal communication, or body language, and so on differ as greatly from one another in morphology and function as the emotional expressions differ from other kinds of motor behavior. Some emotional expressions, like crying, provoke an immediate, highly predictable, and almost automatic response from the social partner, but they are frequently caused by organismic variables and their onset does not depend critically on what the partner does. Other expressions, however, depend critically on a "turn taking" between at least two social partners; they never occur in a social vacuum, and they are usually not caused by internal organismic variables (Stern 1977; Trevarthen 1979; Papoušek and Papoušek 1982). Moreover, they are probably never seen as coherent motor patterns when the infant is alone, and cannot be meaningfully analyzed except as components of a larger action-context (Fentress 1982). A subset of motor patterns commonly identified as expression of emotions therefore exhibits properties that emerge only in a social context, and that necessarily involve at least two persons or two "psychologically independent centers of causality" (Piaget 1956). Typical examples of such "emergent" motor patterns seen during the first six months are eye-to-eye contact, nonverbal vocal exchanges, the imitations of gesture, and the laughter that results from tickling. Their "causation" and occurrence differ categorically from those of crying, not only because of their dependence on a cooperative social partner, but also because of their dependence on the precise reciprocal timing of action components contributed by each of the two or more partners (Kaye and Vogel 1980). The fact that the motor syntax resulting from such interactions cannot be reduced to stimulus-response sequences, transition probabilities, or simple Markov chains may be one crucial reason why "mother-child interactions" appear to be so difficult to study objectively. Such methodological difficulties are likely to persist as long as the appropriate units of analysis, i.e., the *interactants* or component motor patterns that emerge as coherent interactive patterns only when they are parts of a larger coordinated unit, have not been properly identified or codified in a coherent method of measurement (Lewis and Lee-Painter 1974; Brazelton et al. 1975).

Whether such social interchanges should even be classified as expressions of emotion, rather than as nonverbal communications, remains a disputed issue. On the other hand, the Platonic problem of classifying behavioral types and subtypes becomes irrelevant when we analyze expressions of emotion as components of "coordinative structures," shifting the focus of investigation from refined kinesic descriptions of the individual to an analysis of patterns of temporal integration among component motor patterns produced by the two independent centers of psychological causality (Wolff 1972b, 1981). Precisely this attribute of selected emotional expressions may then be a factor that contributes critically to the infant's growing awareness of differences between persons and things (see also Piaget 1956).

The Problem of "Meaning"

While theories of motor coordination provide important and useful units of measurement for investigating the *expression* of emotions in infancy, they do not address the topic which is probably of primary interest for cognitive, neurological, and particularly humanistic theories of psychology, namely, the "underlying" feelings and the "organizing" or disorganizing functions of affects on behavior. A study limited to observations of infants during the first six months is hardly the appropriate context for attempting to deal with this enduring problem. Nevertheless the observations summarized in earlier chapters may also provide an indirect entry point for exploring the "meanings" associated with expressions of emotion in early infancy.

For example, emotional expressions were found to be particularly sensitive to behavioral state. As proposed earlier, state and expression share organizational features when examined in terms of the coordination of motor patterns. Changes of behavioral state altered not only the probability and frequency but also the *form* or *quality* of emotional expression to the same social encounter. Assuming that each waking behavioral state comprises a partially unique ensemble of component variables, any social event (or for that matter, any "intellectual encounter") that elicits a particular motor expression with some consistency should also have a specifiable effect on the behavioral-state context in which the expressive movements occur. At the same time, the organizational characteristics of waking behavioral states should influence the particular form of emotional expression observed. Each behavioral waking state might then be construed as a framework that confers a somewhat specific functional significance (i.e., "meaning") on motor expression. Various behavioral states may confer several discontinuous but not mutually exclusive meanings on the same social encounter, at least to the extent that "meanings" can be inferred from the way in which the infant responds to a series of encounters in different behavioral states. Using a method of "stimulus equivalence" (Klüver 1965) to investigate the variations of emotional expression or nonverbal communication in response to an array of socially meaningful encounters in each of the differentiated waking states, one might then examine the meanings (in this restricted sense) conferred on various expressive movement patterns by virtue of their state dependence.

In parallel with the stabilization of waking behavioral states, the envelope of "meanings" inherent to each waking state is likely to increase its internal coherence and structural stability, so that state variations will predictably modulate the value or meaning attributed to any discrete action, as well as altering the nature of the transactions with persons and objects. However, only some of the behavioral states of the young infant are transformed during ontogenesis. Others, like sleep states, undergo relatively minor organizational changes (Roffwarg et al. 1966). Since states of wakefulness are fully represented in all normal adults, one would expect them to be most extensively differentiated during development. At the same time, waking states are perhaps the most immediately relevant as ontogenetic preparations for dispositions of the adult that are clinically classified as altered states of consciousness, moods, ego states, and affect states, although the hypothesized relation between behavioral states of infants and reversible dispositions of the adult (e.g., ego states) has not been systematically examined.

State and *stage* were categorically distinguished according to their different properties of temporal reversibility as contrasted with directional transformation. Yet, even during the first six months the behavioral states undergo directional developmental transformations, so that a taxonomy of behavioral states found to be sufficient for cataloguing discontinuous dispositions in newborn infants no longer sufficed for characterizing behavior in six-month-old infants; likewise, a taxonomy of states that is adequate for six-month-olds would presumably be grossly inadequate for characterizing behavioral states in five-year-old children or adults. Moreover, the initially orthogonal juxtaposition between reversible states and directional stage successions cannot be considered as developmentally invariant when we assume that the initially fluid composition over time of behavioral state ensembles achieves structural stability during the later growth years. Yet, even normal adults exhibit periodic fluctuations in disposition, mood, "contemplative" mode, action-oriented mode, emotional state, and the like that are totally reversible in any one person. Anecdotal accounts suggest that such fluctuating dispositions confer somewhat different contexts of meaning on the same experiences in a physically constant environment. However, the magnitude of presumed changes in "meaning" within state have rarely been examined systematically in normal adults, so that most of our information comes from clinical observations.

Experiments in state-dependent learning seem to bear some resemblance to what is proposed here, but in such cases the state variable is usually defined pragmatically in terms of arbitrary physiological conditions, drug effects, and so on, and there are no theoretical constraints on the number of different "states" that might be examined. Consequently the state concept, when used in this sense, loses its heuristic value as a term referring to self-organizing conditions whose dynamic characteristics are determined by the interaction among component functions and structures, and which regulates input-output relations. Yet, dynamic variables similar to the behavioral states of infants also regulate the organization of goal-directed action and thought throughout development, although their observable effects may be less dramatic and less discontinuous in adult life than during infancy. By extrapolating from the direct observations on infants, one might therefore expect an analysis of the variations in input-output relations associated with state transitions to become one means for investigating psychological meanings "from the outside" in adults as well.

The findings of this report have generated more questions than definitive answers. Nevertheless, they constituted the basis for a program of empirical investigations formulated in analytic categories derived from the phenomenology of infant behavior, rather than being imported categories from theoretical notions about behavioral organization in the adult. In this sense, the human "ethogram" becomes a point of departure for the causal analyses of behavioral categories that are relevant for species-typical development and adaptation.

More generally, behavioral states served not only as a unifying concept for ordering spontaneous and event-related sensorimotor patterns of emotional expression and goal-directed actions on things and persons; they were also a frame of reference for investigating the induction of novel behavioral forms and the self-organizing as well as self-equilibrating properties of behavioral organization in the infant. The preceding discussions imply that a developmental analysis of waking behavioral states over the growth years should, in principle, constitute one theoretical context for reconciling competing perspectives on the essential mechanisms of development. As suggested earlier, one of these perspectives assumes that development is ultimately controlled by extrinsic executives acting on behavior in a hierarchic top-down mode, and directing ontogenesis toward end states that are specified a priori. The other, which has rarely been applied to studies of human development, assumes that ontogenesis comprises a sequence of discontinuous "catastrophes" controlled in a heterarchic "bottom-up" mode and generating dynamically stable ensembles within the behavioral repertory. The formation of such ensembles is not controlled by extrinsic agencies that anticipate the developmental end states but by self-organizing processes. Since the latter do not necessarily or invariably move from a condition of relative disorganization to one of greater coherence, the finer details of human behavioral development may also be essentially unpredictable.

Both perspectives on development are probably useful and perhaps indispensable for investigating and explaining the phenomena of development at different levels of organization. Neither, however, is sufficient by itself. The proposed program of investigations may thus help to specify under what conditions the competing perspectives can be applied most productively. Further, the program provides a broader context within which complex psychological phenomena can be investigated in terms of biological mechanisms, and biological mechanisms explained by natural laws, without distorting such phenomena by reducing them to their constituent elements.

Bibliography

Ahrens, R. 1954. Beitrag zur Entwicklung des Physiognomie und Mimikerkennens. *Ztsh. Exp. Angew. Psychol.* 2, 412–54; 599–633.

Ainsworth, M. D. S. 1973. The development of infant-mother attachment. In B. M. Caldwell and H. N. Ricciuti, eds., *Review of Child Development Research*, vol. 3. Chicago: University of Chicago Press.

Allport, D. A. 1980. Attention and performance. In G. Claxton, ed., *Cognitive Psychology*. London: Routledge and Kegan Paul.

Ambrose, J. A. 1963. The age of onset of ambivalence in early infancy: indications from the study of laughing. *J. Child Psychol. Psychiatr.* 4: 167–81.

Anders, T., Emde, R., Parmalee, H. A., eds. 1971. *A Manual of Standardized Terminology, Techniques and Criteria for Scoring States of Sleep and Wakefulness in Newborn Infants.* UCLA:BIS.

Argyle, M. and Cook, M. 1976. *Gaze and Mutual Gaze.* Cambridge: Cambridge University Press.

Ashton, R. 1973. The state variable in neonatal research: a review. *Merrill-Palmer Quart.* 1, 3–20.

Baldwin, J. M. 1895. *Social and Ethical Interpretations in Mental Development.* New York: Macmillan.

Belen'kii, V. Y., Gurfinkel, V. S., and Pal'tsev, Y. L. 1967. Elements of control of voluntary movements. *Biophysics,* 12, 135–41.

Bergson, H. 1928. *Creative Evolution.* London: Methuen.

Berlyne, D. 1960. *Conflict Arousal and Curiosity.* New York: McGraw-Hill.

Bernal, J. 1972. Crying during the first 10 days of life and maternal responses. *Develop. Med. Child Neurol.* 14, 362–71.

Bernstein, N. 1967. *The Coordination and Regulation of Movements.* London: Pergamon.

Bertalanffy, L. von. 1933. *Modern Theories of Development.* Oxford: Oxford University Press.

―――. 1968. *Organismic Psychology and Systems Theory.* Barre, Mass.: Clark University Press.

Birns, B., Blank, M., Bridger, W. H., and Escalona, S. K. 1965. Behavioral inhibition in neonates produced by auditory stimuli. *Child Develop.* 36: 639–45.

Bishop, G. H. 1946. Neural mechanisms of cutaneous sense. *Physiol. Rev.* 26, 77–102.

Blurton-Jones, N. G. 1972. *Ethological Studies of Child Behavior.* New York: Cambridge University Press.

Boismier, J. D. 1977. Visual stimulation and wake-sleep behavior in human neonates. *Develop. Psychobiol.* 10, 219–27.

Bower, T. G. R. 1966. Heterogeneous summation in infants. *Anim. Behav.* 14, 395–98.

———. 1974. *Development in Infancy.* San Francisco: Freeman.

Bowlby, J. 1969. *Attachment and Loss.* Vol. 1. London: Hogarth.

Brackbill, Y., Adams, G., Crowell, D. H., and Gray, M. L. 1966. Arousal level in neonates and older infants under continuous auditory stimulation. *J. Exp. Child Psychol.* 4, 178–88.

Brändl, K. and Szekely, G. 1973. The control of alternating coordination of limb pairs in the newt (*Triturus vulgaris*). *Brain, Behav. Evol.* 8, 366–85.

Brazelton, T. B. 1962. Crying in infancy. *Pediat.* 29, 579–88.

Brazelton, T. B., Tromik, E., Adamson, L., Als, H., and Weise, S. 1975. Early mother-infant reciprocity. In *Parent-Infant Interaction.* Ciba Foundation Symposium, 33. Amsterdam: Elsevier.

Bridges, K. M. B. 1932. *The Social and Emotional Development of the Pre-school Child.* London: Kegan Paul.

Bronson, G. 1965. Hierarchical organization of the central nervous system. *Behavioral Science.* 10, 7–25.

Bruner, J. S. 1968. *Processes of Cognitive Growth: Infancy.* Worcester, Mass.: Clark University Press.

Bühler, C. and Hetzer, H. 1928. Das erste Verstandniss für Ausdruck im ersten Lebensjahr. *Z. Psychol.* 107, 50–61.

Buytendijk, F. J. J. 1950. The phenomenological approach to the problem of feelings and emotions. In M. L. Reyment, ed., *Feelings and Emotions: The Mooseheart Symposium.* New York: McGraw-Hill.

Campos, J. J., Barrett, K. C., Lamb, M. E., Goldsmith, H. H., Stenberg, C. 1983. Socioemotional development. In P. H. Mussen, ed., *Handbook of Child Psychology.* Fourth Edition. New York: Wiley.

Capute, A. J., Accardo, P. J., Vinning, P. E. G., Rubenstein, J. E., Harryman, S. 1978. *Primitive Reflex Profile.* Baltimore: University Park Press.

Carmichael, L. 1970. The onset and early development of behavior. In P. H. Mussen, ed., *Carmichael's Manual of Child Psychology.* Third edition. New York: John Wiley.

Casaer, P. 1979. *Postural Behaviour in Newborn Infants: Clinics in Developmental Medicine.* London: Heinemann.

Changeux, J. P. 1980. Genetic determinism and epigenesis of the neuronal network: is there a biological compromise between Chomsky and

Piaget? In M. Piattelli-Palmarini, ed., *Language and Learning.* Cambridge, Mass.: MIT Press.

Changeux, J. P. and Mikoshiba, K. 1978. "Genetic" and "epigenetic" factors regulating synapse formation in vertebrate cerebellum and neuromuscular junction. *Prog. Brain Res.* 48, 43–66.

Chomsky, N. 1959. A review of Skinner's *Verbal Behavior. Language* 35, 26–28.

Cicchetti, D. and Sroufe, L. A. 1978. An organizational view of affect: illustration from the study of Down's syndrome infants. In M. Lewis and L. Rosenblum, eds., *The Development of Affect.* New York: Plenum.

Cobb, S. 1950. *Emotions and Clinical Medicine.* New York: W. W. Norton.

Corman, H. H. and Escalona, S. K. 1969. Stages of sensorimotor development. *Merrill-Palmer Quart.* 15, 351–61.

Crain, S. M. 1976. *Neurophysiological Studies in Tissue Culture.* New York: Raven Press.

Crook, C-K. and Lipsitt, L. P. 1976. Neonatal nutritive sucking: effects of taste stimulation upon sucking rhythm and heart rate. *Child Develop.* 47, 518–22.

Crystal, D. 1980. Prosodic development. In D. Fletcher and M. Garman, eds., *Language Acquisition.* Cambridge: Cambridge University Press.

Darwin, C. R. 1873. *The Expression of Emotions in Man and Animals.* London: Murray.

———. 1877. A biographical sketch of an infant. *Mind* 2, 285–94.

Dawkins, R. 1976. Hierarchical organization: a candidate for ethology. In P. P. G. Bateson and R. A. Hinde, eds., *Growing Points in Ethology.* Cambridge: Cambridge University Press.

Dennis, W. 1934. A description and classification of the responses of the newborn infant. *Psychol. Bull.* 31, 5–22.

Dennis, W. and Dennis, M. G. 1937. Behavioral development in the first year as shown by forty biographies. *Psychol. Rec.* 1, 349–61.

De Rivera, R. 1977. A structural theory of emotion. *Psychol. Issues.* Monograph. 40, New York: International Universities Press.

Dittrichová, J. and Lapačkova, V. 1964. Development of waking states in young infants. *Child Develop.* 35, 365–70.

Dreier, T., Wolff, P. H., Cross, E. E. and Cochran, W. D. 1979. Patterns of breath intervals during non-nutritive sucking in full-term and "at risk" preterm infants with normal neurological examinations. *Early Human Dev.* 3/2: 187–99.

Easter, S. S., Purves, D., Rakic, P. and Spitzer, N. C. 1985. The changing view of neural specificity. *Science* 230: 507–11.

Edelman, G. M. 1984. Modulation of cell adhesion during induction, histogenesis and perinatal development of the nervous system. *Ann. Rev. Neurosci.* 4: 339–77.

Eibl-Eibesfeldt, I. 1970. *Ethology, the Biology of Behavior.* New York: Holt, Rinehart and Winston.

Eigen, M. 1971. Self-organization of matter and the evolution of biological macromolecules. *Naturwissenschaften.* 58: 465–523.

Eisenberg, R. B. 1976. *Auditory Competence in Early Life: The Roots of Communicative Behavior.* Baltimore: University Park Press.

Ekman, P., ed. 1979. *Darwin and Facial Expression: A Century of Research in Review.* New York: Oxford University Press.

Ekman, P. and Friesen, W. V. 1978. *Facial Action Coding System.* Palo Alto, Calif.: Consulting Psychologists Press.

Emde, R. N. and Koenig, K. 1969. Neonatal smiling and rapid eye movement states. *J. Amer. Acad. Child Psychiat.* 8, 57–67.

Emde, R. N. and Harmon, R. J. 1972. Endogenous and exogenous smiling systems in early infancy. *J. Amer. Acad. Child Psychiat.* 11, 77–100.

Emde, R. N., Swedberg, J. and Suzuki, B. 1975. Human wakefulness and biological rhythms after birth. *Arch. Gen. Psychiat.* 32, 780–83.

Emde, R. N., Gaensbauer, T. J., Harmon, R. J. 1976. Emotional expressions in infancy. *Psych. Issues Monogr.* Series X. New York: International Universities Press.

Erikson, E. H. 1950. *Childhood and Society.* New York: Norton.

Fantz, R. L. 1966. Pattern discrimination and selective attention as determinants of perceptual development from birth. In A. H. Kidd and J. L. Rivoire, eds., *Perceptual Development in Children.* New York: International Universities Press.

Fentress, J. C. 1976. Dynamic boundaries of patterned behavior: interaction and self-organization. In P. P. G. Bateson and R. A. Hinde, eds., *Growing Points in Ethology.* Cambridge: Cambridge University Press.

———. 1982. Ethological models of hierarchy and patterning of species-specific behavior. In E. Satinoff and P. Teitelbaum, eds., *Handbook of Neurobiology: Motivation.* New York: Plenum.

Field, T. 1979. Visual and cardiac responses to animate and inanimate faces by young term and preterm infants. *Child Develop.* 50: 188–94.

Flavell, J. H. 1963. *The Developmental Psychology of Jean Piaget.* Princeton: Van Nostrand.

Fleming, P. J., Goncalves, A. L., Levine, M. R. and Woollard, S. 1984. The development of stability of respiration in human infants. Changes in ventilatory responses to spontaneous sighs. *J. Physiol.* 347, 1–16.

Fodor, J. A. 1983. *The Modularity of Mind.* Cambridge, Mass.: MIT Press.

Fontaine, R. 1984. Imitative skills between birth and six months. *Infant Behav. Develop.* 7, 323–33.

Freud, S. 1905. Wit and its relation to the unconscious. In A. A. Brill, transl., *The Basic Writings of Sigmund Freud.* New York: Modern Library.

Gaensbauer, T. and Emde, R. N. 1973. Wakefulness and feeding in human newborns. *Arch. Gen. Psychiat.* 28, 894–97.

Gel'fand, I. M., Gurfinkel, V. S., Tsetlin, M. L. and Shik, M. L. 1971. Some problems in the analysis of movements. In I. M. Gel'fand, V. S. Gurfinkel, S. V. Formin and M. L. Tsetlin, eds., *Models of the Structural-*

Functional Organizations of Certain Biological systems. Cambridge, Mass.: MIT Press.

Goldman, P. S. and Nauta, W. J. H. 1977. Columnar distribution of cortico-cortical fibers in the frontal association, limbic and motor cortex of the developing Rhesus monkey. *Brain Res.* 122: 393–413.

Golub, H. L. and Corwin, M. J. 1985. A physioacoustic model of the infant cry. In B. M. Lester and C. S. Z. Boukydis, eds., *Infant Crying: Theoretical and Research Perspectives.* New York: Plenum.

Gottlieb, G. 1976. The roles of experience in the development of behavior and the nervous system. In G. Gottlieb, ed., *Development and Neural and Behavioral Specificity.* New York: Academic Press.

Gould, S. J. 1977. *Ontogeny and Phylogeny.* Cambridge, Mass.: Harvard University Press.

Graefe, O. 1963. Versuche über visuelle Formwahrnehmung im Säuglingsalter. *Psychol. Forsch.* 27, 177–224.

Greene, P. H. 1972. Problems of organization of motor systems. In R. Rosen and F. Snell, eds., *Progress in Theoretical Biology.* New York: Academic Press.

Haith, M. 1976. Visual competence in early infancy. In R. Held, H. Leibowitz and H. L. Teuber, eds., *Handbook of Sensory Physiology.* Vol. 3. New York: Springer.

Hamburg, D. 1963. Emotions in the perspective of human evolution. In P. H. Knapp, ed., *Expressions of Emotions in Man.* New York: International Universities Press.

Hamburger, V. and Oppenheim, R. W. 1982. Naturally occurring neuronal death in vertebrates. *Neuroscience Commentaries* 1, 39–55.

Harlow, H. F. and Harlow, M. K. 1969. Effects of various mother-infant relationships on rhesus monkey behaviours. In B. M. Foss, ed., *Determinants of Infant Behaviour.* Vol. 4. London: Methuen.

Haroutunian, S. 1983. *Equilibrium in the Balance.* New York: Springer.

Harris, P. L. 1983. Infant cognition. In P. Mussen, ed., *Handbook of Child Psychology.* Fourth Edition. New York: Wiley.

Hartmann, H. 1939. *Ego Psychology and the Problem of Adaptation.* New York: International Universities Press, 1958.

Hebb, D. O. 1946. On the nature of fear. *Psychol. Rev.* 53, 259–302.

Hillman, J. 1964. *Emotion.* Evanston: Northwestern University Press.

Hinde, R. A. 1983. Ethology and child development. In P. Mussen, ed., *Handbook of Child Psychology.* New York: Wiley.

Holst, E. v. 1935. Über den Prozess der Zentral-nervösen Koordination. *Pflüger's Arch. ges. Physiol. Mensch. Tiere* 236, 149–58.

Hooff, J. A. R. M. A. van. 1972. A comparative approach to the phylogeny of laughter and smiling. In R. A. Hinde, ed., *Non-verbal Communication.* Cambridge: Cambridge University Press.

Hopkins, B. and Prechtl, H. F. R. 1984. A qualitative approach to the development of movements during early infancy. In H. F. R. Prechtl, ed.,

Continuity of Neural Functions from Prenatal to Postnatal Life. Oxford: Blackwell.

Hutt, C. and Ounsted, C. 1966. The biological significance of gaze aversion: with special reference to childhood autism. *Behav. Sci.* 11, 346–56.

Hutt, S. J., Lenard, H. G. and Prechtl, H. F. R. 1969. Psychophysiological studies in newborn infants. In H. W. Reese and L. P. Lipsitt, eds., *Advances in Child Development and Behavior.* Vol. 4. New York: Academic Press.

Irwin, O. C. and Weiss, A. P. 1930. A note on mass activity in newborn infants. *J. Comp. Psychol.* 14, 415–28.

Izard, C. E. 1977. *Human Emotions.* New York: Plenum.

Izard, C. E. and Dougherty, L. 1982. Two complementary systems for measuring facial expressions in infants and children. In C. E. Izard, ed., *Measuring Emotions in Infants and Children.* New York: Cambridge University Press.

Jakobson, R. 1940. Kindersprache, Aphasie und allgemeine Lautgesetze. In R. Jakobson, *Selected Writings.* The Hague: Mouton.

Jeannerod, M. 1985. *The Brain Machine,* D. Urion, trans. Cambridge: Harvard University Press.

Kagan, J. 1970. Determinants of attention in the infant. *Amer. Scient.* 58, 289–306.

––––––. 1974. Discrepancy, temperament and infant distress. In M. Lewis and L. A. Rosenblum, eds., *The Origins of Fear.* New York: Wiley.

Kagan, J., Henker, B. A., Hen-Tov, A., Levine, J. and Lewis, M. 1966. Infants' differential reactions to familiar and distorted faces. *Child Develop.* 37, 519–32.

Kahnemann, D. 1973. *Attention and Effort.* Englewood Cliffs, N.J.: Prentice-Hall.

Katchalsky, A. K., Rowland, V. and Blumenthal, R. 1974. Dynamic patterns of brain cell assemblies. *Neuroscience Res. Progr. Bull.* Vol. 12, no. 1. Boston, Mass.

Kaufman, R. and Kaufman, F. 1980. The face schema in 3- and 4-month-old infants: The role of dynamic properties of the face. *Infant Behav. Develop.* 3, 331–39.

Kaye, K. and Vogel, A. 1980. The temporal structure of face-to-face communications between mothers and infants. *Develop. Psychol.* 16, 454–64.

Kelso, J. A. S. and Tuller, B. 1981. Toward a theory of apractic syndromes. *Brain and Language.* 13, 224–45.

Kelso, J. A. S., Holt, K. G., Rubin, P. and Kugler, P. N. 1981. Patterns of interlimb coordination emerge from properties of non-linear, limit cycle oscillatory processes: theory and data. *J. Mot. Behav.* 13: 226–61.

Kelso, J. A. S. and Tuller, B. 1983. A dynamical basis for action systems. In M. S. Gazzaniga, ed., *Handbook of Cognitive Neuroscience.* New York: Plenum Press.

Kendon, A. 1967. Some functions of gaze direction in social interaction. *Acta Psychol.* 26, 22–63.

Kessen, W., Haith, M. M., Salapatek, P. H. 1970. Human infancy. In P. H. Mussen ed., *Carmichael's Handbook of Child Psychology*. New York: Wiley.

Kleitman, N. 1963. *Sleep and Wakefulness*. Chicago: University of Chicago Press.

Klüver, H. 1965. Neurobiology of normal and abnormal perception. In *Psychopathology of Perceptions*. New York: Grune and Stratton.

Koepke, J. E., Hamm, M., Legerstee, M. and Russell, M. 1983. Neonatal imitation: two failures to replicate. *Inf. Behav. Develop.* 6, 97–102.

Konner, M. 1983. *The Tangled Wing*. New York: Harper and Row.

Korner, A. F. and Grobstein, R. 1966. Visual alertness as related to soothing in neonates: implications for maternal stimulation and early deprivation. *Child Develop.* 37, 867–76.

Kugler, P. N., Kelso, J. A. S. and Turvey, M. T. 1982. On coordination and control in naturally developing systems. In J. A. S. Kelso and J. B. Clark, eds., *The Development of Movement Coordination and Control*. New York: Wiley.

Langer, J. 1970. Werner's comparative organismic theory. In P. Mussen, ed., *Carmichael's Manual of Child Psychology*. New York: Wiley.

Lashley, K. S. 1951. The problem of serial order in behavior. In L. A. Jeffries, ed., *Cerebral Mechanisms in Behavior*. New York: Wiley.

Lazarus, R. S. 1968. Emotions and adaptation: conceptual and empirical relations. In W. Arnold, ed., *Nebraska Symposium on Motivation*. Lincoln: University of Nebraska Press.

————. 1984. On the primacy of cognition. *Amer. Psychol.* 39, 124–29.

Leach, E. 1972. The influence of cultural context on non-verbal communication in man. In R. H. Hinde, ed., *Non-verbal Communication*. Cambridge: Cambridge University Press.

Lehrman, D. S. 1971. Behavioral science, engineering, and poetry. In E. Tobach, L. R. Aronson and E. Shaw, eds., *The Psychobiology of Development*. New York: Academic Press.

Lenard, H. G., von Bernuth, H., Prechtl, H. F. R. 1968. Reflexes and their relationship to behavioral states in the newborn. *Acta Paediat. Scand.* 57: 177–85.

Lenneberg, E. H. 1967. *The Biological Foundations of Language*. New York: Wiley.

Lewis, E. B. 1978. A gene complex controlling segmentation in *Drosophila*. *Nature* 276: 575–70.

Lewis, M. and Lee-Painter, S. 1974. Interactional approach to the mother-infant dyad. In M. Lewis and L. A. Rosenblum, eds., *The Effect of the Infant on Its Caregiver*. New York: Wiley.

Leyhausen, P. 1967. Biologie von Ausdruck and Eindruck. *Psychol. Forsch.* 31, 113–76.

Lieberman, P. 1984. *The Biology and Evolution of Language.* Cambridge, Mass.: Harvard University Press.

Lieberman, P., Ryalls, J. and Rabson, S. 1982. On the early imitation of intonation and vowels. In *Handbook of the 7th Annual Boston University Conference on Language Development,* 34–35.

Lipton, E. L., Steinschnerder, A. and Richmond, J. B. 1965. Swaddling, a child care practice: historical, cultural and experimental observations. *Pediat.* 35 (suppl.), 521–67.

Lorenz, K. 1971. *Studies in Animal and Human Behavior.* Vol. I. Cambridge: Harvard University Press.

Marler, P. and Hamilton, W. J. 1967. *Mechanisms of Animal Behavior.* New York: Wiley.

McDougall, W. 1926. *Outline of Abnormal Psychology.* New York: Scribner.

Meier-Koll, A., Hall, U., Hellwig, U., Kott, G., Meier-Koll, V. 1978. A biological oscillator system and the development of sleep-waking behavior during early infancy. *Chronobiologia* 5, 425–40.

Meltzoff, A. N. and Moore, M. K. 1977. Facial and manual imitation by human neonates. *Science* 198, 75–78.

Michon, J. A. 1967. *Timing in Temporal Tracking.* Assen, Netherlands: van Gorkum.

Monod, J. 1972. *Chance and Necessity.* London: Collins.

Montague, A. 1978. *Touching: The Human Significance of the Skin.* New York: Harper.

Moore, K. C. 1896. The mental development of a child. *Psychol. Rev. Monogr. Suppl.*

Murray, A. D. 1979. Infant crying as an elicitor of parental behavior: an examination of two models. *Psychol. Bull.* 86, 191–215.

Mussen, P. H., ed. 1970. *Carmichael's Manual of Child Psychology.* Third Edition. New York: Wiley.

Nijhuis, J. G., Martin, C. B. Jr. and Prechtl, H. F. R. 1984. Behavioral states of the human fetus. In H. F. R. Prechtl, ed., *Continuity of Neural Functions from Prenatal to Postnatal Life.* Oxford: Blackwell.

Oller, D. K. 1981. Infant vocalizations: exploration and reflexivity. In R. Stark, ed., *Language Behavior in Infancy and Early Childhood.* New York: Elsevier.

Olson, G. M. and Sherman, T. 1983. Attention, learning, and memory in infants. In P. H. Mussen, ed., *Handbook of Child Psychology.* New York: Wiley.

Oppenheim, R. W. 1981. Ontogenetic adaptations and retrogressive processes in development of the nervous system and behavior: a neuroembryologic perspective. In K. J. Connolly and H. F. R. Prechtl, eds., *Maturation and Development: Biological and Psychological Perspectives.* London: Heinemann.

Osofsky, J. D. 1979. *Handbook of Infant Development.* New York: Wiley.

Oster, H. and Ekman, P. 1978. Facial behavior in child development. In W. A. Collins, ed., *Minnesota Symposia on Child Psychology.* Vol. II. Hillsdale, N.J.: Erlbaum.

Ostwall, P. H. and Murry, T. 1985. The communicative and diagnostic significance of infant sounds. In B. M. Lester and C. S. Z. Boukydis, eds., *Infant Crying: Theoretical and Research Perspectives.* New York: Plenum.

Oswald, I. 1962. *Sleeping and Waking.* Amsterdam: Elsevier.

Papoušek, H. and Papoušek, M. 1982. Integration into the social world: survey of research. In P. Stratton, ed., *Psychobiology of the Human Newborn.* New York: Wiley.

Parmalee, A. H. and Stern, E. 1972. Development of states in infants. In C. D. Clemente, D. P. Purpura and F. E. Mayer, eds., *Sleep and the Maturing Nervous System.* New York: Academic Press.

Parmalee, A. H. and Sigman, M. D. 1983. Perinatal brain development and behavior. In P. H. Mussen, ed., *Handbook of Child Psychology.* Fourth Edition. New York: Wiley.

Paul, K., Dittrichová, J., Paplikova, E. 1973. The course of quiet sleep in infants. *Biol. Neonat.* 23: 78–89.

Pavlidis, T. 1973. *Biological Oscillators: Their Mathematical Analysis.* New York: Academic Press.

Pavlov, I. P. 1928. *Lectures on Conditioned Reflexes.* New York: Liveright.

Peiper, A. 1963. *Cerebral Function in Infancy and Childhood.* New York: Consultants Bureau, pp. 76, 147–247.

Pepper, S. 1946. *World Hypotheses.* Berkeley: University of California Press.

Piaget, J. 1932. *The Moral Judgment of the Child.* New York: Harcourt.

———. 1951. *Play, Dreams, and Imitation.* London: Heinemann.

———. 1952. *The Origins of Intelligence.* New York: International Universities Press.

———. 1954. *The Construction of Reality in the Child.* New York: Basic Books.

———. 1956. Equilibration and the development of logical structures. In J. M. Tanner and B. Inhelder, eds., *Discussions on Child Development IV.* New York: International Universities Press.

———. 1970. Piaget's theory. In P. H. Mussen, ed., *Carmichael's Manual of Child Psychology.* Third edition. New York: Wiley.

———. 1975. *The Equilibration of Cognitive Structures.* Chicago: University of Chicago Press.

Piattelli-Palmarini, M. 1980. *Language and Learning.* Cambridge, Mass.: Harvard University Press.

Popper, K. R. and Eccles, J. C. 1977. *The Self and Its Brain—An Argument for Interactionism.* Berlin: Springer.

Posner, M. I. and Rothbart, M. K. 1980. The development of attentional mechanisms. In J. H. Flowers, ed., *Cognitive Processes, Nebraska Symposium on Motivation.* Vol. 28. Lincoln: University of Nebraska Press.

Pratt, K. C. 1937. The organization of behavior in the newborn infant. *Psychol. Rev.* 44: 470–90.

Prechtl, H. F. R. 1958. The directed head-turning response and allied movements of the human baby. *Behavior* 13, 212–42.

———. 1974. The behavioral states of the newborn infant (a review). *Brain Research* 76, 184–212.

Prechtl, H. F. R., Vlach, V., Lenard, H. G. and Kerr Grant, D. 1967. Exteroceptive and tendon reflexes in various behavioral states in the newborn. *Biol. Neonat.* 11, 159–75.

Prechtl, H. F. R., Theorell, K. and Blair, A. W. 1973. Behavioral state cycles in abnormal infants. *Develop. Med. Child Neurol.* 15, 606–15.

Prechtl, H. F. R., Fargel, J. W., Weinmann, H. M., Bakker, H. H. 1975. Development of motor function and body posture in preterm infants. *Institut National de la Santé et de la Recherche Médicale* (INSERM). 43: 55–66.

Prechtl, H. F. R. and O'Brien, M. J. 1982. Behavioral states of the full term newborn. Emergence of a concept. In P. Stratton, ed., *Psychobiology of the Human Newborn.* New York: Wiley.

Preyer, W. 1882. *Die Seele des Kindes.* Leipzig: Grieben.

Prigogine, I. 1980. *From Being to Becoming.* San Francisco: Freeman.

Prigogine, I. and Stengers, I. 1984. *Order out of Chaos.* New York: Bantam.

Purves, D. and Lichtman, J. W. 1985. *Principles of Neural Development.* Sunderland, Mass.: Sinauer Associates.

Rapaport, D. 1951a. States of consciousness: a psychopathological and psychodynamic view. In *Transaction of Second Conference on Problems of Consciousness.* Vol. II. New York: Josiah Macy Foundation.

———. 1951b. *Organization and Pathology of Thought.* New York: Columbia University Press.

———. 1953. On the psychoanalytic theory of affects. *Internat. J. Psychoanal.* 34: 177–98.

———. 1954. The conceptual model of psychoanalysis. In R. P. Knight and C. R. Friedman, eds., *Psychoanalytic Psychiatry and Psychology.* New York: International Universities Press.

———. 1960. Psychoanalysis as a developmental psychology. In B. Kaplan and S. Wapner, eds., *Perspectives in Psychological Theory: Essays in Honor of Heinz Werner.* New York: International Universities Press.

———. 1967. Edward Bibring's theory of depression. In M. M. Gill, ed., *The Collected Papers of David Rapaport.* New York: Basic Books.

Richmond, J. B., Grossman, H. J. and Lustman, S. L. 1953. A hearing test for newborn infants. *Pediats.* 11, 634–38.

Rinn, W. E. 1984. The neuropsychology of facial expression: a review of the neurological and psychological mechanisms for producing facial expressions. *Psychol. Bull.* 95, 52–77.

Robson, K. S. 1967. The role of eye-to-eye contact in maternal infant attachment. *J. Child Psychol. Psychiatr.* 8, 13–25.

Roffwarg, H. P., Muzio, J. N., Dement, W. C. 1966. Ontogenetic development of the human sleep-dream cycle. *Science* 152: 604–19.

Rothbart, M. K. 1973. Laughter in young children. *Psychol. Bull.* 80, 247–56.

Saint-Anne Dargassies, S. 1977. *Neurological Development in the Full-Term and Premature Neonate.* Amsterdam: Elsevier.

Salk, L. 1962. Mother's heartbeat as an imprinting stimulus. *Trans. N.Y. Acad. Sci.* 24, 753–63.

Salzarulo, P., Fagioli, I., Salomon, F., Ricour, C., Rimbault, G., Ambrosi, S., Cicchi, O., Duhamel, J. F. and Rigoard, M. T. 1980. Sleep patterns in infants under continuous feeding from birth. *Electroenceph. Clin. Neurophysiol.* 49: 330–36.

Sameroff, A. J. 1979. Learning in infancy: a developmental perspective. In J. Osofsky, ed., *Handbook of Infant Development.* New York: Wiley.

Sander, L. W., Stechler, G., Burns, P., Julia, H. 1970. Early mother-infant interaction and 24-hour patterns of activity and sleep. *J. Amer. Acad. Child Psychiat.* 9: 103–23.

Sartre, J.-P. 1948. *The Emotions: A Sketch of a Theory.* New York: Philosophical Library.

Schachter, S. and Singer, J. E. 1962. Cognitive, social, and physiological determinants of emotional state. *Psychol. Rev.* 69: 379–99.

Schneider, G. E. 1979. Is it really better to have your brain lesion early— revision of the Kennard principle. *Neuropsychol.* 17, 557–84.

Sheldrake, R. 1981. *A New Science of Life.* Los Angeles: Tarcher.

Skinner, B. F. 1938. *The Behavior of Organisms.* New York: Appleton-Century-Crofts.

———. 1953. *Science and Human Behavior.* New York: Macmillan.

Sokolov, E. N. 1963. *Perception and the Conditioned Reflex.* London: Pergamon.

Sollberger, A. 1965. *Biological Rhythm Research.* Amsterdam: Elsevier.

Solomon, R. C. 1983. *The Passions: The Myth and Nature of Human Emotion.* Notre Dame, Ind.: University of Notre Dame Press.

Sosteck, A. M. and Anders, T. A. 1975. Effects of varying laboratory conditions in behavioral state organization in two- and eight-week-old infants. *Child Develop.* 46, 871–78.

Sperry, R. W. 1951. Neurology and the mind-brain problem. *Amer. Sci.* 40: 291–312.

———. 1963. Chemoaffinity in the orderly growth of nerve fiber patterns and connections. *Proc. Nat. Acad. Sci., USA.* 50, 703–10.

Spitz, R. 1950. Anxiety in infancy: a study of its manifestations in the first year of life. *Internat. J. Psychoanal.* 31, 138–43.

Spitz, R. and Cobliner, W. G. 1965. *The First Year of Life: Normal and Deviant Object Relations*. New York: International Universities Press.

Sroufe, A. 1982. The organization of emotional development. In M. Mayman, ed., *Infant Research: The Dawn of Awareness*. Psychoanalyt. Inquiry Monogr. Vols. 1–4. New York: International Universities Press.

Sroufe, L. A., Waters, E. 1976. The ontogenesis of smiling and laughter. *Psychol. Rev.* 83: 173–89.

Sroufe, L. A. and Wunsch, J. P. 1977. The development of laughter in the first year of life. *Child Develop.* 43, 1326–44.

Stark, R. E. and Nathanson, S. N. 1973. Spontaneous cry in the newborn infant, sounds and facial gestures. In J. F. Bosma, ed., *Oral Sensation and Perception*. Fourth Symposium. Bethesda, Md.: U.S.P.H.E.W.

Stark, R. E., Rose, S. N. and Benson, P. J. 1978. Classification of infant vocalization. *Brit. J. Disord. Communic.* 13, 41–47.

Stern, D. N. 1977. *The First Relationship: Mother and Infant*. Cambridge, Mass.: Harvard University Press.

Stich, S. 1983. *From Folk Psychology to Cognitive Science*. Cambridge, Mass.: MIT Press.

Stone, L. J., Smith, H. T. and Murphy, L. B. 1973. *The Competent Infant*. New York: Basic Books.

Strumwasser, F. 1974. Neuronal principles organizing periodic behavior. In F. O. Schmitt and F. G. Worden, eds., *The Neurosciences: Third Study Program*. Cambridge, Mass.: MIT Press.

Szentagothai, J. 1984. Downward causation? *Ann. Rev. Neurosci.* 7: 1–11.

Thelen, E. 1985. Developmental origins of motor coordination: leg movements in human infants. *Develop. Psychobiol.* 18, 1–22.

Theorell, K., Prechtl, H. F. R., Blair, A. W., Lind, J. 1973. Behavioral state cycles of normal newborn infants. *Dev. Med. Child Neurol.* 15: 597–605.

Thom, R. 1972. *Structural Stability and Morphogenesis*. New York: Benjamin.

Thoman, E. B. 1975. Sleep and wake behaviors in neonates: consistencies and consequences. *Merrill-Palmer Quart.* 21, 293–313.

Thomas, H. 1973. Unfolding the baby's mind: The infant's selection of visual stimuli. *Psych. Review.* 80: 468–88.

Tinbergen, N. 1951. *The Study of Instinct*. Oxford: Clarendon Press.

Trevarthen, C. 1979. Communication and cooperation in early infancy: A description of primary inter-subjectivity. In M. Bullowa, ed., *Before Speech*. New York: Cambridge University Press.

Truby, H. M. and Lind, J. 1965. Cry sounds of the newborn infant. *Acta Paeditr. Scand.* 163, 7–59.

Turvey, M. T., Shaw, R. E. and Mace, W. 1978. Issues in the theory of action: degrees of freedom, coordinative structures and coalitions. In J. Pequin, ed., *Attention and Performance*, vol. 7. Hillsdale, N.J.: Erlbaum.

Uzgiris, I. C. and Hunt, J. McV. 1975. *Assessment in Infancy: Ordinal Scales of Psychological Development*. Champaign, Ill.: University of Illinois Press.

Vinh-Bang. 1966. La méthode clinique et la recherche en psychologie de l'enfant. In *Psychologie et Epistemologie Génétiques*. Paris: Dunod.

Vries, J. I. P. de, Visser, G. H. A. and Prechtl, H. F. R. 1984. Fetal motility in the first half of pregnancy. In H. F. R. Prechtl, ed., *Continuity of Neural Functions from Prenatal to Postnatal Life*. Oxford: Blackwell.

Vygotsky, L. S. 1962. *Thought and Language*. Cambridge, Mass.: MIT Press.

Waddington, C. H. 1969. The basic ideas of biology. In C. H. Waddington, ed., *Towards a Theoretical Biology*. Chicago: Aldine.

Wasz-Höckert, O., Michelsson, K. and Lind, J. 1985. Twenty-five years of Scandinavian cry research. In B. M. Lester and C. F. Z. Boukydis, eds., *Infant Crying: Theoretical and Research Perspectives*. New York: Plenum.

Watson, J. B. 1919. A schematic outline of the emotions. *Psychol. Rev.* 26, 165–96.

———. 1928. What the nursery has to say about instincts. In C. Murchison, ed., *Psychologies of 1925*. Worcester, Mass.: Clark University Press.

Watson, J. S. 1972. Smiling, cooing and "the game." *Merrill-Palmer Quart.* 18, 323–39.

Weiss, P. A. 1941. Self differentiation of the basic patterns of coordination. *Comp. Physiol. Monogr.* 17: 1–96.

———. 1955. Nervous system (neurogenesis). In B. H. Willier, P. Weiss and V. Hamburger, eds., *The Analysis of Development*. Philadelphia: Saunders.

———. 1967. 1 + 1 ≠ 2 (one plus one does not equal two). In G. C. Quarton, T. Melnechuk and F. O. Schmitt, eds., *The Neurosciences*. New York: Rockefeller University Press.

Werner, H. 1947. The concept of development from a comparative and organismic point of view. In D. B. Harris, ed., *The Concept of Development*. Minneapolis: University of Minnesota Press.

Werner, H. 1957. *Comparative Psychology of Mental Development*. Revised Edition. New York: International Universities Press.

Werner, H. and Kaplan, B. 1968. *Symbol Formation*. New York: Wiley.

Wilson, E. O. 1975. *Sociobiology: The New Synthesis*. Cambridge, Mass.: Harvard University Press.

Wohlwill, J. 1973. *The Study of Behavioral Development*. New York: Academic Press.

Wolff, P. H. 1959. Observations on newborn infants. *Psychosomatic Medicine* 21: 110–18.

———. 1960. The developmental psychologies of Jean Piaget and psychoanalysis. *Psychological Issues Monograph Series*. Vol. 2, no. 1. New York: International Universities Press.

———. 1963a. Observations on the early development of smiling. In B.

Foss, ed., *Determinants of Infant Behaviour*. Vol. 2. London: Methuen.

———. 1963b. Developmental and motivational concepts in Piaget's sensorimotor theory of intelligence. *J. Amer. Acad. Child Psychiat.* 2, 225–43.

———. 1966. The causes, controls and organization of behavior in the neonate. *Psychological Issues Monograph Series*. Vol. 5, no. 1. New York: International Universities Press.

———. 1967. The role of biological rhythms in early psychological development. *Bulletin of the Menninger Clinic* 31: 197–218.

———. 1968a. The serial organization of sucking in the young infant. *Pediatrics* 42: 943–56.

———. 1968b. Sucking patterns of infant mammals. *Brain Behavior and Evolution* 1: 354–67.

———. 1968c. Stereotypic behavior and development. *Canadian Psychologist* 9: 474–84.

———. 1969. The natural history of crying and other vocalizations in early infancy. In B. Foss, ed., *Determinants of Infant Behaviour*. Vol. 4. London: Methuen, pp. 81–109.

———. 1970. Motor development and holotelencephaly. In R. Robinson, ed., *Brain and Early Behavior*. London: Academic Press, pp. 139–69.

———. 1972a. The interaction of state and non-nutritive sucking. In J. Bosma, ed., *Third Symposium on Oral Sensation and Perception: The Mouth of the Infant*. Springfield, Ill.: Thomas, pp. 293–310.

———. 1972b. Operational intelligence and psychological development. In M. Piers, ed., *Play and Development: A Symposium*. New York: Norton.

———. 1973. The organization of behavior in the first three months of life. *Association for Research in Nervous and Mental Disease* 51: 132–53.

———. 1981. Theoretical issues in the development of motor skills. In M. Lewis and L. Taft, eds., *Developmental Disabilities: Theory, Assessment and Intervention*. Jamaica, N.Y.: SP Medical and Scientific Books.

———. 1984. Discontinuous changes in human wakefulness around the end of the second month of life: a developmental perspective. In H. F. R. Prechtl, ed., *Continuity of Neural Functions from Prenatal to Postnatal Life*. Oxford: Blackwell.

———. 1985. Epilogue. In B. M. Lester and C. F. Z. Boukydis, eds., *Infant Crying: Theoretical and Research Perspectives*. New York: Plenum.

Wolff, P. H. and White, B. 1965. Visual pursuit and attention in young infants. *Journal of the American Academy of Child Psychiatry* 4: 473–84.

Wolff, P. H. and Simmons, M. 1967. Non-nutritive sucking and response thresholds in young infants. *Child Development* 38: 631–38.

Wolff, P. H. and Ferber, R. 1979. The development of behavior in human infants, premature and newborn. *Ann. Rev. of Neurosci.* 2: 291–307.

Yates, F. E. and Iberall, A. S. 1973. Temporal and hierarchical organization in biosystems. In J. Urquart. and F. E. Yates, eds., *Temporal Aspects of Therapeutics*. New York: Plenum.

Zazzo, R. 1957. Le problème de l'imitation chez le nouveau-né. *L'Enfance*. 10, 135–42.

Zelazo, D. 1972. Smiling and vocalizing: a cognitive emphasis. *Merrill-Palmer Quart*. 18, 349–65.

Index

Accommodation, 245, 247
Active inhibition, 45
Adults: behavioral states in, 19–20, 54, 55, 95, 97; crying in, 160; emotions in, 254, 265; eye-eye contact in, 212–13; myoclonic jerks in, 53; non-nutritive sucking in, 37; sleep pattern in, 33; smiling in, 105, 125–26; study of, and infant studies, 1–5, 14, 15; tickling in, 145, 149, 150; volitional actions in, 238–40
Affectivity, Piaget on, 255–56
Ahrens, R., 126, 128, 130, 260
Ainsworth, M. D. S., 168
Alert activity: defined, 25, 55, 70; dual task performance in, 25, 61–62, 70–78; duration of, 60–61; laughter in, 146; in wakefulness state sequences, 62–63. *See also* Wakefulness
Alert inactivity: crying and, 83; defined, 23–24, 55; difficulty of distinguishing alert activity from, 70; duration of, 60–61; laughter in, 146; in wakefulness state sequences, 62–63. *See also* Wakefulness
Allport, D. A., 71, 75
Ambrose, J. A., 138

Anders, T. A., 26, 67
Anger, and crying, 155
Animals: crying and, 152–53; emotional expressions in, 257; laughter and, 140; smiling and, 105; sucking in, 37
Aquinas, St. Thomas, 101
Argyle, M., 212, 213
Ashton, R., 110
Assimilation, 245, 247
Attentional processes, 54
Auditory pursuit, of objects, 194
Augustine, St., 101

Babbling. *See* Noncry vocalizations
Baldwin, J. M., 5
Behavioral states, 7, 13–15, 19–98; defined, 19–22, 96–97; developmental stages versus, 244–45, 264–65; emotional expressions and, 103, 189–91, 231–32, 263–65; hunger and, 90–95, 159–60; induction of new, 234–53; noncry vocalizations and, 185; object relations and, 203–4; of premature infants, 106–7; quantitative dimension of, 87–96, 98; sensorimotor theory and, 245–46; smiling and, 125–26, 133–34; sucking and,

283

.

A